THE POSTAGE STAMPS
OF GREAT BRITAIN

H.M. KING GEORGE V

From the photograph by W. and D. Downey

THE POSTAGE STAMPS
OF GREAT BRITAIN

PART FOUR
THE ISSUES OF KING GEORGE V

by K. M. BEAUMONT
and J. B. M. STANTON

LONDON
THE ROYAL PHILATELIC SOCIETY
1957

Preface

WHEN the revision of Part II of J. B. Seymour's classic work was carried out by Major Beaumont and the late Mr Adams it was decided to extend the story of the Surface-Printed Stamps to the end of the reign of King Edward VII. This was published in 1954 as *The Postage Stamps of Great Britain, Part III.*

The complete study of the stamps of Great Britain has now been carried a stage further with the preparation of this volume on the issues of King George V, in which Major Beaumont has collaborated with Lieutenant Colonel J. B. M. Stanton.

The illustrations in the text have been reproduced from material in the Royal Collection at Buckingham Palace, the collection presented by the late Mr Adams to the Society, and the collection of Mr Thomas E. Field. As in Part III, there is a complete set of illustrations of all the postage stamps issued in the reign.

The Appendixes contain all the information known to the authors at the time of going to press on the markings of the printing plates, leading to the plating of the values. The opportunity has also been taken of including the correspondence between G. W. Eve and the authorities at Somerset House, the General Post Office, and the Royal Mint.

The Editorial Panel is still engaged in the preparation of Part II, which deals with the perforated Line Engraved issues of Queen Victoria.

April, 1957

JOHN EASTON
ARNOLD STRANGE
Publications Committee

Editorial Note

THE Editors of this volume desire to place upon record their indebtedness to the late H. C. V. Adams, Sir John Wilson and Messrs R. H. Sampson, Cecil G. Shaw, Thomas E. Field and Charles Nissen & Co. Ltd for valuable assistance.

In connection with the previous volume in this series, some people have suggested that information which might have been included was omitted. Some others, on the contrary, considered that too many matters of detail were included. On this occasion we have thought it wisest to supply the fullest possible information, including matters of detail which some may consider to be of minor importance, since this appears to be better than omitting matter which may be of interest to some specialists and collectors.

Some of the material is technical, and may be found complicated by those who have not made a careful study of the subject; and it is possible that advanced specialists may not be in agreement with all the facts stated or the deductions and conclusions advanced.

Nevertheless, we hope that any errors which may have crept in will not prove to be serious. We have done our best in handling a subject of considerable complexity.

Finally, the first-named Editor desires to give to the second-named all the credit for Appendixes A to D, for the detailed contents of which the latter is wholly responsible.

K. M. BEAUMONT
J. B. M. STANTON

Contents

CHAPTER

Illustrations

At end

Illustrations showing types of the Postage Stamps
issued in the reign of King George V

Illustrations

Chapter One

The Low Values

PREPARATORY STAGES OF PRODUCTION

KING Edward VII died on May 6, 1910. On July 1 of that year the
Postmaster General issued an invitation to certain artists, including
Mr, later Sir Bertram, Mackennal and Mr George W. Eve, to submit designs of stamps for the new reign, with a stipulation that at
least one of the designs should include the figure of a lion *couchant*
at the foot of the stamp. Before the first issue of the new Halfpenny and One Penny stamps on Coronation Day, June 22, 1911, a
great deal of preparatory work was undertaken. This work is exem-
plified in a remarkable manner by means of artists' sketches and
drawings for designs, essays, die and plate proofs, colour trials, etc.,
comprised respectively in the Royal Collection at Buckingham
Palace and in a collection presented by the late Mr H. C. V. Adams
to the Royal Philatelic Society. A considerable part of the latter
collection originally belonged to Colonel A. S. Bates, D.S.O.,
T.D., for whom it was formed by the late Mr Charles Nissen, who
acquired artists' original drawings by Mr G. W. Eve and obtained
information from Mr Seymour Bennett, who was head of the
Stamping Department of the Inland Revenue at Somerset House.
After its acquisition by Mr Adams, the collection was added to by
him and made as complete as possible with the help of Mr Charles
Nissen. It is probable that there is nothing of any consequence, in
connection with the preparatory work leading to the issues of 1911,
1912 and 1913, which is not represented in one or other of the two
great collections referred to; and obviously a number of items are
unique in the true sense. In many cases, when the only existing
item is included in the Royal Collection at Buckingham Palace, a
photographic reproduction thereof is included in the collection pre-

13

sented by Mr Adams to the Royal Philatelic Society, where it has a permanent home and is available to members for study.

Generally speaking, there was a single underlying principle in the stages of production of these stamps, and this only varied with the artist designing the frames. Those for the Halfpenny to Fourpence values were designed by Sir Bertram Mackennal, though it would appear to have been the original intention that the Fourpence should have been designed by Mr Eve, who designed the frames for the Fivepence to One Shilling values. The figures and lettering of the values on all the stamps were designed by Mr Eve.

From time to time three different heads were adopted and die proofs of these were taken in varying stages of completion. Primarily for the Halfpenny and One Penny stamps of 1911, the head, which was three-quarter face, was taken from a photograph by Messrs W. and D. Downey, which was chosen personally by King George V. Later, for the issues of 1912 and 1913, the Mackennal (profile) head was in use, taken from his design for the coinage or for the Coronation medal. The head on the stamps designed by Mr Eve is often referred to as the 'Improved Medal head', from the fact that, at Mr Eve's suggestion, the size of the head was slightly reduced so that its width was 47·4 per cent of the total width of the stamp design.

Photography played a large part in the preparatory stages, one of its most important uses being the photographing of the frames, whether designed by Mackennal or by Eve, with head inserted, and the painting upon those photographs by Mr Eve of the figures and lettering of the value.

Another part played by photography was the preparation of temporary dies for the production of a series of colour trials. For the values from Fourpence upwards the Motley process was employed. This process is a method of photo-engraving by which temporary plates in blocks of four were made. These were made from Die Engraver's sketches with a profile head.

For the values from Halfpenny to Threepence, single dies were made from the Mackennal sketches with the Downey head inserted. Although the actual process of manufacture is not known, there can be no doubt that these dies were made by one of the photo-engraving processes then in use. Colour trials were made from the above upon large pieces of paper with the printed heading 'Essays for colour only – not design' and many of the examples known are cut down from these.

For the values from Threepence upwards further colour trials were taken from what are known as the 'Eve electro-blocks'. These were supplied by Mr Eve, by arrangement with the Royal Mint, and closely resembled both his 'Pillar' design, subsequently accepted for the Fivepence to Eightpence values, or his 'Wreath' design, subsequently accepted for the Ninepence to One Shilling values. Those of his 'Pillar' design are known with or without value inserted. The process was undoubtedly photographic, since these electro-blocks were made by the half-tone process and appear very similar to zinco-blocks. In each case a Downey type head was (photographically) inserted, both a small and a large head being used, the background to which was either white, shaded or solid.

The colour trials, of which there were many, were produced from ink manufactured by various colour merchants, and were superscribed with a letter or letters, denoting the colour merchant, above a figure or figures denoting the number of the trial. The following code letters are known: S.P. denoting Slater and Palmer; M.B., Manders Bros., and W, Winstone. Further code letters, which are M.H., S.D., and occasionally H and J.K., were also employed, but it is not known to whom or to what these referred, though it is believed that S.D. stood for Stamping Department. Often these trials were endorsed with the official colour name, such as 'Bartolozzi Brown No 22186', 'Special Green No 150', etc. Normally these trials were on white paper, but occasionally trials were made on coloured paper, including yellow, green, blue, rose, mauve, etc.; and these are sometimes endorsed with the paper tinter's code, such as 'Jones Yellow No 139', 'Spicer's Blue No 6440', etc.

It is believed that the actual dies used for the preparation of the printing plates of the approved design, which were made at the Royal Mint, were all engraved by Mr J. A. C. Harrison, though it has been suggested that the Fourpence was engraved by Mr H. P.

PLATE I

Huggill. The latter could not have engraved the die for the frame, because a die proof of this is known endorsed '1st Proof from Die of design 2d. and 3d. 16.3.11. J.A.C.H.', the latter being Mr Harrison's initials, which was the same design as the Fourpence.

It is not within the scope of this work to describe or enumerate the mass of material, of which that referred to above forms only a part, comprised in the two great collections mentioned above, or to describe in detail the manner in which designs of the various stamps were adopted, or in some cases changed, though some reference to the preparatory stages will be made in more detail hereafter in connection with the particular stamps concerned.

The two collections include trials taken on card or on paper, the latter being either unwatermarked or watermarked either Crown or Simple Cypher. These trials were in various stages of completion culminating in the approved die proofs. For obvious reasons many, if not most, of the items cannot be duplicated. It is therefore gratifying to know that they are all in permanent safe-keeping.

PLATES, PRINTERS AND PAPER

Originally for the values from Halfpenny to One Shilling, the plates, which were made at the Royal Mint, consisted of 240 stamp images arranged in two panes of ten rows of twelve images, the panes being separated horizontally by a row of lined pillars or blocks, four to the width of each stamp image. At first each pane was surrounded by co-extensive lines of marginal rule, which crossed the row of lined blocks between the two halves of the plate. Above the centres of the sixth and seventh stamp images in the top row and below the sixth and seventh stamp images in the bottom row there was a break but there was no break between the stamp images concerned. This arrangement of the marginal rule appeared on all plates used for printing the Halfpenny and One Penny stamps of Dies 1A, 1B and 2. On the production of the plates for printing the stamps with the profile head the rule became truly co-extensive with breaks opposite the gutters between each and every stamp image and without any breaks opposite the centres of the sixth and seventh stamp images. On at least two plates of the One Penny value the marginal rule above the control was much thinner than the normal lines. There was an ornament above the centre of the top row and below the centre of the bottom row.

When Waterlow and Sons, Ltd took over the printing in 1924, each plate consisted of a single pane of 240 stamp images in twenty rows of twelve, with no division between the halves, but there was an arrow in each side margin between the tenth and eleventh rows. This arrangement continued unchanged for the Harrison provisional printing of 1934.

In 1912 and 1913, the Stamping Department at Somerset House marked the plates with white dots in the marginal rule above both panes in order to identify individual printings made by them when testing electros before they were handed over to the contractors, Messrs Harrison and Sons; and this practice was also employed with the Sixpence value until 1934 (though after 1924 only in the top margin) when this value ceased to be printed at Somerset House. For the other values, very nearly every electro, though not always for their early printings, had cuts or dots or a combination of both, made by the printers, so that printings from each plate could be identified. But it is by no means easy to make a record of all the plates used, especially in the case of the One Penny and Sixpence values owing to the lack of pieces with plate markings adjacent to the control on these values. The markings usually appear towards the left of the sheet in the bottom row.*

The first Georgian stamps were printed on plate-glazed paper, with watermark Imperial Crown of 1880, manufactured by Messrs R. D. Turner and Co. The marginal watermarks were the same as for the Edward VII stamps. In 1911 a specially coated paper ('Austrian chalk-surfaced') was used experimentally at Somerset House for printing the One Penny Die 1A with control A.11. This paper shows a reflection under the quartz-lamp similar to that of the Edward VII Sixpence 'Magenta on chalky paper', that is the paper appeared yellowish green and the printed portion brown. Examples are rare.

* A list of the electros, with the marks and characteristics by which printings from each can be recognized, and of the controls under which they were put to press, appears in Appendix A, pages 161, et seq.

In August 1912 paper with 'Simple' Royal Cypher watermark, manufactured by Messrs William Joynson and Son, came into use. The Cyphers were arranged in columns, one column to each vertical row of stamps. The paper supplied to Messrs Harrison was highly plate-glazed; that supplied to Somerset House for printing the Sixpence stamp with control C.13 onwards was coated. The printing of the other values at Somerset House, with controls A.12, B.13 and C.13, and later the Twopence Halfpenny with control J.17, was on normal plate-glazed paper. The Eightpence was on yellow paper. With controls J17 and K18 some of the stamps were printed upon paper adulterated by foreign matter, which is known as 'granite' paper. It is sometimes a little difficult to recognize the granite paper, though under the quartz lamp it appears grey with a distinct brown tone, whereas the ordinary paper is grey with little trace of yellowish brown.

The 'Simple' Cypher watermark is divided into three groups: *Type I* (from August 1912 until late 1913). The left of the 'V' of the Cypher joins the 'G'. *Type II* (from 1913 – concurrently with Type I in that year – until the end of the contract with control W24). The left of the 'V' is unattached and is larger than in Type III. *Type III* (from 1917 – concurrently with Type II – until the end of the contract). The 'V' is smaller than in Type II. Types II and III remained in use at Somerset House up to the early part of the B.24 control period.

Sometimes the watermark 'bits' became deformed or broken, causing the following varieties:

'G   R'   with 'v' omitted.
'G v P'   with tail of 'R' missing.
'G v R'   with Crown missing.
'   v R'   with 'G' omitted.
'G   '   with 'v R' omitted.
'G v   '   with Crown and 'R' omitted.
'G v R'   with long tail to 'G'.
'G v R'   with no curl to top of 'G'.
'G v R'   with no left curl to 'R'.

'G v R'   with no loop to 'R'.
'G v R'   with long right tail to 'R'.
'G v R'   with deformed left tail and raised right
              tail to 'R'.
The entire crown and Cypher missing.

Occasionally stamps are found without watermark, or showing part of the marginal watermark only, owing to misplacement of the sheet in relation to the dandy roll. But in two cases (one with the Threehalfpence and the other with the Fivepence) a complete sheet was issued upon which no watermark appeared. This was probably due to an accidental increase in the flow of the pulp during the manufacture of the paper used for the sheets concerned.

Sometimes the watermarks, in relation to the stamps, are inverted, reversed or inverted and reversed. These varieties occurred when the sheets were fed into the press upside down, wrong side up or both upside down and wrong side up. The Joynson paper was not gummed until after printing. In the case of stamps issued in booklets one half of the stamps on the complete booklet sheet invariably had the watermark upright and the other half inverted. Further reference to this appears hereafter.

In December 1912 plate-glazed paper made at the Basted Mills was used temporarily. This had what is known as the 'Multiple' script Cypher watermark, each successive horizontal line of Cyphers being staggered, so that portions of as many as seven Cyphers might appear on a single stamp. The Cypher watermarks, however, did not extend to the side margins of the sheet, which bore the watermark 'POSTAGE'. The use of this paper was very limited, and was confined to printings of the Halfpenny and One Penny Die II with control B12 in December 1912, and to printings of the same values, but from Die III, in August 1913 with control C13. The latter were originally intended for use in coils for automatic slot machines; but subsequently a few complete sheets were issued. Blocks and horizontal pairs of these latter stamps with the multiple watermark are rare.

In 1924, when Waterlow & Sons Ltd obtained the contract for

printing the stamps, the design of the Royal Cypher watermark was changed to 'Multiple' Roman or block capitals. This paper was manufactured by Samuel Jones & Co., Ltd. It was highly plate-glazed, and the gum was very smooth. That supplied to Somerset House for the Sixpence stamps was at first coated, but during the latter part of the supply of stamps with control D.25 the paper was unsurfaced. In the latter part of the issue with control E.26 the paper was highly plate-glazed, as was that for the emergency printing of the Threehalfpence at Somerset House with that control. This continued up to the issue with control T.33, when the printing of the Sixpence stamps at Somerset House ceased.

In 1924 and 1925 a small supply of experimental paper was used. This had the watermark spaced rather wider than normal, and the Cypher was more compact. Its use is only known with the Threehalfpence with controls A24 and D25 and with the One Penny with control B24.

Although the variety of displaced watermark could no longer occur, a complete sheet of the Twopence and of the Twopence Halfpenny values were found without watermark under circumstances similar to those of Threehalfpence and Fivepence sheets during the first Harrison contract referred to above.*

When the printing contract passed to Messrs Harrison in 1934, the paper was supplied by Portals (John Allen) Ltd of Ivybridge. It had the normal 'Multiple' block Cypher watermark. Usually it was highly plate-glazed, with rather streaky gum; but during a period in 1936 and 1937 for printings of the Sixpence stamps, no longer printed at Somerset House, it was coated.

At one time it was suggested that, in some cases, the 'Provisional typographed printings' of Messrs Harrison and the printings of Messrs Waterlow in 1934 could be distinguished by a difference in the gum used respectively by Messrs Samuel Jones and Messrs John Allen. But this is not the case. It is true that, when the

---

* The Samuel Jones paper supplied to Messrs Waterlow was gummed before printing; but that supplied to Somerset House for the chalk-surfaced Sixpence stamps was not gummed until after printing. Consequently no Waterlow or Somerset House printings on unsurfaced paper stamps are known with watermark reversed or inverted and reversed.

contract passed from Messrs Waterlow to Messrs Harrison, the former assisted the latter in the printing of the Halfpenny, One Penny, Threehalfpence and Twopence values, and the Waterlow prints were on Samuel Jones paper with control U34. But these 'provisional printings' were very small. The Editors have heard of very few control blocks of the Threehalfpence; a block of the One Penny was recorded by the late Captain J. A. Perkins. Messrs Harrison also printed these four values with control U34, but not only on John Allen paper. The existing stock of Samuel Jones paper remaining from the Waterlow contract was used up by Messrs Harrison. It follows that the gum on the paper with control U34 is not a distinguishing feature between the work of the two contractors. But the prints can be distinguished by the perforation, since the pin irregularities of the perforating machines used by Messrs Waterlow and Messrs Harrison differed. In all cases (except that of the One Penny Die 1A experimental printings referred to above), and whatever the paper employed, unsurfaced paper shows a dirty yellow under the quartz-lamp, plate-glazed paper shows a very clear white, and coated paper a bluish-violet colour.

In 1924 and again in 1925 special commemorative stamps were issued for the British Empire Exhibition at Wembley, the size of which (29·5 by 25 mm) differed from the normal issue. The dies and plates were made and the stamps printed by Messrs Waterlow by the line-engraved process. Each plate consisted of 120 impressions laid down in two panes of sixty impressions each, in ten horizontal rows of six.

Plates made for printing the stamps for issue in booklets did not have the same layout as those in use for printing the Post Office sheets. Owing to the necessity for a binding margin on the left whilst the stamps were upright, it was necessary to arrange the images on the plates with the first three vertical rows upright, those in rows 4 to 6 inverted, those in rows 7 to 9 upright and those in rows 10 to 12 inverted. Rows 6 and 7 were separated by a narrow bisecting gutter. In both outer margins there were vertical marginal rules and the bisecting gutter was filled with short horizontal rules. Consequently the watermarks on stamps in vertical rows 1 to 3 and 7 to 9 were upright and in vertical rows 4 to 6 and 10 to 12 they were inverted. It is, therefore, possible to distinguish from which vertical rows the panes in the booklets were printed. Those in vertical rows 1 to 3 had single marginal rule and watermark upright, those in rows 4 to 6 had cross rules and watermark inverted, those in rows 7 to 9 had cross rules and watermark upright and those in rows 10 to 12 had single rule and watermark inverted.

Special plates were made to print stamps with *se-tenant* advertisements. The layout was similar but instead of 240 stamp images they consisted of only 160 and 80 blank spaces.

When coils were first issued no special printing plates were necessary, since the coils were made up from strips separated from Post Office sheets joined together, but in 1921, and later in the Waterlow contract, 'continuous' coils, that is coils made up without joins, were issued. These stamps were produced by Reel Printing, a process in which the plates were attached to cylinders and printing took place, not upon separate sheets, but upon paper unwound from a continuous roll. There was no transverse gutter on sheets from these plates.

After Messrs Harrison obtained the contract in 1934, it was not until August 20 that the first stamps printed by the photogravure process were issued.

This process was economical, and a rapid and efficient method of providing, continuously if required, the enormous number of stamps required daily, estimated at twenty million. It had the additional advantage that, since the ink was very volatile, it was practically impossible to clean the surface.

The production of stamps by the rotary photogravure process is a development of normal photogravure. The photogravure system involves the etching of a copper cylinder, not only with the stamp images, but also with a 'screen' or grid consisting of a network of fine lines which break up the surface of the etched cylinder into minute square cells of varying depth to hold the printing ink. For stamp printing a multipositive is photographed on to a gelatine sheet (carbon tissue), which is wrapped round the cylinder; through the medium of etching acid eating through the tissue the design appears in proportion to the light and shade of the original. Finally the cylinder is chromium-plated to make it as durable as possible. The printing ink from the wells is transferred to the minute depressions on the cylinder caused by the etching, and the surface ink is mechanically wiped off prior to printing. More detailed information about this process, and indeed about all methods of stamp production, will be found in *Postage Stamps in the Making* by Mr John Easton, published by Messrs Faber and Faber in 1949.

The layout of the stamp images on the cylinders was the same as on the typographed plates, but each cylinder printed two Post Office sheets side by side. Printings from a few cylinders are known in which only one of the normal two panes was issued. These are not single-pane cylinders, which were not introduced until 1938, and then only temporarily, but printings from two-pane cylinders of which one of the two panes was faulty. They are in all cases, except cylinder 3 of the Threepence and Fourpence, extremely rare, and were probably registration sheets which were eventually perforated and put into circulation. The cylinders in question are 24 of the Halfpenny, 9R of the One Penny and 63 of the Three-halfpence, and also later cylinder 2 of the Silver Jubilee Three-halfpence.

Etched opposite the gutter between the tenth and eleventh rows in both side margins of both panes were divisional arrows similar to those on the typographed issues. Various marginal markings were engraved upon the cylinders such as perforation register marks and key guide marks, the former being open-sided squares and the latter small crosses. No printer's marginal rule was used in this process, since it was unnecessary.

The cylinder number, being the printer's record of every cylinder made, though not necessarily put to press, was engraved twice on each cylinder, and appeared on the printed sheets opposite either the 20th or 18th rows to the left of each pane, that on the left being without period and that on the right with period. Consequently the left pane is generally known as the 'no stop' pane and that on the right the 'stop' pane. The two panes were separated prior to issue to Post Offices.

After the initial printings it was found that the gutter between the stamps was too narrow to allow for accurate perforation, and it was decided to make a small reduction in the size of the stamps. This reduction was later found to be inadequate and a further reduction was made. These three sizes of stamps are usually referred to as the 'large', the 'intermediate' and the 'small' size images.

The control was no longer screwed in but was etched upon the cylinder and appeared on both 'no stop' and 'stop' panes. Its position varied. Originally it was below the second stamp in the bottom row, but only upon printings with control U34 and early printings with control V34 of the Threehalfpence value. It was then etched opposite the left of the 19th row in fractional form with the letter above the figures. The final position was opposite the 18th row.

When it became necessary to change the control the minute cells on the cylinder upon which the control was etched were filled in and the new control etched over the filling, the cylinder being then again chromium-plated. This process was apparently fraught with difficulties which became evident in connection with later George VI cylinders, though in the case of the George V stamps only once can traces of the previous control be seen. This occurred on the One Penny cylinder 50. In this case traces of the X of X35 can be seen to the right of the Y of Y36. Occasionally the control was etched too lightly and was engraved to deepen it. Only one good example of this occurred during this period, namely upon the Halfpenny cylinder 4 with control W35. These difficulties led to the practice in connection with cylinders used for printing the lesser used stamps of higher value, which were in use over a longer period, of 'boxing' the control. Instead of changing the control a horizontal line was engraved below it, the 'quarter box', to represent the first change; for the second change a vertical line was engraved to the left of the control, the 'half box'; for the third change a vertical line was added to the right of the control, the 'three-quarter box';

and finally a horizontal line was added above the control, the 'whole box'.

Timson rotary presses were employed for the printing, which was upon John Allen paper, but before a sufficient supply could be obtained Messrs Harrison used German presses, the cylinders for use in which had the stamp images etched sideways. Some of these cylinders were worked the reverse way round. These are denoted by the letter 'R' following the cylinder number. These presses, unlike the Timson presses, were fed sheet by sheet, and from these printings come the error of the One Penny printed on the gummed side and the variety with watermark inverted.

The cylinders for printing the stamps of the Silver Jubilee issue were similarly etched except that, as these stamps were double the width of the normal issue, each pane consisted of only 120 stamp images in twenty horizontal rows of six images each.

The layout of cylinders for printing stamps for booklets, except those of the Silver Jubilee issue, and for coils, was similar to that of the typographed stamps, but two panes were printed side by side. The cylinder numbers in both cases were preceded by a letter. In this case it is not possible to identify by their margins the vertical rows from which the panes for the booklets were printed.

The cylinders for printing the Silver Jubilee issue stamps in booklets comprised three panes side by side, each pane consisting of twenty horizontal rows of four images each. The first two vertical rows in each pane were upright, and the third and fourth inverted. The cylinder number, which was not preceded by a letter, only appeared on the left of the left-hand pane.

There are differences between the design of the stamps printed in sheets and those issued in booklets, and between the booklet panes with watermark upright and watermark inverted, which indicates that different multipositives are used. It is believed that this was caused by the designer, Mr Barnett Freedman, having multiplied his design on litho stones. The differences which, though marked, are small, are fully described in an article by Mr Harry Nissen in Volume XXXIII of the *British Philatelist* (December 1940 and January 1941).

CONTROLS AND PERFORATION

The system of having a control letter in the bottom margin of the sheet, which started with the One Penny value in 1884, and was followed by the Halfpenny in 1888 and subsequently by the Halfpenny and One Penny values (with a date figure added from 1904 onwards) of the Edward VII stamps, was continued for all values of the George V stamps up to the One Shilling, with the exception of the first issue of the Twopence. The last control of the Edward VII stamps – A11 – remained in use for the first issue of the Halfpenny and One Penny stamps of the new reign; and this was followed by B11, A12, B12, C12, B13, C13, C14, D14, E14, F15, G15, H16, I16, J17, K17, K18, L18, M18, M19, N19, O19, O20, P20, Q20, Q21, R21, S21, S22, T22, U22, U23, V23, W23, W24, A24, B24, C25, D25, E26, F26, G27, H27, I28, J28, K29, L29, M30, N30, O31, P31, Q32, R32, S33, T33, U34, V34, W35, X35, Y36, Z36, A37, B37, C38 and D38.

It will be noticed that in 1912, 1914 and from 1918 to 1924 inclusive there were three controls for each year, unlike the system which had prevailed during the previous reign, when each control covered a six-monthly period. The controls should be regarded as relating to issues, rather than printings, because frequently more than one printing from the same plate was made with the same control. This is obvious from cases in which printings from the same plate have the control in different positions, showing that the control piece was unscrewed from the plate and replaced in a different position for a subsequent printing either with the same, or another similar, control piece.

The types of letters and figures of the controls varied from time to time; and Somerset House controls had a period between the letter and the figures, whereas those of the contractors did not. One of the D.14 control pieces in use with Plate 1 of the Sixpence had a faulty period which appeared like a comma; and one of the Somerset House L.18 control pieces in use with Plate 4 had the period so faulty that it failed to print. The Somerset House controls A.11, B.11 and B.12 had bold letters and figures without serifs; but for controls A.12, B.13 and C.13 to T.33, when printings of the Sixpence at Somerset House ceased, the letters and figures were fine with serifs.

The Harrison controls for their 1911 contract, were tall without serifs from A11 to K18, but from L18 to W24 the letters and figures, which remained tall, had serifs. Under the Waterlow contract, the controls A24 to U34, and, under the provisional printing of the Harrison contract of 1934, the controls U34 to D38, had letters and figures which were short with serifs. Four controls existed in two widths as follows:

A11	Narrow – space between the figures measuring 1 mm
A11	Wide – space measuring	$1\frac{1}{2}$ mm
A.12	Narrow – overall measurement $11\frac{1}{2}$ mm
A.12	Wide – overall measurement	13 mm
B12	Narrow – overall measurement $14\frac{1}{2}$ mm
B12	Wide – overall measurement	$16\frac{1}{2}$ mm
Q21	Narrow – overall measurement $16\frac{1}{2}$ mm
Q21	Wide – overall measurement	$18\frac{1}{2}$ mm

Of these varying controls A11 and B12 only appeared on the Halfpenny and One Penny values. A.12 was used in two widths on the Threehalfpence and Threepence and with the narrow control on the Twopence Halfpenny. The Q21 in both widths was used on the Halfpenny, One Penny, Threehalfpence, Twopence and Tenpence; with the narrow type only on the Twopence Halfpenny, Threepence and Fourpence; and with the wide type only on the Fivepence. There was no printing of the Ninepence or One Shilling with control Q21.

For the first issue of the Twopence in orange-yellow the control was purposely omitted from all three plates used. In the case of the Halfpenny Die II with watermark Crown certain sheets printed from Plate 17 bore no control. This was an error. On one day the Inland Revenue Authorities forgot to screw in the control piece before printing began. Evidently this was soon noticed and the omission rectified before many sheets were printed. Consequently examples of this error are not common.

The control '18' alone, which occurred on the Threehalfpence, is

not an error in the omission of the letter 'K'. It was omitted purposely. In 1918 the Threehalfpence was printed from two plates
side by side simultaneously. At the beginning of the K18 period
Plates 2c,* 3b and 4b were still at press. In June of that year the
minimum inland letter rate was increased from 1d to 1½d and, in
preparation for the increased demand for the Threehalfpenny
stamp, it was decided to print that value in multiples of four plates
simultaneously. It was apparently intended to begin such printing
with four new plates 5, 6, 7 and 8; but at the time of going to press
Plate 8 was not ready, and Plate 2c was temporarily used in its
place. It was for Plate 2c only that the control '18' without letter
was used. It is presumed that this was done so that the sheets from
Plate 2c could be recognized. Its use thus was short-lived, because
Plate 8 was soon substituted; and this variety is rare.

The One Penny, also printed in 1918, is known with the control
'M' only and this somewhat distorted in position. It is believed
that this occurred through something having obscured or damaged
the '18' of the control piece during the printing of a few sheets.
This variety is of extreme rarity, only one or two examples having
been recorded.†

The controls in use with the photogravure stamps were U34,
V34, W35, X35, Y36, Z36 and A37. Of these control X35 with the
Ninepence is known quarter, half, three-quarter and wholly boxed
as is control Y36 on the Fourpence and Tenpence and control Z36
with the Fivepence and One Shilling values. Control Z36 on the
Threepence is known quarter and half boxed only.

The normal perforation of the George V surface-printed stamps
was 15 by 14, that is to say the horizontal rows had 15 holes and
the vertical rows 14 holes to every two mm. There were two excep- *cm.*
tions to this and one error. At least one machine used during the
first Harrison contract, between 1913 and 1915, had a pin setting
in the horizontal row of 14½ gauge. And in 1920 and 1921 the 15
by 14 machine used at Somerset House for the Sixpence was

---

* For the meaning of the letter following a plate number, see page 162.

† The halfpenny with K omitted from the K17 control, the Threehalfpence with
M omitted from the M19 control and the Threehalfpence with 23 omitted from the
V23 control are also known. See footnotes on pages 48 and 72.

temporarily superseded by a machine with 14 by 14 gauge. The error was the use of a machine with 14 by 14 gauge on a few sheets of the Halfpenny and One Penny stamps of 1911, Die 1A with watermark Crown. Examples of this are very rare, more especially in the case of the One Penny. Two unused examples of the Halfpenny are known to the Editors. Four unused copies of the One Penny are known, but no used copies. Proofs with this perforation are known. They differ in colour and texture from the issued stamps.

For normal perforation of the Post Office sheets comb-heads with six different pin settings were used. In the description of each type the long arm of the comb-head is regarded as horizontal with the perforation spurs rising at right angles to it. Most comb-heads had an extension spur, that is further pins in extension of the long arm at one or other end.

Type I

There was an extension spur on the left of the comb-head and a single extension pin on the right. This machine was set to perforate the unsevered width of the mill sheet, that is two Post Office sheets side by side, from bottom to top or top to bottom. The perforation spurs were of 17 pins. Three different lengths of extension spur are known, one of 15 pins, one of 12 pins and one of 9 pins. Control blocks with wide side margins exist showing part of the spur, the gap between the side perforation and the right of the extension spur being 14·1 and 17·1 mm respectively in the first two cases. No gap commensurate with the 9-pin extension spur machine has been found. It is, however, not known whether the 9-pin machine perforated the entire width of the mill sheet or only single Post Office sheets.

(a) When set to perforate from bottom to top the bottom margin would be imperforate, the top margin perforated through, the left margin perforated through and the right margin with a single extension hole.

(b) When set to perforate from top to bottom the bottom margin would be perforated through, the top margin imperforate, the left margin with a single extension hole and the right margin perforated through.

These machines had a very short life and were used at Somerset House and by Messrs Harrison only on some sheets of the Halfpenny and One Penny values printed from electros made from the first three master-plates (Dies 1A, 1B and 2).

Type II

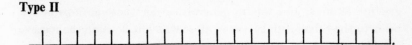

This machine also had an extension spur on the left and a single extension pin on the right, but differed from Type I by the perforation spurs only being of 14 pins. This machine was set to perforate the single sheets from side to side.

(a) When set to perforate from left to right the bottom margin would have a single extension hole, the top margin perforated through, the left margin imperforate and the right margin perforated through.

(b) When set to perforate from right to left, the bottom margin would be perforated through, the top margin with a single extension hole, the left margin perforated through and the right margin imperforate.

This machine was in general use throughout the period of the typographed stamps and was normally set to perforate from left to right, though no printings of the Ninepence with control E14 were perforated with this feed. When set to perforate from right to left its use was limited, but such use is known with all the Somerset House printings up to the end of 1913 with the exception of the Ninepence with control B.13 and the Sevenpence and Eightpence with control C.13. Beginning with the Sixpence D.14 right feed was the exception to the general rule and is only found with controls E.14, F.15, L.18, N.19, S.21 and T.22. Messrs Harrison used both feeds for all their printings, with the exception mentioned above. Messrs Waterlow used left feed on all printings, the use of right feed being exceptional and only known with the Halfpenny with controls A24, C25 and E26, the One Penny with control C25, Threehalfpence with controls F26 and I28, Twopence with control B24 and Threepence with control G27. The same machine was also in use by Messrs Harrison for their provisional printing of 1934 with left feed, the use of right feed being limited to the Halfpenny with control V34, the Sixpence with controls W35, X35, B37 and D38 and the One Shilling with control V34.

This machine was also in use on the introduction of the photogravure stamps, and was in general use for those stamps issued prior to the Silver Jubilee issue, after which it became the reserve machine and its use restricted to some printings of the Halfpenny with controls W35, X35 and Y36, the One Penny with controls X35 and Y36, the Threehalfpence with controls W35, X35, Y36 and Z36, the Twopence with controls W35 and Z36, the Twopence-halfpenny with controls W35 and Y36, the Threepence with controls W35, Y36 and Z36, the Fourpence with controls W35 and X35, the Fivepence with controls Y36 and Z36, single box, and the Tenpence with control Y36, single box. The 'no stop' pane was normally perforated from left to right and the 'stop' pane from right to left.

From time to time this machine had the single extension pin broken off, so that no single extension hole appeared in the left or bottom margin. This first occurred in the provisional Edward VII printings under control A11. Under subsequent controls it appeared as follows:

With control A.11. A few sheets of the One Penny Die 1A perforated at Somerset House.

With control A11. A few sheets of the Halfpenny and One Penny Die 1A and One Penny Die 1B perforated by Messrs Harrison.

With control C.13. Nearly all the Twopence and a few sheets of the Sixpence (reddish-purple) perforated at Somerset House.

With control C13. A few sheets of the Threehalfpence perforated by Messrs Harrison.

With control C14. A few sheets of the Twopence Halfpenny perforated by Messrs Harrison.

With control J17. A few sheets of the Threehalfpence and Fourpence perforated by Messrs Harrison.

With control A.24. Nearly all sheets of the Sixpence perforated at Somerset House.

With control B.24. All sheets of the Sixpence on script watermark paper and nearly all sheets on block watermark paper perforated at Somerset House.

With control B24. A few sheets of the Threehalfpence, Threepence and Fourpence perforated by Messrs Waterlow.

With control C.25. A few sheets of the Sixpence perforated at Somerset House.

With control E26. A few sheets of the One Penny and Fourpence perforated by Messrs Waterlow.

With control H27. A few sheets of the Halfpenny perforated by Messrs Waterlow.

There was also a pin breakage of the fifth pin of the extension spur, which also first appeared during the provisional Edward VII printing with control A11. Printings, all of which were perforated by Messrs Harrison with this variety, were as follows:

With control B11. A few sheets of the Halfpenny and One Penny Die 2.

With control B12. A few sheets of the One Penny printed on Basted Mills paper.

With control C13. A few sheets of the One Penny, Threehalfpence and Threepence (blue-violet).

With control F15. A few sheets of the Halfpenny.

With control G15. A few sheets of the Twopence and Fourpence.

With control P20. A few sheets of the Halfpenny.

Other pin breakages have been noted. These are the sixth pin (Twopence D14, Sevenpence G15), tenth pin (One Shilling J17, Threehalfpence Q20) and thirteenth pin (Halfpenny B11), but these were not common.

A machine, with the same pin setting, but in 14 by 14 gauge, was used only at Somerset House for some sheets of the Sixpence with controls Q.20 and R.21. The only other use of a perforator with 14 by 14 gauge was by Messrs Harrison on a very few sheets of the Halfpenny and One Penny Die 1A. As mentioned above, this was an error. Presumably Messrs Harrison inadvertently used one of the machines formerly used for the Edward VII stamps before the gauge was changed late in 1911, thus providing varieties of great rarity.

Type III

This machine had the extension spur on the right and the single extension hole on the left. It was set to perforate the sheets from side to side.

(*a*) When set to perforate from left to right, the bottom margin would be perforated through, the top margin with a single extension hole, the left margin imperforate and the right margin perforated through.

(*b*) When set to perforate from right to left, the bottom margin would be with a single extension hole, the top margin perforated through, the left margin perforated through and the right margin imperforate.

With left feed this machine was confined to sheets of the Twopence and Sixpence (dull-purple) at Somerset House with control C.13 and the Sixpence with controls I.28, J.28 and M.30; sheets perforated by Messrs Harrison of the Halfpenny and One Penny Die 1B with control A11 and the Halfpenny Die 2 with control B12 on Crown watermark paper; sheets perforated by Messrs Waterlow of the Halfpenny with controls A24, G27, H27 and L29, the One Penny with control A24, the Threehalfpence with control A24, the Twopence with control B24 and the Fivepence, Ninepence, Tenpence and One Shilling with control A24; and sheets perforated by Messrs Harrison during their provisional printing of the Halfpenny with control V34.

With right feed its use was extremely limited. It was in use for some sheets perforated at Somerset House of the Sixpence (dull purple) with control C.13, after which it was not used until 1935 for some sheets of the photogravure stamps of the Halfpenny cylinder 4 with control W35, Threepence cylinder 1 with control W35 and Twopence cylinder 10 with control Y36, in each case only from the stop pane. The only known example of the Half-penny is with the extension pin broken off.

Type IV

This machine only differed from Type II in that there were two extension pins instead of one. With left feed the bottom margin had two extension holes. This machine was used by Messrs Harrison during their provisional printings of 1934 and is known on the Halfpenny with control U34, and with control V34 on the Half-penny, One Penny, Threehalfpence, Twopence, Threepence, Four-pence, Fivepence, Ninepence and One Shilling, and with control W35 on the Sixpence.

This machine continued in use during the early photogravure period and its use is known with controls U34 and V34 on the Half-penny, One Penny and Threehalfpence, but not later than cylinders 4, 25 and 107 respectively.

All the above machines had single-row comb-heads.

Type V

This comb-head, which was not introduced until the photo-gravure period, was a single-row comb-head, set to perforate the undivided web from bottom to top. There were no extension spurs but at each end of the comb-head, on both 'no stop' and 'stop' sides, there was a single extension pin. The bottom margin was imperforate and the top margin perforated through. Both side margins on both 'no stop' and 'stop' panes had a single ex-tension hole.

Examples of the use of this machine were first found on the Threehalfpence stamps printed from cylinder 98 with control V34, but this was experimental. Its use prior to the Silver Jubilee issue is rare. Just before that issue one of the machines had a breakage of the single extension pin on the left of the 'no stop' pane. A unique example on the Threehalfpence cylinder 116 with control

W35 has been found without any extension hole in either left side or bottom margin.

For the Silver Jubilee issue some of these machines, including the machine with the broken extension pin, were adapted to the double width of the stamp by the removal of the middle legs. Later in this issue the broken pin was repaired. One extra machine was also brought into use which differed from the normal machines by having two extension pins on the left of the 'stop' side. It was only in use with the Threehalfpence stamps printed from cylinder 7, 'stop' pane. The extra pin was soon removed and examples of such perforation are rare.

After this issue these machines remained in general use for the normal stamps.

Type VI

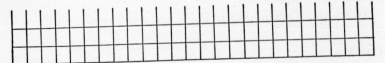

This machine was not introduced until the photogravure period and was a continuous web perforator with a triple-row comb-head. It was set to perforate the continuous web from top to bottom. The two outer ends of the comb-head were without extension pins, but the pins crossed the interpane gutter. On both panes the top and bottom margins were perforated through. On the 'no stop' pane the left margin was imperforate and the right margin perforated through. On the 'stop' pane the left margin was perforated through and the right margin was imperforate.

This machine was first used on Threehalfpence stamps printed from cylinders 46 and 47 with control V34, after which it was in supplementary use.

Sheets perforated thus with the bottom and left side margins perforated through can be distinguished from those perforated by the Type II machines by the irregularity of the pin setting.

This machine was later modified by the removal of the pins of the interpane gutter, with the exception of a single pin on the right of the 'no stop' pane and a similar pin on the left of the 'stop' pane. Such perforation was first found on the Threehalfpence cylinder 98 with control V34. It was also used for the Silver Jubilee issue.

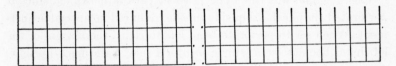

The perforators used for the British Empire Exhibition commemoratives were first a line machine which was only in use with the 1924 stamps. Later a comb machine was in use for both the 1924 and 1925 issues.

The following types were used for perforating sheets issued in booklet form.

Type B I

This machine was set to perforate the sheets from bottom to top or from top to bottom and had the perforation spurs specially adjusted to allow for the narrow bisecting gutter. There was a single extension pin at each end of the comb-head and also on each side of the bisecting gutter.

Booklet panes so perforated invariably have a single extension hole in the margin. This machine was used by Messrs Harrison for the Halfpenny and One Penny Die 1B, with both crown and script Cypher watermarks, also for the 1912 issue, and up to the latter part of 1918. Its use for the Threehalfpence is rare. It was never used on the Twopence stamps.

Type B II

This was similar to Type B I, but the perforation spurs were specially adjusted to the bisecting gutters of the Silver Jubilee issue. All booklet panes had a single extension hole in the margins.

Type B III

This machine was the Type II sheet perforator which, since it perforated the sheets from side to side, required no special adjustment. When set to perforate from left to right, the margin of the left-hand booklet pane (single printer's rule, watermark upright) was imperforate and all the other panes were perforated through. When set to perforate from right to left, the right-hand booklet pane (single rule, watermark inverted) was imperforate, and all the other panes perforated through.

This machine was in use by Messrs Harrison for printings of the Halfpenny and One Penny Die 1B, but only on paper with watermark Crown. It was the perforator in general use from the end of 1918 to 1924, both feeds being used. It was exclusively used by Messrs Waterlow and by Messrs Harrison in their 1934 contract. The use of right feed by Messrs Waterlow is rare; it is unknown for Messrs Harrison's provisional printing. When the photogravure stamps were introduced this machine was the reserve perforator, and its exceptional use was rare. The 'no stop' pane was invariably perforated from left to right and the 'stop' pane from right to left.

Both these machines had single-row comb-heads.

Type B IV

A new machine was introduced on the issue of the photogravure stamps. It was set to perforate the whole width of the web from bottom to top. There was a single extension pin on the outer ends of the comb-head, but there were no extension pins in the interpane gutter. The pins were continuous across the bisecting gutters. On the 'no stop' pane the left-hand booklet pane had a single extension hole in the margin and on the right-hand pane the margin was imperforate, both bisecting gutter panes being perforated through. On the 'stop' pane the left-hand booklet pane was imperforate and on the right-hand pane the margin was imperforate, both bisecting gutter panes being perforated through.

In June 1936, one of these machines was modified by the introduction of a single extension pin on both sides of the interpane gutter. The perforation only differed in that the right-hand booklet

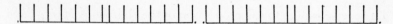

pane of the 'no stop' pane and the left-hand pane of the 'stop' pane both had single extension holes.

On the issue of stamps in coils no special perforators were necessary since the coils were made up of strips from Post Office sheets joined together. However in 1921, when experiments were carried out at Somerset House, and later, during the Waterlow and subsequent contracts, coils were produced by reel printing, and some form of continuous perforator was required to perforate the continuous web. Little is known about the early machines, but it is

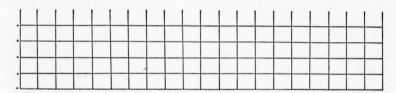

known that during the photogravure period they had five-row comb-heads for perforating the sideways coils.

Chapter Two

The Halfpenny

THE steps leading to the production of the Halfpenny stamp have been referred to in Chapter I. The frame was designed by Sir Bertram Mackennal, the lettering by Mr Eve and the head was taken from a photograph by Messrs W. and D. Downey.

The die existed in three states. Stamps printed from plates made from each of the three states of the die can be recognized as follows:

Original Die (known as Die IA)

The left of the bottom ornament below the oval has two thin curved vertical lines; and the three upper scales of the right-hand dolphin form a complete triangle. The snout of this dolphin is just clear of the horizontal line below it. The fronts of both dolphins' heads are shaded by only a single line.

Deepened Die (known as Die IB)

The bottom ornament and right-hand dolphin remained unchanged, except that the upper of the three top scales is broken and the three do not form a complete triangle.

Redrawn Die (known as Die II)

The left of the bottom ornament has only one curved vertical line, which is thick. Further shading has been added to the front of both dolphins' heads and the snout of the right-hand dolphin runs into the horizontal line below it.

DIE IA

Colour trials are known in nine shades of green taken from the Mackennal sketch die with the Downey head inserted.* This die

---

* For a full list of the colours used in the extensive series of essays for colours, together with their official notations, see Appendix D, page 212.

can be recognized by its coarseness and by the fact that the dolphins' snouts are much longer than in the issued stamp. One of these colour trials is known endorsed 'Specimen for colour for George V unified stamp' and is initialled by Mr Seymour Bennett, the then Inspector of Stamping at Somerset House.

Die proofs of the Die IA frame with the Downey head, but without value, are known in three colours, with the figure '2' above the image, and die proofs in varying stages of adding the value are known in black and green.

The die after approval was numbered '5A', and proofs are known in three colours, one of which bears the endorsement 'From Mint. 7 Apr. 1911'. The first master plate was struck from this die.

Imperforate plate proofs were taken in green on thin card, on unwatermarked glazed paper in black and on paper watermarked Crown in green. Perforated stamps are known overprinted 'Specimen'.

The stamps from Die IA were issued on Coronation Day, June 22, 1911, on Crown watermark paper, in shades of green, pale green, dark green, bright green (yellow tone), yellowish-green, pale yellow-green, intense green and bluish green, although actually variations in the green colour were not great. Printing was done by Messrs Harrison with control A11, both wide and narrow types, but the narrow control is known only with some printings from one plate, and it is rare. Sheets are known with watermark inverted, owing to error of feeding into the press. Six plates (electros), from the first master-plate, can be identified by lack of marking or marks in the marginal rules to the right of the 17th, 18th, 19th and 20th rows. None of the plates concerned were printed from at Somerset House. Copies with the very rare 14×14 perforation are known, used from Brighton (9/8/11), Crowborough (14/8/11), Great Yarmouth (18/8/11), Gorleston (21/8/11), Caister-on-Sea (30/8/11) and Middlesborough (25/8/11). Two unused copies have been recorded. Some proofs on thick paper were also perforated with this comb. The colour of these differs from that of the issued stamps.

DIE IB

The die in its original state was considered unsatisfactory. It was therefore deepened, and a second master-plate therefrom was made. There is a proof of this die in green. Twelve plates (electros) from the deepened die (Die IB) have been identified, which can be recognized by cuts, etc. in various lines of the marginal rule. Printing from the new plates was done later in 1911, with control A11, both wide and narrow, on Crown watermark paper, in shades of green, pale yellow-green, bright green (yellow tone), deep yellow-green, dull green, deep bright green, dark green, intense green, bluish-green and blue-green. The variations in colour and shade are much more marked than in the case of the stamps from Die IA, and there is a very rare variety in dark green printed in booklet form in experimental colour varnish or varnished ink, which caused the printed portions of the stamps to shine or glisten. Similar ink was used experimentally for the One Penny Dies IA and III, the Fivepence with control H16 and the Shilling with controls G15 and I16. Sheets are known with watermark inverted, owing to error in feeding into the press. On one plate there is a variety on the third stamp in the bottom row of the sheet which shows the 'F' and 'P' of 'Halfpenny' joined at the top; and there was a small printing on paper with thick yellowish gum. Copies exist overprinted 'Cancelled'. There was also a printing on William Joynson paper with 'Simple' Cypher watermark, but this was only from electros made for printing sheets for issue in booklet form.

Among the plate flaws which have been recorded is one appearing on the second stamp of the bottom row of Plate 3. Shortly after the plate had been put to press it sustained damage which is clearly evident at the adjacent ends of the marginal rules below the second and third stamps. At the same time there was a fine split in the plate surfacing which showed as a thin white line running down slightly diagonally from the left bottom of the central ornament at the bottom, through the 'F' of Halfpenny and the base line of the stamp. This flaw was never repaired. Early printings without the flaw are easily recognized, because the control piece, A11 wide, is very distinctive, having the first figure 1 not only shorter, but also higher than the second.

DIE II

The die in its deepened state was still considered unsatisfactory and steps were taken to improve it. The Downey head was redrawn. A die proof of the original head is known dated 3.10.11, upon which a cut-down proof of the redrawn head was pasted. This proof is endorsed 'Old die' and 'Altered die' opposite these heads respectively.

Die proofs of the improved frame, with or without the insertion of the altered die (Die II) head, were taken in three colours. In this design the right-hand dolphin's snout runs into the horizontal line below it, as in Die II, but the left of the lower ornament was still with two fine curved lines of shading and the front of the dolphins' heads with a single line of shading, as in Die I. This die, which was known as the 'Amended die', was never used for striking leads, though it was used for colour trials.

Die proofs in black similar to the above are also known, but the left of the lower ornament has one thick line of shading.

Finally, further die proofs are known in black with the shading added to the front of the dolphins' heads. This die is known as the 'Modified die' and is very similar to the approved die for Die II. A copy of Die II is known cut down and pasted on card endorsed 'Die used for making leads for Master Plate. 7th Dec. 1911.', though this die must have been completed before this date. This master plate was the third master plate from which the Die II electros were made.

Colour trials were made from proofs, taken from both the Amended and Modified dies, on October 20 and November 13, 1911. They were in several colours, probably ten in all, and were on paper either unwatermarked or watermarked Crown, either upright or sideways.

Imperforate plate proofs were taken in green upon paper watermarked Crown, either upright or sideways. Perforated stamps are known overprinted 'Specimen' in upright type measuring $12\frac{1}{2}$ mm; and 'Cancelled', also in upright type measuring 15 mm; a sheet of the first is known with the control B12 narrow. Twenty-four plates have been identified.

Stamps from the redrawn die (Die II) were issued on January 1, 1912, on paper with watermark Crown, with control B11, in green, pale green and pale yellowish-green; with control B12, narrow, in green, pale green and bright green; and with control B12, wide, in green and bright green. There were also deep green, dark green, blue-green and intense green shades. Seventeen plates have been identified as put to press on this paper. Copies are known with watermark inverted, owing to an error in feeding sheets into the press. There was a small printing on paper which had thick yellowish gum. A small printing was made from Plate 17, from which the control piece (B12) was omitted in error. There was a variety which occurred on some electros in which the cross at the top of the Crown surmounting the stamp failed to print, or only printed partially. This was probably due to the nickel surface of the plate flaking off at the point concerned.

In August 1912 the stamps appeared printed upon William Joynson paper with the 'Simple' Cypher watermark, although, from a study of the plates put to press, it would seem that this paper was not used until after printing had taken place upon the Basted Mills paper with 'Multiple' Cypher watermark. Controls B12, both wide and narrow, and B13 were used. The stamps are known overprinted 'Specimen' ($12\frac{1}{2}$ mm) and 'Cancelled' (15 mm), a sheet of the former being known with Control B12 narrow.

The shades with control B12 were green, pale green, yellowish-green, dark green and deep green. Those with control B13 were green and bright green. Nineteen plates have been identified as put to press on this paper. The watermark was normally Type I; but with control B13 Type II is found, but rarely. Sheets are known with the watermark inverted, reversed or inverted and reversed. The variety 'No Cross on Crown' occurs also in this printing.

In October 1912 the stamps appeared on Basted Mills paper with 'Multiple' script Cypher watermark, with Control B12, both wide and narrow, in green, pale green, yellowish-green, pale yellowish-green and dark green. Eight plates have been identified as put to press on this paper. Sheets are known with the watermark inverted, reversed or inverted and reversed. The variety 'No Cross on Crown' appears also in this printing. Some sheets were issued imperforate in error.

At least one plate (Plate 9) was put to press at Somerset House on the Basted Mills paper with the 'Multiple' script Cypher water-mark. The control was B.12 in two slightly differing types. The colour was distinct shades of yellow-green and blue-green. Examples of this control with the 'Multiple' Cypher watermark are very rare.*

ISSUES OF 1912-23

The Die II stamps were still considered to be unsatisfactory, and an entirely new stamp (Die III) was made, based upon a design of both frame and profile head prepared by Sir Bertram Mackennal.

Die proofs in black, green and red, either on glazed card, unwatermarked paper or paper watermarked Crown, are known in varying stages of completion.

A Die III proof in the approved state is known in black dated 8.10.12. This die was numbered '31A'. A proof of this die is also known endorsed 'Die proof – New Design. See my Report 6 Nov. 1912', which was initialled by Mr Seymour Bennett.

The differentiation and grading of the colours and shades of the Halfpenny Die III, both by natural light and under the lamp, is a fascinating study. During the war period 1914-18, when the printers were making experiments to overcome difficulties, some of the colours and shades produced are no doubt rare, and some are very rare. Certain dyes, which had previously been obtained from Germany, were no longer available and under date 1916 there were three colour trials, which were perforated and overprinted 'Cancelled', of an experimental nature in connection with the use of British dyes manufactured by The Imperial Chemical Dyestuffs Group in an admixture of yellow lake and Prussian blue. Some of the experiments made to resolve these problems resulted in some

---

* In the Brocklehurst collection there was a strip with this control with side and bottom margins perforated through, and another showing the side margin imperforate and bottom margin with a single extension hole. The latter was badly misplaced. The type of the perforating machine was the same. The first example was fed right side first and the second left side first.

extraordinary colours and shades, and in phenomena of a remarkable character emanating from certain stamps under the quartz lamp. These are referred to hereafter under their respective values.*

Stamps of Die III are known with 'Specimen' overprint measuring 12½ mm, both imperforate and perforated (controls B.13 and C13); and with 'Cancelled' overprint measuring 15 mm, all perforated, with controls D14 (from Plate 2b) and E14 (from Plate 14b). A small portion of a sheet from Plate 21b, with control G15, was doubly printed.

The fourth master-plate was struck from Die III, and stamps in the new design, printed on William Joynson paper, with watermark 'Simple' Cypher, were issued on January 31, 1913. The colours of the stamps issued between 1912 and 1923 vary greatly and the shades are innumerable. They can be classified as follows:

Basic Colours	Shades	Remarks
Green		
	Pale	Various Controls 1913-23
	Dark	
	Dull	
	Deep	
	Bright	
Yellow-green		
	Bright	Controls D14, G15, etc.
		Highly fluorescent, Control D14
	Paler	
	('Cyprus green')	Slightly fluorescent, Control D14
	Bright	Not fluorescent
	Pale	Not fluorescent
Blue-green		
	Deep	Controls B.13, G15, H16, L18, etc.
	Dull	

* An explanation of the phenomena, that is to say altered reflected colour, Flash-up and Fluorescence, seen when stamps are viewed under the quartz lamp, appears in Appendix C, page 207.

Basic Colours	Shades	Remarks
Grey-green	Dull	
Apple-green		Control G15
Olive-green	Pale	Control H16. Three distinct
	Deep	shades. Under lamp all
		appear dark mahogany
Pale dull olive-green		Booklet (probably 1916).
		Not mahogany under
		lamp
Dark sage-green or		
'myrtle-green'		Control M18

There are many variations in most of the colours and shades
listed above. The 'Cyprus green' listed under S.G. 355 is actually
rather pale yellowish green.† These stamps show a slight fluorescent emission under the quartz lamp, that is to say, a radiant
greenish-yellow colour, indicating the presence of fluorescin dye
mixed with the pigment. This emission has not the brilliant golden
effect of a copy belonging to one of the Editors, the natural colour
of which is deeper yellowish green. Some specimens with control
G15 resemble the 'Cyprus green', but they do not fluoresce.

It was stated by the late Mr Ewen, who discovered this 'Cyprus
green' colour, that it only occurred on one sheet in a batch which
he had purchased, and that the sheet below was of a colour intermediate between 'Cyprus green' and the colour of all the remainder
of the sheets in that batch. He considered this to be due to the in-
sufficient mixing of the ink in the wells. It seems probable that
fluorescin dye rose to the surface so that the first sheet thus printed
was the brightest and had the most brilliant fluorescent emission,
the second sheet being less bright with a less brilliant fluorescence,
and so on as the inking rollers mixed the ink in the wells. The
Editors have no record of any used copies of this variety. It is
probable that no stamp from Mr Ewen's sheet was ever used
postally.

† This description is an attempt to convey the impression created by specimens
in the possession of Mr Robson Lowe, of Messrs Wingfield and Co., and in the collection of Mr H. C. V. Adams (obtained from Mr Charles Nissen), all probably from
the same sheet.

The three types of 'Simple' Cypher watermark were respectively in use during the various control periods as follows: B.13 Types I and II (small printing); C13 Types I and II; C14 Types I (small printing) and II; D14 Types I (very small printing) and II; E14, F15, G15, H16, I16 Type II; J17 Types II and III; K17* Types II (small printing) and III; K18 Types II (small printing) and III; L18, M18, M19 Type III; N19 Types II (small printing) and III; O19 Type II (small printing) and III; O20 Types II and III; P20 Types II (small printing) and III; Q20 Type III; Q21 (wide), Q21 (narrow), R21 Types II and III; S21, S22 Type III; T22, U22, U23, V23, W23 Types II and III; W24 Type II.

Errors of watermark, owing to sheets being fed incorrectly into the press, were as follows:

Watermark Inverted with controls B.13, C13, C14, E14, F15, G15, H16, I16, J17, K17, K18, L18, M18, M19, N19, O19, O20, P20, Q20, Q21, R21, S21, T22, U23, V23, W23, W24.

Watermark Reversed with controls B.13, C13, C14, F15, G15, H16, J17, K17, L18, M19, P20, S21, T22.

Watermark Inverted and Reversed with controls B.13, C13, C14, D14, E14, F15, G15, H16, I16, J17, K17, K18, L18, M18, M19, N19, O19, O20, P20, Q20, Q21, R21, S22, T22, U22, U23, V23. Eighty-three plates, made from the fourth master-plate, and used for printing the Die III stamps, have been identified. They can all be differentiated by cuts, dots, etc. in the marginal lines of rule. They were all put to press on William Joynson paper with 'Simple' Cypher watermark.

Among the plate flaws which have been recorded is one appearing on the twelfth stamp of the nineteenth row of Plate 16. This plate had been at press with controls E14, F15 and the early printings with G15 without the flaw, which is progressive. It developed on later printings with G15 and appeared like a white letter J lying on its side, hook downwards, to the right of the 'Y' of 'Halfpenny' in later G15 printings. Later it appeared like the letter O, and finally the coloured centre wore away leaving a large white blot, all with

* One instance is known with J17 control in which the J of the control failed to print, as did a portion of the bottom frame of the stamp above the control. The plate is 34, which establishes that the missing letter could not have been K.

control G15. Printings with control H16 showed the flaw in its final stage, after which the plate was taken from press. Printings without the flaw may be recognized, *inter alia*, by the dot under the 'PE' of 'Halfpenny' in the rule below the second stamp.

As above-mentioned, there was a very small printing with control C13 upon the Basted Mills paper with the 'Multiple' script Cypher watermark. The plate or plates used for this are not known. The colour was green. The printing was originally intended only to provide stamps for issue in coils; but actually a very few complete sheets were issued under circumstances which are unknown. Blocks and horizontal strips or pairs are very scarce. Inverted watermarks, due to error of feeding, are known.

THE WATERLOW PRINTINGS AND HARRISON (PROVISIONAL) PRINTINGS OF 1924-34

Perforated stamps are known overprinted 'Specimen' in sloping type.

The following is a list of the Waterlow Controls, with colours, which appeared first in April 1924:

A24 green, B24 green, bright green, C25 and D25 bright green, E26 bright green, pale green, G27 bright green, H27 bright green, green, pale green, I28 bright green, J28 bright green, green, K29 bright green, L29 bright green, green, M30 and N30 bright green and paler shade, O31 pale shade of bright green, P31 and Q32 green, bright green and paler shade, R32 bright green, S33, T33 and U34 bright green with a paler shade. Controls A24, B24, C25, F26, G27, H27 and L29 exist with perforated, as well as imperforate, bottom margins. All these controls, except A24, with perforated margins are scarce.

The Harrison provisional printing (prior to production of the stamps by the rotary photogravure process) under their 1934 contract was as follows:

U34 green, but less bright than the Waterlow shade, V34 bright green.

Sheets with controls A24, B24, C25, D25, E26, F26, G27, H27, I28, J28, K29, L29, M30, N30, O31, R32, T33, U34 and V34 are known with watermark inverted. Part of a sheet under the Harrison provisional printing with control U34, from Plate 32, was doubly printed. Thirty-three plates made from the fifth masterplate, and used for the 1924-34 issues, have been identified. They were put to press at first with 'Multiple' block Cypher watermark, on Samuel Jones paper, and later on John Allen paper, in the same manner as the plates, paper and controls were used during the first Harrison contract.

POSTAL UNION CONGRESS

For the Postal Union Congress issue of May 10, 1929, the stamps were designed by Mr J. W. Farleigh, and were printed by Messrs Waterlow on Samuel Jones paper with 'Multiple' block Cypher watermark. Die proofs in black on glazed card are known. The colour was green and the stamps were issued under controls K29 and L29. Eight plates, made from the sixth master-plate, have been identified, and printings were made from all except Plate 8 with both the controls. Sheets with controls K29 and L29 are known with watermark inverted. Control blocks with this variety are very rare.

THE PHOTOGRAVURE STAMPS 1934-36

On November 19, 1934, the Halfpenny stamp produced by a rotary photogravure process was first issued. The designs differed materially from those of the previous issue, and the backgrounds to the heads in the ovals appeared solid. The colour was described officially as 'dark green', but by the Printers as 'Russian Green'. The controls and cylinder numbers were as follows:

V34 cylinders 3 and 4; W35 cylinders 4, 11, 13, 18, 22, 24, 25, 27; X35 cylinders 30, 31, 32, 36, 39, 40, 41, 42; Y36 cylinders 39, 41, 42, 44, 45, 48, 49; Z36 cylinder 48. Printings from cylinder 24 are known only from the 'stop' pane. They are rare.

Printings from the stop pane of cylinder 25 with control W35 with left and bottom margins perforated through are rare. Printings from the stop pane of cylinder 4 with left margin perforated through and bottom margin imperforate exist perforated by the

Type III comb-head with right feed with the extension pin broken off. The example known is believed to be unique.

The V34 control was opposite the left of the 19th row, and controls W35 onwards were opposite the left of the 18th row. Cylinder numbers 3 and 4 were engraved opposite the left of the 20th row, but cylinder numbers 11 onwards were opposite the 18th row.

The Halfpenny stamp, which was not issued until November 19, 1934, was not produced in the large size. Cylinders 3 and 4 were etched in the intermediate size, and cylinder 11 onwards in the small size.

On cylinder 36 of the Halfpenny, with Control X35, the twelfth stamp in the first row shows the 'Horns' variety, which was constant. To the left of the 'P' of 'Postage' there are two short strokes (instead of one) which bifurcate upwards at an angle, near the end of the scroll enclosing 'Postage'. The Halfpenny stamp is known on double paper, where a join occurred in the roll.

SILVER JUBILEE

The stamps issued on March 7, 1935, to celebrate the Silver Jubilee of the King's reign included the Halfpenny value.

Three sets of imperforate essays for the Halfpenny, One Penny, Threehalfpence and Twopence Halfpenny are known, number 1 being an upright rectangular design and numbers 2 and 3 oblong. Numbers 1 and 2 had the King's head three-quarter face and number 3 in profile. Number 3 was selected. The colours were as for the issued stamps, except that the Twopence Halfpenny in so-called 'Prussian Blue' was also submitted as an alternative for the blue colour of the normal issue. They were designed by Mr Barnett Freedman and printed by Messrs Harrison by means of the photogravure process on paper with the 'Multiple' block cypher watermark, and perforated 15 × 14. The control in every case was W35. Although the issue was not made officially until May 7, copies are known postmarked May 6, and a few even on May 4.

The cylinder numbers for the Halfpenny were 18, 20, 47, 55, 60, 61 and 62. Printings from cylinder 20 are rare and those from cylinder 62 are scarce.

PLATE II

Essays for the Silver Jubilee Commemorative issue of 1935 by Barnett Freedman.

Both the oblong (1) and upright (2) format were submitted with a three-quarters face, head and shoulders, but these were not adopted. (3) with profile head, was accepted.

These essays are in the Royal Collection, and are reproduced by gracious permission of Her Majesty.

1

2

3

PLATE II

Chapter Three

One Penny

THE frame design was that of Sir Bertram Mackennal, and the head was taken from a photograph by Messrs W. and D. Downey. As in the case of the Halfpenny, there were three states of the die. Stamps from the plates prepared from each are identifiable as follows:

Original Die (known as Die IA)

The lion is only partially shaded; the second line of shading on the ribbon to the right of the Crown extends completely across it; and the right-hand full leaf below the centre ribbon has three distinct lines of shading.

Deepened Die (known as Die IB)

There was no change in the shading of the lion; no complete line crosses the ribbon to the right of the Crown; and the right-hand full leaf has only one distinct line of shading.

Redrawn Die (known as Die II)

The lion is completely shaded.

DIE IA

Colour trials are known, in eleven shades of red, taken from the Mackennal sketch die with the Downey head inserted. This die can be recognized by its coarseness and the irregularity of the lines of shading of the frame.

The die, after approval, was numbered '6B', and proofs are known in black and red, one of which, on watermarked paper, was pasted upon card endorsed 'Crown watermark. From Mint 7 Apr. 1911'. A further proof in red is known cut down, pasted on card endorsed 'Specimen for colour of George V 1d unified stamp' and initialled by Mr Seymour Bennett. Imperforate plate proofs are known in red, and perforated stamps overprinted 'Specimen' exist.

The stamps, on R. D. Turner paper with Crown watermark, were issued on Coronation Day, June 22, 1911. The Somerset House printings, with control A.11, were in carmine. The Harrison prints, with control A11, were in pale rose-red, rose-red, deep rose-red, bright rose-red, intense rose-red, pale misty rose-pink, rose-pink, deep rose-pink and carmine. The last, which appeared only with the narrow type of control, is rare, especially with perforated bottom margin. Examples are known printed in the experimental varnished ink or colour varnish, referred to in Chapter II. Similar ink was used for the Halfpenny Die IB, One Penny Die III, Five-pence (control H16) and One Shilling (controls G15 and I16). Presumably this was the result of experiments which were numerous during the period concerned. (See correspondence on the subject in the *London Philatelist* of July 1943.) A flaw occurred on the first stamp of the sixteenth row on Plate 4, the right-hand *fleur-de-lys* failing to print and appearing as a large white mark.

The 'No Cross on Crown' variety is known in this issue, but it is rare. Copies perforated in error with a 14 × 14 gauge comb are of great rarity, but four unused examples are known. The Editors have no record of any used copy. Some proofs on rather thick paper were perforated with this comb.

Thirteen plates (electros) made from the first master-plate from Die IA have been identified by dots, cuts, etc. in the lines of marginal rule. It has only been possible to identify two of the plates printed at Somerset House with control A.11. Messrs Harrison used both the wide and narrow types of control A11, and all the plates can be identified with the wide type. But the narrow type is rare in this issue, especially with perforated bottom margin, and only three plates can be identified with this.

There was an experimental printing on coated paper. The Postmaster General had enquired if paper similar to the 'Austrian chalk-surfaced' could be used. The method of coating this paper was entirely different from that employed by Messrs De La Rue for some of the Edward VII stamps. Under the quartz lamp it shows the same greenish-yellow colour as that of the Edward VII Sixpence 'Magenta on chalky' printed at Somerset House, and of some of the later imperforate proofs of the George V Penny from Die IB, though the coating of the latter is heavier than that of the Sixpence 'Magenta'. The Head of the Stamping Department at Somerset House (Mr Seymour Bennett) took some sheets of plain paper, with Crown watermark, which had been specially coated, and an experimental printing was made on these,* but the coating was so thick that the watermark was invisible. The late Mr Charles Nissen saw sheets, or part sheets, of this printing, all with Somerset House control A.11. Each was marked in manuscript A.B.C. or D. Printing took place from Plate 10. Later, several types of paper made in Austria were obtained, and experimental printings were made upon them from plates from the third master-plate (Die II), as recorded later.

Owing to public disapproval of the Die IA stamps, suggestions for improvement were sent by Messrs Harrison to the Inland Revenue, with stamps pasted on a card, as follows:

(a) As designed, but with diagonal shading to the background of the head.

(b) As designed, but with a white background to the head.

(c) Frame as designed, but with a full-face portrait on a dark background.

This card, which was illustrated in the *British Philatelist*, was signed by Sir Cecil Harrison, but none of the suggestions was adopted.

DIE IB

The Die was deepened and a second master-plate was struck. There is a Die Proof on paper with Crown watermark in the colour adopted; and Plate Proofs in the adopted colour. These latter are on heavily coated paper without watermark, but gummed. Under

---

* One of the Editors has a control block (A.11) of this variety from the Brocklehurst Collection, and there was another similar block in the Per Gjerding Collection, which was acquired by Chas. Nissen & Co. Ltd.

PLATE III

1   Halfpenny Mackennal sketch die.

2   Halfpenny die proof (almost similar to Die 1A) without value.

3   Eve's Lion Couchant essay for the One Penny.

4   One Penny Mackennal sketch die.

5   The Mackennal Plaster Cast in which form the design for the profile issue One Penny of 1912 was approved by King George V.

6   One Penny die proof (almost similar to Die 2) without head or value.

1

2

3

4

5

6

PLATE III

the lamp this paper shows the same greenish-yellow reflection as that of the Edward Sixpence 'Magenta' and that of the experimental printing of Die IA stamps referred to above.

The stamps from the deepened die (Die IB) were issued on R. D. Turner paper with watermark Crown later in 1911. The Somerset House printings with control A.11 were in shades of carmine. The Harrison prints with control A11 (wide and narrow) were in pale carmine, carmine, pale rose-red, rose-red, bright rose-red, pale misty rose-pink, pale crimson, crimson and deep crimson. The wide control is scarce and, with perforated bottom margin, rare. The stamps were also issued in scarlet, but only in booklets. The so-called 'aniline scarlet', listed as S.G. 333, can be identified by the fact that, under the lamp, it is fluorescent and appears as bright yellow on bluish paper. It is scarce. Of all identifiable stamps issued as Post Office Sheets examined by the Editors under the lamp, those which were printed at Somerset House give a plum colour reflection, and those printed by Harrison appear pinkish, with a greater or lesser degree of flash-up. This feature is referred to in Chapter XVI in connection with the Die IB stamps issued in booklet form.

Sometimes sheets printed at Somerset House with wide bottom margins have one or two red lines printed horizontally across the margins.

The 'No Cross on Crown' variety occurs also in this printing; and there was a small printing upon paper with thick yellowish gum.

Fifteen plates from the second master-plate (from Die IB) can be identified by marginal markings, of which three can be identified as having been printed at Somerset House. Plate 9 had scoops, without dots therein, cutting the 47th and 48th pillars between the panes. All the plates were used by Messrs Harrison with control A11, narrow type; only three plates have been identified as having been used with the wide type of control.

A printing was made on William Joynson paper with 'Simple' Cypher watermark, but only from booklet plates.

Although it cannot be classed as a plate flaw, a variety occurs on printings from Plate 2. In the margin below the right of the twelfth stamp in the bottom row appears a mark resembling the figure 4 reversed. Printings of this are known with two different A11 control pieces, both narrow, and the variety is constant on all printings.

DIE II

Die IB was still considered unsatisfactory and steps were taken to improve it. The Downey head was redrawn and was used with a new die, which was numbered '42A', without value and very similar to the original die, but, whereas in that die the second line of shading of the upper right-hand ribbon extended across it, it was the third line which extended thus in the new die.

A plate proof of Die IB in red is known upon which new lines of shading on the lion's body were painted in in magenta.

Colour trials were taken from two further dies, which were known respectively as the 'Amended die' and the 'Modified die'. There was little difference between these. In the former only the second line of shading of the right-hand upper ribbon is complete, but in the latter both the second and fourth lines are complete. The Amended die is very similar to the approved die, but has more shading in the foliage of the surround.

Colour trials in blue geranium were taken from the Modified die on October 20, 1911, and in the approved colour and Royal Scarlet from the Amended die on October 24 and November 29, 1911, respectively.

Die proofs of a further die are known in black and stone, in varying stages of completion of the lion's body, the lines of which differed from those of the accepted die. In each case there was a white patch on the lion's haunches. This die was not adopted.

Further progressive die proofs, with and without value, and also in varying stages of completion of the lion's body, are known. This die was accepted as Die II. Colour trials were taken from this in red-maroon, pink, yellow, blue, crimson and in the accepted colour for the Die IB stamps. A proof of the latter was endorsed 'This is the colour used at Somerset House for printing the present issue of 1d unified stamps. M.B. 23201', and was initialled by Mr Seymour

Bennett under date November 24, 1911. Eighteen electros have been identified.

The Die II stamps were issued on January 1, 1912, on R.D. Turner paper with watermark Crown in the following shades according to controls:

Somerset House printings under control B.11 and B.12, scarlet and pale scarlet.

Harrison printings under control B11, bright scarlet, scarlet, pale scarlet and intense scarlet; under control B12, scarlet, deep rose-scarlet, bright rose-scarlet, pale rose-scarlet, geranium and shades of 'aniline' scarlet and bright 'aniline' scarlet.

There is also a rare outstanding shade of bright scarlet-vermilion, with orange tone, under controls B11 and B12. The B11 control in this shade is abnormal in that the first figure '1' is much shorter than the other and has hardly any serif (Plate 1). The two 'aniline' scarlet shades were printed in ink which fluoresces with a true golden emission. The scarlet stamps, but not those printed in rose-scarlet or intense scarlet, were printed in ink which fluoresces only slightly with a brown emission. Many of the stamps of this issue fluoresce to some degree under the lamp.

At least one sheet with control B12, narrow type, was over-printed 'Specimen'. Sheets are known with watermark inverted. The 'No Cross on Crown' variety occurs in this printing. There was a small printing on paper with thick yellowish gum. Sixteen plates have been identified as put to press on this paper.

Among the plate flaws which have been recorded is one appearing on the tenth stamp in the bottom row of Plate 5. This plate was one of those originally put to press with control B11, and later in this period a coloured blot developed on the 'O' of 'One', which also appeared with control B12 narrow. This plate had a short life and was not at press after the later period on Crown paper.

In August 1912 the stamps appeared on William Joynson paper, with watermark 'Simple' script cypher, although these were prob-ably printed after those on Basted Mills paper. The controls were B12, wide type only, and B13, both printings sometimes having a horizontal line along the bottom margin. The shades were palish scarlet, and with the B13 control there was a pinkish-scarlet shade. There was also a rare outstanding shade of bright scarlet-vermilion with orange tone. The paper had watermark Type I only. Stamps are known overprinted 'Cancelled'. The 'No Cross on Crown' variety is known; and varieties of watermark inverted, reversed and inverted and reversed. Seven plates have been identified as put to press on this paper.*

In October 1912 the stamps appeared on Basted Mills paper with watermark 'Multiple' script Cypher under control B12, wide type only, in palish scarlet, pinkish-scarlet and red. Four electros have been identified as having been put to press on this paper. Some of the stamps were printed in ink which fluoresces under the lamp. A very small printing was made also at Somerset House with control B.12. The 'No Cross on Crown' variety is known; and watermarks inverted, reversed and inverted and reversed. Some sheets are known with watermarks sideways. The explanation of this is not known, but the stamps may have been printed on paper intended for National Health Insurance stamps, which could account for this variety. They cannot have been printed on 'Currency' paper (which, however, was subsequently used for a proof from the fourth master-plate or for use in coils) because the texture of this paper is quite different. Copies with the control (B12) are very rare. Some sheets were issued imperforate by mistake.

During this period many experimental printings were made on various papers. These were as follows, all the specimens concerned being imperforate:

A. Printed at Somerset House or by Messrs Harrison in sheets of 240 or 480.

(a) On the Austrian coated paper in carmine and scarlet. The effect of viewing the scarlet stamps under the lamp is extraordinary. The ink appears so brilliant that the white paper

---

* One of the Editors has a block with B12 control on which the watermark is reversed and widely displaced. The cyphers are wide in the right margin and on the right of the stamps in the 12th vertical row. On the left of the 11th and 12th vertical rows the watermark is 'POSTAGE' reading downwards. In the 10th row it reads upwards, and the 10th row is only just touched by the cyphers.

of the stamp is made to appear black, giving the impression of the stamp having been turned into a negative.

(b) On John Dickinson paper – extra superfine rag paper – in carmine.

(c) On John Allen (Ivybridge) paper.

  (i) On very thin special paper, in carmine, endorsed 'C 54299, special stamp paper'.

  (ii) On cream wove litho paper, plate-glazed one side, in carmine, endorsed '54 cream wove litho-Plate-glazed one side only' or 'Cream wove litho P.G.1. Plate-glazed one side only. Ivybridge. (Allen & Sons)'.

  (iii) Cream wove litho paper, plate-glazed both sides, endorsed 'Cream wove litho. P.G. Plate-glazed both sides. Ivybridge. (Allen & Sons)'.

  (iv) Special finish, machine finish, in scarlet, endorsed '109 Ivybridge F (Allen & Sons). Surface, special finish, machine finish' or '68 Ivybridge – A. special finish', or 'John Allen. Ivybridge B. special finish' or '88 John Allen. Ivybridge (C). M.F. underside. Special finish top side'.

  (v) Special finish as (iv) but thinner paper, endorsed '96 John Allen. Ivybridge D. special finish top side' or 'John Allen. Ivybridge (F). M.F. underside. Special finish top side'.

B. Printed at Somerset House in sheets of 240.

(a) Under control B.11 without gum; on John Allen paper with special finish, in original 'red', used with the first and second master plates. Six sheets were printed, some of which, according to Mr Charles Nissen, were numbered 70, 71, 72 and 73.

(b) Under control B.12 with gum. There was no numbering, and no other particulars are available.

The above list has been recorded in *The British Philatelist*.

For a long time it was believed that all electros made from the third master-plate (Die II) were tested at Somerset House before being handed over to Messrs Harrison for use. In fact, only the first eight of the eighteen plates concerned were tested. Of these eight, only three (Nos. 2, 6 and 8) were tested at Somerset House, and the printings there were from Plate 2 under control B.12, and from Plates 6 and 8 under controls B.11 and B.12. The other five plates (Nos. 1, 3, 4, 5 and 7) were tested by Messrs Harrison, and the prints from these tests were issued to the public under control B11. They can be recognized from the fact that they had no plate markings. They are rare.

The Die II design was considered to be unsatisfactory, and an entirely new design (Die III) was adopted for the

1912-23 ISSUES

The design of the new frame and large profile head was by Sir Bertram Mackennal, whose actual approved design was in the form of a plaster cast. Die proofs were taken in varying stages of completion in black, blue or red, on paper either unwatermarked or watermarked 'Simple' Cypher.

Colour trials were taken in eight different tints of red on paper watermarked 'Simple' Cypher. They were printed from plates of 240 stamps each, and a complete sheet of each tint is in the Royal Collection. Each sheet, which was perforated, bore the control $\frac{C}{X} \frac{8}{12}$ under the eleventh stamp in the bottom row. In the margin below the tenth stamp was printed a One Penny stamp of King Edward VII, which was left imperforate. The following is a list of these Colour Essays, with their official names (where known) and their unofficial colour names:

Official Colour Names	*Unofficial Colour Names*
1. M/B Scarlet 25568	
2. M/B Scarlet 25569	Shades ranging from rose-pink to pale scarlet
3. Unknown	
4. Unknown	
5. M/B Scarlet 25602	
6. S.E. 3181	Shades of scarlet and red, merging into bluish carmine
7. Unknown	
8. Blue geranium	

No. 5 (M/B Scarlet 25602) was selected on September 6, 1912, as the colour for the Die III One Penny stamp, and it was issued thus on October 8, 1912, on the Joynson paper with 'Simple' script Cypher watermark Type I.

Stamps overprinted 'Specimen' in upright type measuring $12\frac{1}{2}$ mm are known. This overprint was on perforated sheets with control C12. Similar sheets, with control C13, were similarly overprinted. Some of these were left imperforate, and some were perforated. Further sheets were overprinted 'Cancelled' in upright type measuring $14\frac{1}{2}$ mm. Some of these were left imperforate, and some were perforated. They were experimental printings, for testing the ink or paper, as follows:

(a) Imperforate sheets with controls D14 or E14, for experiments with war-time paper.

(b) Perforated sheets (from Plate 10b) with Control E14.

(c) In March 1915 there was an experimental imperforate printing on 'Currency' paper, made by William Joynson & Son, watermarked with the same 'Simple' Cypher as that on the issued stamps; but the 'Currency' paper was of better quality. The sheets (from Plate 28a) had no control. The paper required more colour to ensure a good print; but eventually it was used, and stamps printed on this were made up into coils for issue in automatic vending machines.

(d) Early in 1916 experiments were carried out with British dyes, because dyestuffs hitherto used in the inks for stamp printing had been obtained from Germany, and the supplies of these were running low. The Imperial Chemical Dyestuffs Group produced various red pigments, such as Monolite Fast Scarlet, Monolite Red, Monolite Fast Red (Paranitraniline Red), and samples of these inks were used to print Penny stamps, which were perforated and overprinted. These experimental printings, however, were not accepted for issue.

The fourth master-plate was struck from Die III. Ninety-nine plates have been identified as used for the issue first made in October 1912 on William Joynson paper. The following is a list of the colours and shades associated with all the controls employed:

PLATE IV
PLATE V (overleaf)

Essays for the British Empire Exhibition Commemorative issue of 1924 by Harold Nelson.

Plate V, (3), was the accepted design. Although Plate V, (1), was rejected for this issue it was accepted, with alteration, for the design of the One Pound value of the Postal Union Congress Commemorative issue of 1929; the head of the King and the figure of St George were transposed.

These essays are in the Royal Collection, and are reproduced by gracious permission of Her Majesty.

1

2

PLATE IV

2

3

1

PLATE V

C12, scarlet, pale scarlet, red; C13, scarlet, red, carmine-red; C14, scarlet, pale scarlet; D14, bright scarlet, deep scarlet, scarlet, rose-red, and an abnormal outstanding shade of very bright orange-vermilion; E14, bright scarlet, scarlet, red, rose-red, and an abnormal outstanding shade of bright orange-vermilion. One sheet with this control was on unmilled paper. The shade of ink was dull.

F15, scarlet, red; G15, scarlet, red, pale rose-red; H16, scarlet, pale scarlet, red; I16, deep scarlet, scarlet, pale rose-red; J17, deep scarlet, scarlet, very pale rose-red and an abnormal outstanding very pale pink shade showing much white; K17, scarlet, pale scarlet, rose-red; K18, scarlet, rose-pink, and two abnormal outstanding shades, the first a very brilliant orange, with reddish tone, in bright and pale shades, and the second in a very pale pink shade with a large amount of white. L18, scarlet, rose-red, and three abnormal outstanding shades, the first vermilion and scarlet-vermilion, the second very bright orange, with reddish tone, in two shades, and the third very pale pink with a large amount of white. M18, bright scarlet, scarlet, pale scarlet, and an abnormal outstanding shade of very brilliant orange, with reddish tone. (There was also a remarkable brick-red shade during the 1914-18 period.) M19, scarlet, red, rose-red; N19, bright scarlet, scarlet, carmine-red; O19, bright scarlet, scarlet; O20, scarlet, dull red, rose-red; P20, scarlet, pale scarlet, very pale scarlet; Q20, bright scarlet, scarlet, red; Q21, bright scarlet, deep scarlet, scarlet, dull red, rose-red; R21, bright scarlet, scarlet, rose-red; S21, scarlet, pale scarlet, S22, scarlet, pale scarlet; T22, deep scarlet, scarlet, rose-red; U22, bright scarlet, scarlet, pale scarlet; U23, scarlet, pale scarlet, rose-red; V23, scarlet, pale scarlet, rose-red, carmine-red; W23, scarlet, rose-red, carmine-red; W24, scarlet, pale scarlet, rose-red. Copies, both in sheet and booklet form, are also known printed in the experimental colour varnish or varnished ink referred to above. These are very rare. In sheet form the colour is scarlet-vermilion, and in booklet form deep scarlet.

The 'Simple' Cypher watermark Type I was used with controls C12 and C13; the Type II watermark with controls C13, C14, D14, E14, F15, G15, H16, I16, J17, K17 (small printing), K18 (small printing), M19, N19, O19 (small printing), O20, P20 (small printing), Q21 (wide), Q21 (narrow), R21, S22, T22, U22, U23, V23, W23 and W24; the Type III watermark was used with controls J17, K17, K18, L18, M18, M only, M19, N19, O19, O20, P20, Q20, Q21 (wide), Q21 (narrow), R21, S21, S22, T22, U22, U23, V23, W23 and W24. The control 'M' only, omitting '18', is very rare.

Among the plate flaws which have been recorded were two which are usually known as the 'QNE' flaws, in which there is a white diagonal line running from the bottom of the 'O' of 'One' giving it the appearance of a 'Q'. On the first the tail runs from N.W. to S.E. This is the stamp listed as S.G. 357A, and occurred on the fourth stamp of the top row of one of the electros, the number of which is not known. It appeared with control E14. In the second the tail runs from N.E. to S.W. and occurred on the ninth stamp of the fifteenth row. It appeared under control T22.

There were two other plate flaws. On Plate 17, with control E14, the right frame line of the twelfth stamp of the nineteenth row became broken towards the top. This plate was first put to press with control D14, but the Editors have not seen an example with the flaw at this period. The other flaw was on Plate 43. Damage occurred to the S.W. corner of the tenth stamp of the nineteenth row which became extensively broken. The plate was at press with controls G15, H16 and I16.

Inverted watermarks are found on sheets with controls C12, C13, D14, E14, F15, G15, I16, J17, K17, K18, L18, M19, N19, O20, P20, Q20, Q21, R21, S21, S22, T22, U23, V23, W24. Reversed watermarks are found on sheets with controls C12, C13, D14, G15, H16, I16, K17, L18, M19, P20, Q20, R21, S21, S22. Inverted and reversed watermarks are found on sheets with controls C12, C13, C14, D14, E14, F15, G15, H16, I16, J17, K17, K18, L18, M18, M19, N19, O19, O20, P20, Q20, Q21, R21, S22, T22, U23, V23. Sheets with a red line along the bottom margin appeared with controls C12, C13, D14, E14, F15, G15 and H16.

The position of many of the controls varied considerably. As they formed no part of the plates, and were screwed in before, and removed after, each printing period, this is comprehensible. Although ninety-nine plates have been identified by plate markings, it is probable that several more existed which have not been identified.

Stamps were also issued with control C13 upon Basted Mills paper with 'Multiple' Script Cypher watermark under circumstances similar to those in connection with the Halfpenny. The colours were scarlet and bright scarlet, the latter showing a bright golden red under the quartz lamp. Blocks and horizontal strips or pairs are very scarce. At least one plate with the thin marginal rule, and one with the thick rule, were at press for this printing. Watermarks inverted, due to error of feeding, are known.

WEMBLEY EXHIBITION COMMEMORATIVES

On April 23, 1924, special One Penny and Threehalfpenny stamps were issued at the British Empire Exhibition, held at Wembley in 1924-25. Essays for these had been submitted by Messrs John D. Barton, Eric Gill (four designs), Noel Rooke, and five designs, including that adopted, by Harold Nelson. One of the unadopted essays by Mr Nelson was later re-submitted in 1929 for the commemorative Postal Union Congress issue, and was accepted for the One Pound value. It is described later.

The die for the One Penny was cut by Waterlow & Sons Ltd and die proofs are known in black on white wove paper and in scarlet on watermarked paper. Imperforate copies are known overprinted 'Specimen' in sloping type measuring 10 mm

Recess plates were laid down by Messrs Waterlow in six rows of ten stamps each, and were put to press on paper watermarked 'Multiple' block cypher without control, and perforated 14 × 14, at first by means of a single line machine and later by a comb.

The original issue, which appeared on April 23, 1924, incorporated the date '1924' in the design. Upon the re-opening of the British Empire Exhibition on May 9, 1925, the commemorative stamps were re-issued, but the date upon them was altered to '1925'. Only the comb perforator was used for these.

THE WATERLOW PRINTINGS AND HARRISON (PROVISIONAL) PRINTINGS 1924-34

Perforated and imperforate copies are known overprinted 'Specimen' in sloping type measuring 10 mm. The stamps were issued in April 1924, typographed by Waterlow & Sons Ltd on paper with watermark 'Multiple' block cypher. The perforation was 15 × 14. The following is a list of the controls, with the colours associated with each:

A24 and B24, scarlet, pale scarlet, very pale scarlet; C25, bright scarlet, scarlet; D25, pale scarlet; E26, scarlet, pale scarlet; F26, pale scarlet; G27, scarlet, pale scarlet; H27 and I28, pale scarlet; J28, scarlet, pale scarlet; K29, bright scarlet, scarlet, pale scarlet; L29, scarlet, pale scarlet; M30, pale scarlet; N30 and O31, scarlet, pale scarlet; P31, bright scarlet; Q32 and R32, scarlet, pale scarlet; S33, scarlet; T33, bright scarlet; and the Harrison controls, for their provisional printing under the 1934 contract, U34 and V34, scarlet, pale scarlet. Controls A24, B24, C25, L29, O31 and V34 exist both with imperforate and perforated bottom margins. With the latter O31 is rare and A24, B24 and L29 are scarce.

Inverted watermarks are found on some sheets with controls A24, B24, C25, D25, E26, F26, G27, H27, I28, J28, K29, L29, M30, O31 and U34. A small printing was made upon the experimental paper, referred to in Chapter I, under control B24.

The number of electros made from the fifth master-plate is not known, and it has been possible to identify only a small number of plates from the marginal plate markings, because, while the control appears on the right of the sheets, the plate markings usually appear towards the left. Therefore, unless complete bottom strips are available, it is not possible to differentiate the various plates and to identify them with the different controls.

THE POSTAL UNION CONGRESS ISSUE

The One Penny stamp, issued on May 10, 1929, was designed by Mr E. Linzell. The stamps were typographed by Waterlow & Sons

Ltd on Samuel Jones paper with 'Multiple' block cypher water-mark, from plates made at the Mint, as usual. Die proofs in black on glazed card are known. The colour was scarlet, and the stamps were printed under controls K29 and L29. The latter with per-forated bottom margin is rare. Two electros were made from the sixth master-plate, and printings were made from both of these under both the controls. Copies are known upon which the print is completely smudged.

THE PHOTOGRAVURE STAMPS 1934-36

On September 24, 1934, the Penny stamp produced by rotary photogravure process was first issued. Imperforate essays are known in a design similar to that of the typographed stamps with a larger head. They were printed in red and blue. Imperforate colour trials in the issued design are known in the approved red colour and also in blue. The paper with 'Multiple' block cypher water-mark was used, and the system of cylinder numbers and controls described in Chapter I was employed. Copies are known imper-forate but these are very rare. Part of a sheet printed on the gummed side of the paper was found, and copies with watermark inverted are known from sheets from the 'no stop' panes of cylinders 2, 5R, 11R and 15. These sheets came from printings in the German presses. They were not made in the continuous web, but were fed sheet by sheet. Both these errors are rare. There are also varieties showing the paper double, where a join occurred in the roll on which the stamps were printed; and some instances of misplaced perforation, providing the variety imperforate between pair, etc. The colour was officially described as 'deep scarlet'.

The cylinder numbers used with the various controls were as follows: V34 cylinders 1, 2, 5R, 6R, 9R, 10R, 11R, 14, 15, 20, 24, 25, 28; W35 cylinders 24 and 32; X35 cylinders 34, 35, 39, 40, 41, 42, 44, 45, 46, 50; Y36, cylinders 50, 53, 54. Printings from cylinders 9R and 40 are known only from the 'stop' pane. Only one copy of 9R was found. Cylinders 10R and 28 are rare, and cylinders 14, 15, 40, 44 and 45 are scarce. Printings from the 'stop' pane of cylinder

28 with control V34, and 35 with control X35 with left and bottom margins perforated through, are extremely rare. The examples seen are believed to be unique. Printings from cylinder 46 with control X35, from the 'no stop' pane with left margin imperforate and bottom margin with a single extension hole, and from the 'stop' pane with left and bottom margins perforated through, are rare. Examples occur where perforation of the 'no stop' pane is with right feed and the 'stop' pane with left feed, the reverse feed to the contractors' almost invariable rule. Examples seen are probably unique. These are from the 'stop' pane of cylinder 2 with control V34, the left margin being imperforate and the bottom margin with a single extension hole; and from the 'no stop' panes of cylinder 25 with control V34 and cylinder 50 with control X35, the left and bottom margins being perforated through.

The control V34 was opposite the left of the 19th row, and W35 onwards opposite the 18th row. The cylinder numbers up to 28 were opposite the 20th row on the left, but from 32 onwards they were opposite the 18th row. Cylinders 1 to 15 were etched in the large size, 20 to 25 in the intermediate size, and 28 onwards in the small size.

SILVER JUBILEE

The stamps issued on May 7, 1935, to celebrate the Silver Jubilee of the King's reign, referred to in the previous chapter, included the One Penny value; and general remarks concerning the Halfpenny apply also to the One Penny, the only control for which was W35.

The cylinder numbers of the One Penny were 14 and 22.

Chapter Four

Threehalfpence

THAT it was the intention to have a frame common to both the Halfpenny and Threehalfpence is shown by the die proofs of the Halfpenny Die IA frame without Downey head, one of which has the figure '½' in the upper left corner with cut upper right corner blank, and the other after the insertion of the figures '1½' in the blank space. Colour trials were made from the Mackennal sketch die, with the Downey (Die IB) head inserted, in four shades of brown, six of purple, one in red, one in claret, one in maroon and one in magenta. Except for the value, this die was similar to the Halfpenny sketch die with long dolphins' snouts. Further colour trials were made from the Harrison Sketch Die, with Downey (Die II) head in three shades of brown, two of purple and one in blue-green. On this die the dolphins' snouts were short and the heads unshaded. The background to the value figures consisted of horizontal lines.

A single colour trial is known in brown from the 'Amended die'. This die only differed from the Harrison Sketch Die in that the background to the value figures was now solid.

There was a further proof similar to that with '½' in the top left corner and '1½' in the top right corner, but with a photograph of the Mackennal plaster cast profile head, which is described under the One Penny value.

The first die proofs with the Mackennal coinage head (profile) known to the Editors were dated May 25, 1912, upon which the dolphins' heads were uncut. Two such dies are known, the first being discarded, as the head was too much to the right. The die, as approved, developed from the second. The dolphins' heads were fully shaded, and die proofs are known in black and brown on unwatermarked paper and in red and brown on paper watermarked 'Simple' Cypher.

There are perforated stamps with 'Specimen' overprinted in upright type measuring 12½ mm from sheets with controls A.12 and

C13, and stamps overprinted 'Cancelled'. The watermark was 'Simple' Cypher, and the perforation 15 × 14. The stamp was issued on October 15, 1912.

The following is a list of the controls of stamps produced from electros derived from the first master-plate, with the colours associated with each: A.12 (wide and narrow), red-brown, reddish-brown; C13 and D14, red-brown; F15 and G15, red-brown, chocolate-brown; H16, pale red-brown, red-brown, chocolate-brown; J17, pale reddish-brown, red-brown, chocolate-brown; K18 and L18, red-brown, chocolate-brown, dull brown. There is also an outstanding shade of very pale greyish-brown, which is a true brown. This, which is scarce, is found also with control M18, the normal shades of which were red-brown, chocolate-brown and dull brown. M19, red-brown, dull brown; N19, yellowish-brown, chocolate-brown, deep chocolate-brown; O19, red-brown, chocolate-brown; O20, yellowish-brown, red-brown, chocolate-brown; Q20, red-brown, chocolate-brown; Q21, red-brown; T22, red-brown, chocolate-brown, deep chocolate-brown; U22 and U23, red-brown; V23, chocolate-brown, deep chocolate-brown; W23 and W24, red-brown, chocolate-brown. Some of the yellowish-brown shades might be classified as orange-brown. Control A.12 (wide) with perforated bottom margin is scarce, and with this margin A.12 (narrow) is rare.

The following is a list showing the three types of 'Simple' Cypher watermark used with the various controls:

Type I. Controls A.12 (wide and narrow) and C13;

Type II. Controls C13, D14, F15, G15, H16, J17, K18 (small printing), L18 (small printing), N19, O19 (small printing), O20, Q21 (wide and narrow), T22, U22, U23, V23, W23 (small printing), W24;

Type III. Controls J17, K18, – 18, L18, M18, M19, – 19,* N19, O19, O20, Q20, Q21 (wide and narrow), T22, U22, U23, V23, W23.

Among the plate flaws which have been recorded is what is known as the 'PENCF' flaw. This occurred on the twelfth stamp in

---

* The K18 control is known in which the K was purposely omitted (see page 29); the M19 control is known in which the M failed to print; and the V23 control is known in which the '23' failed to print.

the fifteenth row of some sheets with controls L18, M19, O19 and Q21 (wide). It consists of the lower bar of the final 'E' of the value being missing. It has only been possible to identify this with Plate 29, but it must have occurred also on at least two other plates. After its first appearance the flaw was repaired, and a new lower bar was added; but this was too long and sloped slightly downwards. Its reappearance after repair indicates that the latter was made on the electro, whereas the source of the flaw was the master-plate, which was not repaired until later.

In the *British Philatelist*, No. 8, Vol. XVII of October 1924, are recorded three specimens from the top of a sheet from which the marginal line and a part of the top frame of the stamp are missing. It is suggested that this was due to damage of the plate.

The error 'no watermark' occurred with controls L18 and M18. This was not due to stamps being printed on a sheet with misplaced watermarks. In this case at least two sheets in quite different shades were found entirely without watermark. The paper was thick, and the probable explanation is that the error was due to the flow of the pulp over the dandy-roll having momentarily increased during manufacture.

Inverted watermarks occurred with controls L18, M18, M19, N19, O19, O20, Q21, T22, U22, U23 and V23. Reversed watermarks occurred with controls L18, N19, Q21, T22, U22 and U23. Inverted and reversed watermarks occurred with controls A.12, C13, D14, F15, G15, L18, M18, M19, N19, O19, O20, Q20, Q21 T22, U22, U23, V23, W23.

Forty-two electros, which can be identified by marginal plate markings, were made from the first master-plate.

WEMBLEY EXHIBITION COMMEMORATIVES

The Threehalfpence Commemorative Stamp issued on April 23, 1924, and again in May 9, 1925, in connection with the British Empire Exhibition at Wembley, has already been described in Chapter III. Die proofs, under date 1924, are known in black and in three shades of brown on white paper, and in scarlet on paper watermarked 'Multiple' block cypher.

THE WATERLOW PRINTINGS AND HARRISON (PROVISIONAL) PRINTINGS 1924-34

The normal Threehalfpence stamp was issued in April 1924. The watermark was 'Multiple' block cypher, and the perforation 15 × 14. The stamps were typographed by Waterlow & Sons Ltd. Perforated stamps are known overprinted 'Specimen' in sloping type.

The following is a list of the controls, with the colours associated with each: A24, pale chocolate-brown, chocolate-brown; B24 and C25, red-brown, chocolate-brown; D25, chocolate-brown; E26, red-brown, chocolate-brown, deep chocolate-brown; E.26, orange-brown; F26, red-brown, chocolate-brown, deep chocolate-brown; G27, red-brown, chocolate-brown; H27, red-brown; I28 and J28, red-brown, chocolate-brown; K29, red-brown, deep red-brown; L29, pale red-brown, red-brown; M30, N30, O31, P31, Q32, R32, S33, red-brown; T33 and U34, red-brown, pale red-brown. The colour of the Harrison (Provisional) Printings, under controls U34 and V34 was pale red-brown. Controls A24, B24, C25, F26, H27, I28, K29, N30 and V34 are known both with imperforate and perforated bottom margins. With the latter B24, F26, H27, I28 and K29 are scarce, and C25, N30 and V34 rare.

Inverted watermarks occurred on sheets with controls A24, B24, C25, D25, E26, F26, G27, H27, I28, J28, K29, M30, N30, O31 and Q32.

A small printing was made on the experimental paper, referred to in Chapter I, with control A24 (Plate 1) and control D25 (Plate 3).

During the General Strike of 1926, it was necessary to augment Messrs Harrison's printings of this value, and a small printing was made at Somerset House, with control E.26, from Plate 15.

A sheet was found printed on the gummed side. This had control U34, and was part of the Harrison (Provisional) Printing made prior to the issue of the photogravure stamps.

Thirty-nine electros, which have been identified by marginal plate markings, were made from the second master-plate. Unsevered blocks and horizontal strips from complete booklet sheets show *tête-bêche* pairs, and also *tête-bêche* pairs with intervening marginal cross rules. These came from complete sheets which had been printed from a booklet plate and which had never been bound into booklets and guillotined into blocks of six.

THE POSTAL UNION CONGRESS ISSUE

The Threehalfpence stamp, issued on May 10, 1929, was designed by Mr E. Linzell. Die proofs are known in black on glazed card. The stamps were typographed by Waterlow & Sons Ltd on Samuel Jones paper with 'Multiple' block cypher watermark, from plates made at the Mint. The colour was purple-brown, and the stamps were printed under controls K29 and L29, only known with imperforate bottom margins. Five electros, made from the third master-plate, have been identified. Printings were made from all five plates with control K29, and from all, except the fourth, with control L29. Some sheets with control K29 are known with watermark inverted. Control blocks with this variety are very rare.

THE PHOTOGRAVURE STAMPS 1934-36

On August 20, 1934, the Threehalfpence stamp produced by the rotary photogravure process was first issued. Imperforate colour trials are known in red, blue, grey-green, green and in the approved colour. Since a few stamps were issued imperforate, owing to an error of perforation, difficulty may be experienced in separating imperforate colour trials in the approved colour from the imperforate error. However, they can easily be distinguished under the lamp by comparison with the perforated stamps, since the reflection is entirely different. The paper with 'Multiple' block cypher watermark was used, and the system of cylinder numbers and controls described in Chapter I was employed. The colour was known officially as 'Brown Lake', but by the printers as 'Murrey Brown'.

Inverted watermarks are known on sheets with cylinder number 68R, 'stop' pane, under circumstances similar to those which occurred with the Penny stamps. Owing to errors of perforation, specimens are known partially imperforate and imperforate between pair. Examples are known with double paper, where the joins occurred in the rolls.

The cylinder numbers used with the various controls were as follows: U34, cylinders 8 and 34; V34, cylinders 13, 17, 34, 38, 42, 43, 45, 46, 47, 49, 54, 55, 63, 68R, 69, 70, 94, 97, 98, 100, 101, 102, 104, 105, 106, 107, 113; W35, cylinders 116, 119, 124; X35, cylinders 127, 128, 130, 132, 133, 135, 137, 141; Y36, cylinders 135, 137, 139, 140, 141, 143, 144, 146, 148, 149; Z36, cylinders 144, 149, 153. Cylinder 63 is known only from the 'no stop' pane, and only two copies of this have been recorded. Examples from cylinders 49 and 70 are also very rare. Only about five copies from each have been found.

Printings from the 'no stop' panes of cylinders 46 and 47 with control V34 with left margin imperforate and two extension holes in the bottom margin, and from the 'no stop' panes of cylinders 98 and 104 with a single extension hole in the left margin and the bottom margin imperforate, are extremely rare. Examples seen are believed to be unique, the two latter being trials for the Type V comb-heads. Printings from the stop panes of cylinders 107 with control V34, 135 with control X35 and 149 with control Y36, with left and bottom margins perforated through, are rare. Examples of reverse feed perforation, described under the One Penny value, occur. These are from the 'no stop' panes of cylinders 45, 68R and 101, all with control V34, the left and bottom margins being perforated through, and from the 'stop' panes of cylinders 139 and 149, both with control Y36, the left margin being imperforate and the bottom margin with a single extension hole.

Among the cylinder flaws recorded is the error of engraving the cylinder number on the 'no stop' pane of cylinder 13. It was originally engraved 'direct' on to the cylinder and hence appeared reversed. It was correctly re-engraved over the reversed number before the cylinder was put to press, and both engravings can be seen clearly.

There was a flaw on multipositive 10 which was used for making both cylinder 116 and cylinder 119. This appeared as a white mark over the top right-hand corner of the inner frame line and extending vertically upwards on the first stamp of the 19th row on the 'no stop' pane of both these cylinders. Later cylinder 116 was rechromed, thus considerably reducing the area of this flaw. Cylinder 119 was never rechromed.

Printings from the 'no stop' pane of cylinder 143 with control Y36 are of interest. After this cylinder had been at press for some time it sustained considerable damage to the left margin, showing as a large irregular coloured mark to the left of the first stamp in the 19th row. This damage must have affected the control image, as it was retouched by engraving. This is clearly visible in the lower part of the figures '36' which appear darker than the rest of the control.

On first issue the control U34 was below the second stamp in the bottom row. This position remained unchanged with control V34 on all cylinders up to 45, with the exception of 17. The cylinder number was opposite the left of the 20th row. On cylinders 17, 46 and onwards to 107 the control V34 was on the left opposite the 19th row. There was no change in the position of the cylinder number. On cylinder 113 the control V34 and cylinder number were opposite the 18th row. These positions were maintained for the remainder of the issues with control W35 onwards. Cylinders 8 to 102 were etched in the large size, 104 to 113 in the intermediate size and 116 onwards in the small size.

SILVER JUBILEE

The Silver Jubilee stamps which, together with their colour trials, have been described in Chapter II, also had the control and cylinder number alongside the third row from the bottom. The control for these was W35, and the cylinder numbers 2 (unique), 7, 21, 27 (scarce) and 48.

The printing from cylinder 2 is extremely interesting. No examples from the 'stop' pane have been found and the only known block from the 'no stop' pane shows that this cylinder was printed from a different multipositive from that used for the other cylinders. The shading in the spandrels is noticeably stronger and that in 'Silver Jubilee' and 'Threehalfpence' varies from that of the other cylinders.

Chapter Five

Twopence

AMONG the original drawings submitted for the design was one by Mr Eve, which was the forerunner of his 'wreath' design and which was later accepted for the Ninepence, Tenpence and One Shilling values.

For the Twopence, Sir Bertram Mackennal's original sketch for the frame, which was without value, had the three value tablets in white. This was later amended, with value tablets in black, and in this form his design was accepted.

Colour trials were made from the Mackennal (second) sketch die with Downey (Die II) head, after the values had been inserted in white. They are known in eight shades of brown, three of yellow, two of blue, five of purple, in red and magenta.

Die proofs in black, brown and red were taken from the die, which was in stage 2, with horizontal lines of shading in the upper corners, with the Downey (Die II) head inserted, but without value. An example in red is known endorsed '1st proof from Die for design 2d and 3d. 16.3.11', and initialled by Mr Harrison, the die engraver, which indicates that it was originally intended to have a frame common to the Twopence and Threepence values, though it was subsequently decided to extend the use of this frame to the Fourpence value.

Further die proofs with the Downey (Die II) head, but without value, are known from the 'Amended die'. This is the die in its third stage with the top corners with solid background.

Die proofs in black are known of the new die with the Mackennal coinage head after the value had been inserted. Proofs of the first die, dated May 30, 1912, have the inner white side lines of the frame not extending above the upper ribbon design. Those of the second die show these lines partially erased, whereas those of the third die have a finer inner white line, not only at the sides but continuing along the top. The die in this state was approved.

Imperforate colour trials on gummed paper were made from a special plate of four stamp images, and are known in 'Fine cadmium orange', 'Brilliant pale green' and in the approved colour.

There were two dies used for the issued stamp. The first was slightly too high, with the result that the perforation of stamps from electros made from the first master-plate was irregular and caused wastage. In the second die the height was in consequence reduced slightly.

Up to 1922, the demand for Twopenny stamps was small. But when, in that year, the initial inland letter rate was increased to twopence, a much greater supply became necessary, and the second die was made. The main differences between the two dies are as follows:

	Die I	Die II
Inner frame line and lines round value tablet	Thin and close to outer frame line	Thick and further from outer frame line
Lines of shading above top of head	Four	Three

Perforated stamps overprinted 'Specimen' in upright type measuring $12\frac{1}{2}$ mm are known.

On first issue on August 21, 1912, the stamps, were printed by Messrs Harrison & Sons in shades of yellow-orange. The perforation was 15×14 and the watermark 'Simple' Cypher Type I. This was the first of the 1912-24 series to be issued, and was without any control. Some sheets are known with watermark inverted and inverted and reversed.*

Three plates from the first master-plate were used for the initial printing. In November 1913 there was a deliberate change of colour to reddish-orange. Normally the shades were pale. The first

* The variety no watermark is known on stamps from Die I due to prints on the sheet margin (watermark displaced). It is also known on Die II stamps, as well as the error no watermark (S.G. 421a).

PLATE VI

PLATE VI

printing in this colour was made at Somerset House with control C. 13.

The following is a list of the Die I controls, with the colours associated with each: C.13, pale reddish-orange; C14, D14, F15, orange, reddish-orange; G15, orange, pale orange; H16, orange, deep orange, pale orange; I16 bright orange, orange, pale orange, and an outstanding shade of brilliant deep red-orange, which is scarce; J17, bright orange, orange, pale orange; K17, orange, pale orange; L18 and M19, bright orange, orange; N19, orange, bright orange, pale orange; O19, orange, pale orange; O20, P20 and Q20, bright orange, orange, pale orange; Q21, bright orange, orange, and an outstanding shade of brown-orange, which is scarce; R21, S21, S22 and T22, orange, pale orange. With perforated bottom margin control H16 is rare and O19 scarce.

The Type I Cypher watermark was used with control C.13 only; Type II with controls C14, D14, F15, G15, H16, I16, J17, K17 (small printing), N19, O19 (small printing), O20 (small printing), P20, Q21, R21, T22; Type III with controls J17, K17, L18, M19, N19, O19, O20, P20, Q21, R21, S21, S22, T22.

Inverted watermarks are known with controls H16, I16, K17, M19, N19, O20, P20, Q20, Q21, S21; reversed watermarks with controls C14, G15, I16 and P20; inverted and reversed watermarks with controls C.13, C14, G15, H16, I16, L18, M19, N19, O19, O20, P20, Q20, Q21, R21, S21, T22. Twenty-one electros, made from the first (Die I) master-plate, have been identified. This total includes the three electros used for the initial printing in yellow-orange which were subsequently put to press in reddish-orange. The William Joynson paper with 'Simple' Cypher watermark was used throughout the above printings.

The first Die II stamps appeared in September 1921. The controls were S21, S22, T22, U22, U23, V23, W23, W24, and the colours orange and shades of pale orange. The Type II watermark is found with controls T22, U22, U23 (small printing), V23, W23, W24; and Type III with controls S21, S22, T22, U22, U23, V23 (small printing) and W23.

Inverted watermarks are known with controls S22, W23 and

F

W24; and inverted and reversed watermarks with controls S21, S22, T22, U23, W23 and W24.

Six electros, made from the Second (Die II) master-plate, have been identified.

THE WATERLOW PRINTINGS AND HARRISON (PROVISIONAL) PRINTINGS 1924-34

Perforated stamps are known overprinted 'Specimen' in sloping type.

The Waterlow Twopence Stamp was issued in October 1924. The watermark was 'Multiple' block cypher and the perforation 15 × 14. The stamps were typographed by Waterlow & Sons Ltd. The colour was shades of orange and pale orange. The controls were A24, B24, C25, D25, E26, F26, G27, H27, I28, J28, K29, L29, M30, N30, O31, P31, Q32, R32, S33, T33. The Harrison controls for the provisional printings were U34 and V34. Inverted watermarks are found with controls A24, B24, C25, D25, E26, F26, G27, H27, I28, J28, K29, M30 and P31. Sixteen electros, made from the third master-plate, have been identified. With perforated bottom margin control B24 is scarce. The other controls are unknown with perforated margin.

A complete sheet was found without any watermark. The control was C25, the control block of which is unique.

THE PHOTOGRAVURE STAMPS 1934-37

On January 21, 1935, the Twopence stamp produced by the rotary photogravure process appeared on 'Multiple' block cypher watermark paper. The colour was known officially as 'Orange Vermilion', and by the printers as 'Deep Orange'. Examples are known on double paper where a join occurred on the paper roll. Owing to errors of perforation, specimens are known partially imperforate and imperforate between pair. The cylinder numbers used with the various controls were as follows: V34 cylinder 5; W35 cylinder 5; X35 cylinders 8, 10 and 12; Y36 cylinders 10 and 12; Z36 cylinders 10, 12 and 13; A37 cylinders 12 and 13. The controls and cylinder numbers in this and all subsequent values were in the margin to the left of the 18th row. Controls V34 and W35 with side and bottom margins perforated are rare. The printing from cylinder 10 with control Y36, with side margin perforated and bottom margin with single extension hole, is very rare. Cylinder 5 was etched with the intermediate size images, and cylinder 8 onwards with the small size images. The figure '5' on the cylinder concerned was small on first issue. Upon change of the control to W35, and consequent rechrome of the cylinder, the figure became very faint. Later it was re-engraved much larger.

Chapter Six

Twopence Halfpenny

THAT it was the original intention to have a frame common to the One Penny and Twopence Halfpenny is shown by a photograph of the die engraver's sketch of the One Penny which was endorsed '1d. & 2½d.', and by a further proof of this design upon which the value in figures '2½' was inserted, though the value in words remained 'One Penny'.

Further, early trials were carried out in this design in which the value in figures and words were both '2½d.' and 'Twopence Halfpenny'.

Colour trials in eight shades of blue and one in green were taken from a die made from the Mackennal sketch with Downey (Die IA) head inserted. This die can be recognized by the roughness of the horizontal lines of shading, and also because the left part of the right-hand figures '2½' is drawn over the lion's haunches.

Later trials took place with a die cut from the engraver's sketch with Downey (Die II) head inserted. This die can be recognized by the evenness of the background shading, and also because the left part of the right-hand figures '2½' is engraved behind the lion's haunches. Proofs from four such dies are known. The first was cut with the word 'TWOPENCE' as one word, the 'P' in 'Twopence' being small and that in 'Halfpenny' being large. The second die had the letters of the value 'OPENC' obliterated, the 'P' in 'Halfpenny' remaining large. The third die had the words 'TWO' and 'PENCE' as two separate words, the 'P' in 'Twopence' still being small and that in 'Halfpenny' large. The fourth die was as the third but the 'P' in 'Halfpenny' was small and the same size as that in 'Two pence'.

However, upon the decision to issue the One Penny stamp in the new design with the Mackennal profile head, trials for the Twopence Halfpenny with the lion *couchant* design were discontinued.

84

A new die was taken up from the profile One Penny die from which the values and base of the design were removed, and proofs of this stage are known in black. Later the new values were cut, and proofs of the completed die are known in blue.

The watermark at first was 'Simple' Cypher, and the perforation 15 × 14. The stamp was issued on October 18, 1912. Imperforate colour trials are known overprinted 'Cancelled' measuring 15 mm; and perforated stamps overprinted 'Specimen' measuring $12\frac{1}{2}$ mm from sheets with controls A.12 and C13. The stamps were printed at first at Somerset House (control A.12) to a limited extent, and thereafter by Messrs Harrison & Sons. The following is a list of the controls of stamps produced from eleven electros derived from the first master-plate which have been identified, with the colours associated with each:

A.12 (narrow type only), light ultramarine, pale ultramarine; C13, bright ultramarine, bright blue, pale blue; C14 and D14, blue, ultramarine; E14, ultramarine, deep blue, blue; G15, deep blue, bright blue; H16, ultramarine, deep blue, bright blue, pale blue; J17, ultramarine, blue, pale blue, milky blue; J.17, blue; K17, ultramarine, blue, pale blue, milky blue; L18, bright blue, blue, milky blue; M18, ultramarine, blue, milky blue, and an outstanding shade of powder blue; M19, deep blue, blue, pale blue; N19, deep ultramarine, ultramarine, blue; O19, ultramarine, deep blue, blue, pale blue; O20, ultramarine, deep blue, blue, pale blue, and an outstanding shade (which occurs also with control R21) which has come to be known as 'Prussian blue'. The Editors prefer the name 'metallic blue' to describe the cold, greyish shades concerned which, under the lamp, appear as very dark dull blue, as compared with the bright blue, green and grey shades which appear under the lamp in connection with the many blue colours and shades which lack the special metallic or steely aspect, which is associated with certain of the Cape De La Rue Fourpenny triangular stamps of 1863-64;* P20, deep ultramarine, deep blue; Q21, deep blue, blue; R21, deep blue, blue, metallic blue; S22, blue,

§ In their 1957 Catalogue Stanley Gibbons refer to these 'metallic blue' shades as 'deep dull blue' and 'Prussian blue'.

deep blue; T22, deep blue, blue; U23, blue, pale blue; V23 deep blue, blue, and an outstanding shade with violet tinge.

Stamps are known also in a colour which has been described as 'aniline blue', although it has not been possible to verify that any pigment used for this value had an aniline dye content. The ink of the stamps in question is very fugitive (like some of the 'metallic' shades), runs when wetted and sometimes turns green if dipped in water. This applies to certain of the stamps under controls O19 and R21 above referred to. The colours and shades of this value are innumerable, ranging from bright whitish blue to dull dark blue, with many intermediate colours and many shades of each. Under the lamp, stamps which look similar to the naked eye often show extraordinary differences, ranging from bright blue and pale grey, through green in various shades, to deep dull navy blue. The 'deep dull blue', now listed as S.G. 373, to the naked eye is very deep dull greyish blue, and would seem to be the darkest shade of the 'metallic' series referred to above in connection with controls O20 and R21. The Editors have not seen an unused copy of the stamp listed as S.G. 373, the Stanley Gibbons reference copy being a used specimen, darker than any other known to the Editors. Incidentally, it is easy to change the colour of many of the surface-printed George V stamps, by exposure to heat, gas, acid fumes, damp or sunshine, by which means curious results can be achieved. It is therefore necessary to be careful about copies which may be faked. The three types of 'Simple' Cypher watermark appeared with the various controls as follows: Type I controls A.12 and C13; Type II controls C13, C14, D14, E14, G15, H16, I16, J17, J.17, K17 (small printing), L18 (small printing), M18 (small printing), Q20, R21 (small printing), U23, V23; Type III controls J17, K17, L18, M18, M19, N19, O19, O20, P20, Q21, R21, S21, S22, T22.

Inverted watermarks are found with controls A.12, C14, J17, L18, N19, O19 O20, Q21 and R21; reversed watermarks with controls G15 and P20; and inverted and reversed watermarks with controls A.12, C13, C14, G15, H16, J17, K17, L18, M18, M19, N19, O19, O20, P20, R21 and T22. With perforated bottom margin control A.12 is rare and K17 scarce.

THE WATERLOW PRINTINGS AND HARRISON
(PROVISIONAL) PRINTINGS 1924-35

The Waterlow stamps appeared in October 1924. The watermark was 'Multiple' block cypher and perforation 15 × 14. Perforated copies are known overprinted 'Specimen'. The stamps were typographed by Waterlow & Sons Ltd.

The following is a list of the controls, with the colours associated therewith:

B24 and C25, dull blue, pale blue; D25 and E26, deep blue, blue, pale blue; G27, H27, I28, K29, M30 and N30 shades of deep blue; O31, deep greyish-blue. The printing under this control was very small, and it is rare; Q32, deep blue; R32, deep blue, blue, pale blue; S33, deep blue, blue; T33, blue, pale blue. The controls and colours of the Harrison (Provisional) Printings were:

V34, deep dull blue, dull blue; W35, dull blue. Inverted watermarks are found on some sheets with controls B24, C25, D25, E26, F26, G27, I28 and M30.

Under control B24 there was found a whole sheet without watermark, the control block of which is unique. Thirteen electros from the second master-plate have been identified. The only one of these controls known with perforated bottom margin is W35.

THE POSTAL UNION CONGRESS ISSUE

The Twopence Halfpenny stamp, designed by Mr. J. W. Farleigh, was issued on May 10, 1929. Die proofs are known in black on glazed card. The stamps were typographed by Waterlow & Sons Ltd on Samuel Jones paper, with watermark 'Multiple' block cypher, from plates made at the Mint. The colour was deep and paler shades of blue. Two electros, from the third master-plate, have been identified and were used with controls K29 and L29. Some sheets with control L29 had the watermark inverted. Control blocks with this variety are very rare.

PLATE VII

PLATE VII

THE PHOTOGRAVURE STAMPS 1935-36

The Twopence Halfpenny stamp produced by the rotary photogravure process appeared on March 18, 1935. The official colour was 'deep ultramarine', described by the printers as 'Royal blue'. Examples are known on double paper, where a join in the continuous roll occurred.

The controls and cylinder numbers were control W35 with cylinders 6 and 7; and Control Y36 with cylinders 8 and 9. With perforated side margin controls W35 and Y36 are scarce.

Among the cylinder flaws recorded there was one on the multipositive used for making the 'no stop' and 'stop' panes of cylinder 8. On the first stamp of the eighteenth row on both panes the left-hand upright pillar was abnormally weak, and before the cylinder was put to press with control Y36 these pillars were retouched by engraving. On the 'no stop' pane these engraved lines ran diagonally downwards from left to right and on the 'stop' pane they ran upwards from left to right.

SILVER JUBILEE

The Twopence Halfpenny Silver Jubilee Stamp had control W35, and the only cylinder 34, alongside the third row from the bottom of the sheet. This issue included another so-called 'Prussian blue', the colour of which incidentally is totally different from that of the 'Prussian blue' of the regular issue listed under S.G. 373[a], referred to above. The circumstances relating to the Silver Jubilee 'Prussian blue', according to the late Mr F. H. Vallancey, were as follows. Imperforate colour trials were made, including some sheets in a so-called 'Prussian blue' shade. Three of these sheets (360 stamps) were perforated, presumably in error, and sent to a sub-post office at Edmonton on June 26, 1935. A few days later a sheet of these (120 stamps) was purchased by a Mr A. at face value, and a Mr B. purchased the rest, except for about 41 copies which had been sold to the general public. Mr A. sold a few dozen copies at 10d each before enquires were made from the General Post

Office and the scarcity of the stamps was realized. The next few dozen were sold at £10 each, since when the price has risen to what would seem to be an exaggerated figure in view of the fact that about 320 copies became available to collectors. One of these sheets was cut abnormally. Instead of being separated from the adjoining sheet down the centre of the marginal paper it was divided down the vertical line of perforation of one sheet, so that the sheet bought by Mr A. had no control or cylinder number, and one of the sheets bought by Mr B. had a control and cylinder number on both sides. One control with cylinder number attached to a single stamp exists, this having been stuck in the Postmaster's Stock Book by the marginal paper bearing the control.

A few used copies are known. These may be either from the 41 specimens sold to the general public or from some of the copies acquired by the above-mentioned two gentlemen which were sent through the post. A copy dated on or about June 26, 1935, would obviously be rare. The Editors have recorded what they believe to be the true facts concerning these stamps, as published by Mr Vallancey, in order that collectors may know the exact status of a stamp which has acquired a high market value. The fact, as mentioned above, that two of those sheets were separated down the line of perforation and not guillotined down the centre of the inter-pane gutter is, in the opinion of the Editors, proof that the 'Prussian blue' stamp was not an authorized issue.

Chapter Seven

Threepence

AMONG the early original sketches was one submitted by Mr Eve, which was the forerunner of his 'Pillar' design, and which was later accepted for the Fivepence, Sixpence, Sevenpence and Eightpence values.

Extensive colour trials were made. The first series was from the Eve zinco-blocks of a design similar to his 'Wreath' design. There were two types of this. The first was with the small Downey type head on a white background. Trials of this are known in eight shades of red or pink, two shades of orange, six shades of brown, ten shades of green, ten shades of blue, six shades of violet, purple or mauve, two shades of grey, and olive-bistre and very pale yellow ochre, all of which were on white paper. There was also a trial on yellow paper in brown.

The second type had a large Downey type head on a solid background. The trials of this were in seven shades of reds and pinks, two shades of orange, four shades of brown, nine shades of green, seven shades of blue, six shades of violet, mauve and purple, and olive-bistre, pale yellow ochre and slate-grey, all of which were on white paper. There was also a trial on yellow paper in brown.

The next series of colour trials was made from the Mackennal sketch die with Downey (Die II) head inserted. They were in six shades of violet and purple, four shades of yellow, seven shades of brown, two of green and two of blue, all of which were on white paper. There were also trials in three shades of purple, three shades of brown and in blue, all of which were on yellow paper. This die can be recognized by the irregular lines of horizontal shading.

A photograph of the engraver's sketch die without head is known in stage 1 with white spaces in both upper corners, upon which were inserted by Mr Eve the figure '2' in the left-hand tablet, the figure '3' in the right-hand tablet and the words 'Two pence' in the bottom tablet, together with an extra tablet below his sketch with the words 'Threepence'.

The Amended die was also used for colour trials. This die was made from the engraver's sketch with Downey (Die II) head inserted. This die can be recognized by the evenness of the horizontal lines of shading, and also from the fact that the spaces in the two upper corners are shaded.

In the first stage of this die the background to the head was white. Colour trials of this are known in five shades of brown, rose and in blue-violet.

In the second stage of this die the background to the head was shaded. A colour trial is known in red.

The Altered die was also used for colour trials. The head and its background were as in the Amended die, but the spaces in the two upper corners were filled with solid colour. Colour trials of this were made on unwatermarked paper in three shades of purple and violet, five shades of brown, two shades of orange, two shades of grey, and also in red, yellow and the officially named 'Blue Geranium'. This latter colour was, in fact, one of the blues. There is another colour trial of the same name which occurred with the One Penny under control $\dfrac{C}{X} \dfrac{8}{12}$, but its colour was a bluish carmine.

Colour trials were also taken on paper watermarked crown, either upright or sideways, in orange, yellow, maroon, blue and pale violet.*

The Threepence value was issued on October 9, 1912, in a red-violet or purple-violet colour. Perforated copies are known over-printed 'Specimen' in upright type measuring $12\frac{1}{2}$ mm from a sheet with control A.12. The printers were again Somerset House at the outset (1912-13) and thereafter Messrs Harrison & Sons. The water-mark was again 'Simple' Cypher, in three types over the period 1912-23; and the perforation 15 × 14. With control C13 copies are

---

* There was a colour trial in the issued design closely resembling the adopted colour, a marginal corner block of which is in the Stothert Collection. It was on watermarked paper apparently in complete sheet form. The Control, which was under the second stamp in the bottom row, was X.13. The block was endorsed 'not accepted' in manuscript.

known on rough unsurfaced paper with no glaze. It is believed that
all these came from the same sheet. Ten plates have been identified,
of which only three were used in this colour.

In November 1913, there was a deliberate change of colour from
reddish-violet to blue-violet, which included shades of lilac. Perforated stamps overprinted 'Specimen' came from sheets with controls C.13 and C13. The controls, and the shades associated with
each, were as follows:

(a) *First Colour* – A.12 (wide and narrow), red-violet and deep
red-violet; B.13, violet; C13, slightly red-violet, purple-violet and
greyish violet.

(b) *Second Colour* – C.13, blue-violet; C13, blue-violet, pale blue-
violet, dull misty blue-violet; D14, slightly deeper blue-violet; E14,
blue-violet, pale blue-violet; G15, H16 and I16, deep to pale shades
of blue-violet; pale mauve and slate-lilac; J17 and L18, deep,
bright and pale shades of blue-violet and lilac; M18, N19, O20,
P20 and Q21, deep to pale shades of blue-violet, sometimes with
reddish tinge; R21, bright blue-violet with redder tone, pale blue-
violet; S21 and S22, blue-violet; T22, pale blue-violet; U22, deep
and bright blue-violet with reddish tinge; U23, deep to pale shades
of blue-violet; V23, blue-violet and bright blue-violet with reddish
tinge; W23, deep and dark blue-violet. During this issue there was
also an outstanding and scarce shade of lavender. With perforated
bottom margin control A.12 (wide) is rare and C.13 scarce.

The Type I watermark was used for the first colour with controls
A.12 (wide and narrow), B.13 and C13. It was used also in the
second colour with control E14, examples of which are very rare.
The Type II watermark was used for the first colour with control
C13, and in the second colour with controls C.13, C13, D14, E14,
F15, G15, H16, I16, J17, N19, O20 (small printing), R21, U22, U23
(small printing), V23 and W23. Type III was used with controls
J17, L18, M18, N19, O20, P20, Q21, R21, S21, S22, T22, U22, U23,
V23 (small printing) and W23.

Inverted watermarks are known with controls B.13 (reddish-
violet), G15, L18, N19 and U23; reversed watermarks with controls
I16 and Q21; and inverted and reversed watermarks with controls

B.13 (reddish-violet) C13 (bluish-violet), E14, F15, G15, I16, J17, L18, N19, O20, Q21, R21, S22 and U22. All ten electros from the first master-plate have been identified in use in bluish-violet.

THE WATERLOW PRINTINGS AND HARRISON (PROVISIONAL) PRINTINGS 1924-34

The Waterlow stamps appeared in November 1924. The watermark was 'Multiple' block cypher and perforation 15 × 14. They were typographed by Waterlow & Sons Ltd. Perforated copies are known overprinted 'Specimen'.

The following is a list of the controls, with the colours associated with each, the colours generally being rather redder than the blue-violet shades of the Harrison stamps: B24, bluish-violet, with pale and very pale shades; C25, D25 and E26, bluish-violet shades, G27, I28, K29, M30 and N30, deep to pale shades of bluish-violet; P31, R32, S33 and T33, bluish-violet, deep bluish-violet. The Harrison provisional printing had control V34 and was in dark bluish-violet, deep bluish-violet and blue-violet with red tone. Inverted watermarks are known with controls B24, C25, D25, E26, G27 and I28. For these printings nine electros from the second master-plate have been identified. Printings with control G27 and perforated bottom margin are rare.

THE PHOTOGRAVURE STAMPS 1935-37

The Threepence stamp produced by the rotary photogravure process appeared on March 18, 1935. Imperforate colour trials are known in orange, grey-green and the accepted violet colour. The official colour was 'Deep Violet', described by the printers as 'Royal purple'. Examples are known on double paper, where a join in the continuous roll occurred.

The controls and cylinder numbers were: W35, cylinders 1, 2 and 3, the last being known only from the 'no stop' pane; X35, cylinder 6; Y36, cylinders 12, 13 and 14; Z36, Z36 single box, and Z36 half box, cylinder 14.

The controls and cylinder numbers were in the margin to the left of the 18th row. Printings from the 'stop' pane of cylinder 1 with control W35 with the left margin perforated through and the bottom margin with a single extension hole are very rare. The Editors have only seen two examples. Printings from cylinder 3 with control W35 are not known from the 'stop' pane. An example from the 'no stop' pane, which has the left and bottom margins perforated through, is believed to be unique. Control Y36 with perforated side margin is scarce.

PLATE VIII

1

2

3

4

5

6

7

8

PLATE VIII

Chapter Eight

Fourpence

It was originally intended that the design for this value should have been the Eve 'Wreath' design, in common with the Five-pence, Sixpence and Sevenpence stamps. This design was, how-ever, later allotted to the Ninepence, Tenpence and One Shilling values.

Early sketches by Mr Eve are known in varying stages of back-ground shading, either with or without a three-quarter face head. Die proofs from the engraver's sketch of this design are known in black with the head on a solid background and in black or yellow with the head on a shaded background. Some examples of the proofs in yellow were on paper watermarked Crown. These die proofs are easily recognized, because they are the only ones with the full size threequarter face head.

Early colour trials were made from the Eve zinco-blocks of the 'Wreath' design, with small Downey type head on a coloured background. These are known in eight shades of green, three shades of red, three shades of brown, three shades of grey, three shades of orange, and in mauve, 'Ruby black', 'Stamp maroon' and amber.

Further essays of the Eve 'Wreath' design are known with the profile head in varying stages. A proof is known in black endorsed by Mr Seymour Bennett 'Design for 4d postage stamp amended by Mr Eve to correspond with the amended 5d design (Motley process)'. There was also a trial in light turquoise-blue on paper watermarked Crown. On both these proofs the shading at the sides of the stamp extended down to the lower corner ornaments.

A series of colour trials was made from a die similar to the above, but with a profile head 12 mm high, which was rather smaller than that employed for the Motley series described below. On these the shading at the sides remained unaltered. These trials are known in five shades of brown, two shades of grey, three shades of mauve and purple, two shades of blue, and also in green, 'Geranium lake' and red-carmine, all of which were on white paper. Trials were also made in blue and 'Bartolozzi brown' on pink paper and in 'Dahlia claret' on blue paper.

The Motley series of colour trials was made from a 'Wreath' design die with a head $12\frac{1}{2}$ mm high. The shading at the sides remained unaltered. Temporary plates of four stamp images, two above two, were made from this die by the Motley process, each plate having a patch of colour below. The trials are known in violet, very deep green, red-brown and azure blue.

There was also a proof from a different die in light blue on paper watermarked 'Simple' Cypher sideways. In this case the shading at the sides stopped at the centre of the wreath, below which the space was filled in with solid colour.

Further trials took place to obtain a head of more suitable size for this design, but this design for the Fourpence was abandoned in favour of the Mackennal design which was common to the Two-pence and Threepence stamps. A composite photograph of this frame is known with the figure 4 in white on a shaded background in the left-hand tablet and the figure 3 in outline on a white back-ground in the right-hand tablet. In the lower tablet are the words 'FOUR PENCE', below which is an extra tablet with the word 'THREEPENCE'.

Die proofs in the approved design are known in black and also in the selected colour, the latter being endorsed 'Pearl Grey'. The Fourpence value was issued on January 15, 1913. The watermark was 'Simple' Cypher, and the perforation 15×14.

Perforated copies exist overprinted 'Specimen' in upright type measuring $12\frac{1}{2}$ mm, from sheets with controls B.13 and C13. At least part of a sheet was printed on unmilled paper. Examples of this are rare. As usual, the stamps were printed at first at Somerset House (control B.13) to a limited extent, and thereafter by Messrs Harrison & Sons.

The following is a list of the controls of stamps produced from the four identified electros derived from the first master-plate, with the colours associated with each: B.13, grey-green, pale grey-green; C13, D14, F15, G15, H16, I16, J17, shades of pale to deep grey-green; K17, pale grey-green; K18, M18, grey-green, pale grey-green; N19, O20, deep to pale grey-green; Q21, pale grey-green shades; R21, S21, S22, grey-green to pale grey-green; T22, dark to pale grey-green; U22, U23, V23, grey-green to pale grey-green.

The three types of 'Simple' Cypher watermark appeared with controls as follows: Type I, controls B.13 and C13; Type II, controls C13, D14, F15, G15, H16, I16, J17, K17, K18 (small printing), O20, R21, S21, U22, U23 (small printing), V23; Type III, J17, K17, K18, M18, N19, O20, Q21, R21, S21, S22, T22, U23.

Inverted watermarks are known with controls B.13, G15, K17, K18 and M18; watermarks reversed with controls C13, J17 and V23; and watermarks inverted and reversed with controls B.13, C13, G15, I16, J17, K17, M18, R21 and U22. Control B.13 with bottom margin perforated is scarce; also control H16 and K17 with perforated margin are rare.

Among the Plate flaws which have been recorded there is one occurring on the second stamp in the 19th row of Plate 1, appearing like an acute accent above the 'o' of 'FOUR'. This plate was originally put to press with control B.13, but it was not until it was at press with control F15 that the flaw appeared. The flaw was never repaired.

Another flaw appeared on the first stamp of the 19th row of Plate 2. This was the cracking of the fine surfacing of the Plate, and appears as a white diagonal line through the marginal rule to the left of the stamp which it enters, by the left hand value tablet running down the lower left hexagonal side of it, through the 'FO' of 'FOUR', and out through the base line below the 'U' of 'FOUR'. This plate was originally put to press with control B.13, but it was not until the Plate was put to press with control I16 that the flaw developed. Before the Plate was put to press with control R21 it was re-surfaced, obliterating all the flaw except a very small portion in the marginal rule to the left of the stamp.

THE WATERLOW PRINTINGS AND HARRISON (PROVISIONAL) PRINTINGS 1924-35

The Waterlow stamps appeared in November 1924. The watermark was 'Multiple' block cypher and the perforation 15 × 14. The stamps were typographed by Waterlow & Sons Ltd. Perforated copies are known overprinted 'Specimen'. Eight electros have been identified.

The following is a list of the controls, with the colours associated therewith: B24, deep grey-green; C25, E26, G27, I28, K29, shades of grey-green, deep grey-green and pale grey-green; M30, O31, grey-green, pale grey-green; Q32, deep grey-green, grey-green; R32, grey-green; T33, deep grey-green, grey-green. The controls and colours of the Harrison (Provisional) Printings were: V34, dark grey-green, deep grey-green; W35 and X35, deep grey-green, black-green.

Inverted watermarks are known with controls B24, C25, D25, E26, G27, I28 and M30. One sheet was found printed in error on the gummed side, which consequently had the watermarks reversed. Control X35 has been recorded with perforated bottom margin. It is rare. Otherwise perforated bottom margins are unknown.

THE PHOTOGRAVURE STAMPS 1935-38

The Fourpence produced by the rotary photogravure process appeared on December 2, 1935. The official colour was 'Deep green slate', described by the printers as 'Royal myrtle-green'. It is almost black. The controls and cylinder numbers were as follows: control W35 with cylinder 3, which is only known from the 'no stop' pane; control X35 with cylinders 8, 9 and 11; control Y36, Y36 quarter box, Y36 half box, Y36 three-quarter box and Y36 whole box, all with cylinder 11. Cylinder 3 was a sideways-etched cylinder, the only one so etched to have small-size images, and only printings from the 'no stop' pane are known. One known example with the left margin imperforate and the bottom margin with a single extension hole is believed to be unique. The remainder had the left and bottom margins perforated through. There can be no doubt that the images were etched sideways and that printings took place sheet by sheet in German presses. An example in the technical collection formed by Mr R. W. Leach of Evanston, Illinois, showing the corner of a sheet turned over and partly printed on the gummed side, is conclusive proof of this.

Chapter Nine

Fivepence

For the original trials, including those for colour, the Eve 'Wreath' frame was used. A die with this frame, with the Downey type head inserted, was made with the side shading extending down to the ornaments in the two lower corners, from which colour trials were made. These are known in four shades of green, three of red, two of brown, and in mauve, light blue, grey-green, grey, orange-vermilion and amber. Die proofs are known in black and blue. The light blue trial is also known on watermarked paper.

Further trials took place with the 'Wreath' frame, but with the profile head inserted and varying shading at the sides, which culminated in a trial dated November 22, 1912. These were in black by the Motley process. Two designs are known, the first had even shading to the head, but in the second the shading was deep at the top and shallow at the bottom.

By April 29, 1913, it had been decided to use the Eve 'Pillar' design for this value, and under that date a die proof of an early type of this frame is known. It had the Downey type head, but without value. There were lines of shading through the upper portion of the words 'POSTAGE' and 'REVENUE', which were without stop after the former and before the latter. Die proofs are known in black on glazed card and in blue on paper watermarked 'Simple' cypher sideways. It had already been decided to use the Mackennal medal head, which had been improved by Eve bringing its width down to 47·4 per cent of the width of the frame. Approved die proofs of this head exist dated April 3, 1913.

Die proofs are known with this head in the amended 'Pillar' frame, with value inserted. There were now no lines of shading through the upper part of 'POSTAGE' and 'REVENUE', but there was a stop after the former and before the latter. These proofs were dated between June 2 and 8, 1913, one of those dated June 8 being approved.

The stamp as issued was similar to the Sixpence, Sevenpence and Eightpence. The watermark was 'Simple' Cypher and the perforation 15 × 14. It was issued on June 30, 1913. Perforated copies are known overprinted 'Specimen' in upright type measuring 12½ mm from sheets with control B.13. The stamps were printed at first at Somerset House (control B.13) to a limited extent, and thereafter by Messrs Harrison & Sons. The following is a list of the controls of stamps printed from the three identified electros produced from the first master-plate, with the colours associated with each: B.13, brown, pale brown; C14, D14, F15, G15, shades of brown, pale brown, yellow-brown, pale yellow-brown; H16, deep brown, yellow-brown. With this control there was a very rare printing in colour varnish or varnished ink in deep shiny brown, notes concerning which appear above in connection with the Halfpenny Die IB and the One Penny Die IA and Die III; I16, deep brown, brown, yellow-brown; J17, deep brown, brown, bright yellow-brown; K17, bright yellow-brown, pale yellow-brown, bistre-brown; L18, deep brown, brown, pale brown, bistre-brown; N19, bright yellow-brown, pale yellow-brown; O19, brown, yellow-brown; Q21, brown, deep bistre-brown; R21, brown; S21, deep bistre-brown; S22, pale brown; T22, brown; U22, brown, pale brown, yellow-brown; V23, brown, pale brown. Some of these shades resemble chestnut and ochre-brown.

The three types of 'Simple' Cypher watermark appeared with the various controls as follows: Type I, control B.13 which is very rare; Type II, controls B.13, C14, D14, F15, G15, H16, I16, K17 (small printing), N19, O19 (small printing), Q21, R21, U23 (small printing) and V23; Type III, controls J17, K17, L18, N19, O19, 21, S22, T22 and U23. Inverted watermarks are found with controls H16, L18 and N19; and watermarks inverted and reversed with controls D14 and N19. A whole sheet was found printed in error upon paper without watermark, under circumstances similar to those which occurred with the Threehalfpence value. Control S22 with bottom margin perforated is rare.

THE WATERLOW PRINTINGS AND HARRISON (PROVISIONAL) PRINTINGS 1924-35

The stamps typographed by Waterlow & Sons Ltd appeared in November 1924. The watermark was 'Multiple' block cypher and perforation 15 × 14. Perforated copies are known overprinted 'Specimen'. The following is a list of the controls, with the colours associated therewith: A24, brown, bistre-brown, C25, F26, H27, I28, brown, yellow-brown; K29, deep yellow-brown, yellow-brown; L29, brown, pale brown, bistre-brown; M30, pale yellow-brown; N30, O31, Q32, shades of brown, pale brown, yellow-brown, pale yellow-brown; S33, yellow-brown, pale yellow-brown; T33, yellow-brown. This printing was very small, and the control is rare. The controls and colours of the Harrison (Provisional) Printings were: U34, yellow-brown, bright yellow-brown; V34, deep yellow-brown, yellow-brown, pale yellow-brown; X35, yellow-brown, deep bistre-brown. Inverted watermarks are found with controls A24, C25, F26 and I28. Three electros have been identified from the second master-plate, and were used for this issue. Except in the case of control A24, perforated bottom margins are unknown.

THE PHOTOGRAVURE STAMPS 1935-38

The Fivepence produced by the rotary photogravure process appeared on February 17, 1936. Imperforate colour trials are known in the accepted brown colour. The official colour was 'orange-brown' described by the printers as 'yellow-brown'.

Only cylinder 5 was used. The controls were X35, Y36, Z36, Z36 quarter box, Z36 half box, Z36 three-quarter box, and Z36 whole box. Control X35 is very rare; Z36 (quarter box) with perforated side margin is rare.

Chapter Ten

Sixpence

THE original sketch for this value was in the Eve 'Wreath' frame with a three-quarter head roughly drawn in. Colour trials are known, taken from a 'Wreath' design similar to that used for the Fivepence colour trials, in four shades of purple and mauve, three shades of green, two shades of red, two shades of brown, three shades of grey, and in maroon, orange and ruby black.

The Eve 'Pillar' design was adopted, and a photograph of this design, incorporating the profile head dated April 25, 1913, was sent to Mr Eve to draw in the values. There is no stop before the word 'POSTAGE' or after 'REVENUE'.

The approved die proof, with stop before 'POSTAGE' and after 'REVENUE', and the Eve improved medal head in black, was dated May 28, 1913.

The watermark was 'Simple' Cypher and perforation 15 × 14. The stamp was issued on August 1, 1913. Perforated copies in dull lilac exist overprinted respectively 'Specimen' in upright type measuring 12½ mm from sheets with control C.13, and 'Cancelled' from sheets with control E.14 in red-purple. Until 1934 the printing of this stamp was done at Somerset House exclusively, and up to 1925 the paper was coated. The watermark was 'Simple' Cypher and the perforation 15 × 14, except in 1921, when some of the sheets were perforated 14 × 14. Almost immediately after the first issue in August 1913, in dull lilac or grey-purple, there was a deliberate change of colour to reddish-purple or bright magenta. At first the stamps were printed on Joynson paper. But in 1924, during the B.24 control period, Sam Jones paper came into use. At first this was coated, but during the D.25 control period unsurfaced paper was employed; very shortly afterwards it was plate-glazed. Two faulty control blocks were used, in each case the faulty portion being the stop between the letter and the figures. The first of these occurred in control D.14, the stop appearing as a comma. This control block was in use with Plate 1. The second occurred on control L.18 in which the stop failed to print. The control block was in use with Plate 4. In 1934 Messrs Harrison took over the printing under their contract of that year, but for this stamp they never made use of the photogravure process. They put the electros to press on plate-glazed John Allen paper. However, during 1936 there was a temporary return to the use of coated paper.

The following is a list of the controls, with the colours associated with each:

SOMERSET HOUSE PRINTINGS ON JOYNSON PAPER 1913-24

C.13 (a) dull lilac, deep grey-purple, pale grey-purple, (b) reddish-purple, bright magenta; D.14, red-purple, pale red-purple; E.14, deep red-purple, red-purple, pale red-purple, bright magenta; F.15, G.15, H.16, I.16, red-purple, pale red-purple; J.17, K.17, L.18, M.18, deep red-purple, red purple, pale red-purple; N.19, red-purple, deep reddish-purple, rose-lilac; O.19, shades of deep reddish-purple; P.20, reddish-purple, deep reddish-purple, bright magenta; Q.20 (Perf. 15 × 14), red-purple (Perf. 14 × 14), deep red-purple, red-purple; R.21 (Perf. 14 × 14), pale red-purple, (Perf. 15 × 14), red-purple, pale red-purple; S.21, reddish-purple, red-purple; T.22, red-purple; U.22, reddish-purple, deep red-purple; V.23, W.23, reddish lilac, dull purple; A.24, B.24, reddish-lilac, pale reddish-lilac, dull purple, grey-purple. The only controls which had bottom margins both imperforate and perforated were C.13, E.14, L.18, N.19, S.21 and T.22. Of these, F.15 with perforated margin is rare, and L.18, N.19, S.21 and T.22 thus are scarce.

Two types of 'Simple' Cypher watermark were used with controls as follows: Type II, controls C.13 (dull lilac and red-purple), D.14, E.14, F.15, G.15, H.16, I.16, J.17, O.19, P.20, Q.20 (Perf. 15 × 14 and 14 × 14), R.21 (Perf. 14 × 14 and 15 × 14), S.21, V.23, W.23, A.24, B.24; Type III, controls J.17, K.17, L.18 (and L18),

M.18, N.19, O.19, P.20, Q.20 (Perf. 15 × 14 and 14 × 14), R.21 (Perf. 14 × 14 and 15 × 14), S.21, T.22, U.22, V.23, A.24, B.24. Inverted watermarks appear with controls C.13, E.14, H.16, L.18, M.18, N.19, O.19, P.20, Q.20 (Perf. 15 × 14), R.21 (Perf. 15 × 14), S.21, V.23, W.23, A.24. Reversed watermarks appear with controls D.14 and O.19; and inverted and reversed watermarks with controls D.14, E.14, K.17, N.19, O.19, P.20, R.21 (Perf. 15 × 14).

SOMERSET HOUSE PRINTINGS ON SAMUEL JONES PAPER
1924-33

Perforated stamps overprinted 'Specimen' are known. The controls and colours were as follows: B.24, reddish-lilac; C.25, reddish-lilac, pale reddish-lilac, greyish-purple; D.25, (a) coated paper, pale reddish-lilac, (b) unsurfaced paper, pale reddish-purple; E.26, F.26, G.27, pale reddish-purple, reddish-purple; H.27 reddish-purple, pale reddish-purple, pale red-purple, pale rose-lilac; I.28, pale red-purple; J.28, rose-lilac, pale rose-lilac; K.29, pale reddish-purple; L.29, reddish-purple; M.30, bright magenta, red-purple; M.30, O.31, P.31, red-purple, pale red-purple; Q.32, R.32, S.33, T.33, red-purple, deep red-purple, pale red-purple. Only controls I.28 and J.28 are known with both imperforate and perforated margins.

Inverted watermarks appear with controls B.24, C.25, D.25 (coated paper), F.26. G.27, H.27, I.28, J.28, K.29, L.29, N.30. Inverted and reversed watermarks appear with controls B.24 and C.25.

HARRISON PRINTINGS ON JOHN ALLEN PAPER
OCTOBER 1934-38

The controls and colours associated with each were as follows: V34, W35, deep red-purple, bright magenta; X35, red-purple, pale red-purple, bright magenta; Y36 (plate-glazed paper), deep red-purple, red-purple; (coated paper) deep red-purple, pale red-purple;

PLATE IX

1   Sevenpence. Eve's Zinco block with small head.

2   Sevenpence. Eve's Zinco block with large head.

3   Comparison of the size of Eve's Zinco blocks with the size of the actual stamp.

4 to 6

Sevenpence. The Motley Trials in wreath frames.

1

2

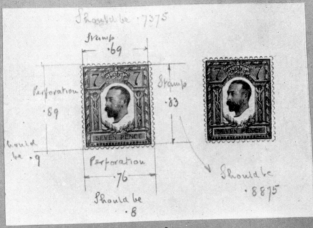

3

4

5

6

PLATE IX

Z36 (coated paper) deep red-purple, red-purple; (plate-glazed paper) deep reddish-purple, red-purple, pale red-purple; A37, deep reddish-purple, red-purple; B37, red-purple; C38, reddish-purple, red-purple, bright magenta; D38, red-purple, pale red-purple.

V34 is known only with imperforate margin and W35 and X35 are known both imperforate and perforated. Y36 on ordinary paper is only known imperforate; on coated paper it is only known imperforate, and this is rare. B37 and D38 are known both imperforate and perforated. The others are only known imperforate.

Plates 1 to 7 inclusive were used with Joynson paper; Plates 7 to 17 inclusive with Samuel Jones paper; and Plates 16 and 18 to 22 inclusive with John Allen paper.

Somerset House did not mark their plates with cuts or dots in the marginal rule, in the manner adopted by the contractors in connection with the other values. They did, however, employ dots in the rule above both upper and lower panes, in the same manner as that adopted in connection with their tests of the early plates of the other values. These dots were never filled in after the initial printings from the electros. Normally they appear only above the first or second stamp in the top rows. But they exist, not only in slightly differing positions, but also on sheets of Joynson paper with watermark Type III, which was not used before 1917. On Samuel Jones and John Allen paper they only appear above the top row, though in the Plate 7 printings they must exist above both panes.

Chapter Eleven

Sevenpence

THERE were extensive colour trials. The first series was made from the Eve zinco-blocks of which there were three types. The first was the 'Wreath' design with the small Downey type head. Colour trials are known in three shades of mauve and violet, five shades of green, three shades of red, four shades of brown, four shades of grey, and in magenta, maroon, orange, ruby-black, blue and black, all on white paper. Further trials were made in art purple on rose and blue paper, bright sage-green on blue paper, brown on green paper and turquoise on blue and yellow paper.

The second series was in the 'Pillar' design with small Downey head inserted. Colour trials are known in nine shades of red, pink or carmine, two shades of orange, eight shades of brown, ten shades of green, ten shades of blue, six shades of violet, mauve or purple, three shades of grey, and in olive-bistre and very pale yellow-ochre.

The third series was also in the 'Pillar' design but with large Downey head inserted. Colour trials are known in two shades of red, brown, purple-brown, violet, olive-green, blue and grey-black. Examples are also known in red and black on paper watermarked Crown.

Examples from the third series are known mounted, together with examples, in the same colour, of the One Shilling colour essays, on a card with the printed heading ' "Essays" for colour only – not design'. A manuscript addition shows the colours favoured for the Eightpence to One Shilling values. These were: for the Eightpence, $\frac{W}{98}$ quick drying black; for the Ninepence, $\frac{SP}{93}$ verdant green; for the Tenpence, $\frac{SP}{95}$ art purple No. 225 on Jones Rose No. 80; and for the One Shilling $\frac{SP}{95}$ art purple No. 225 on Jones Blue No. 91.

Further colour trials were made, from 'Wreath' design stamps with profile head made by the Motley process, of which there were four different types. In the first three of these the shading at the sides does not extend below the middle of the wreath, the variation being in the shading of the background of the head. In the first the shading in the upper left background is solid and that in the lower right is shaded. A colour trial is known in brilliant yellow-green. In the second the background is all solid, and colour trials are known in deep bistre-brown, greenish-grey, purple-brown, reddish-brown, vermilion and black. In the third the background is all shaded and a colour trial is known in black. In the fourth type the shading at the sides extends down to the lower ornaments. The background to the head is all shaded. Colour trials are known in bistre-brown, turquoise-blue, magenta and black. Examples in magenta and bistre-brown are known overprinted 'ESSAY' in upright sans-serif capitals measuring $7\frac{3}{4}$ mm.

Die proofs in black of the accepted 'Pillar' design with improved medal head are known dated June 5, 1913.

The watermark was again 'Simple' Cypher, and the perforation 15×14. The stamp was issued on August 1, 1913. Perforated copies are known overprinted 'Specimen' in upright type measuring $12\frac{1}{2}$ mm from sheets with control C.13. The stamps were printed at first at Somerset House (control C.13) to a limited extent, and thereafter by Messrs Harrison & Sons.

The controls and colours were as follows: C.13, pale olive; C13, D14, greyish-olive, greenish-olive; F15, deep greyish-olive, greyish-olive; G15, dark greyish-olive, greenish-olive; H16, pale greenish-olive, very pale greenish-olive; J17, sage green, greenish-olive, pale greenish-olive; L18, sage green.

Inverted watermarks are known with controls J17 and L18. Type I watermark was used with control C.13, but it is rare; Type II with control C.13, C13, D14, F15, G15, H16, J17 (small printing); and Type III with controls J17 and L18. Three electros have been identified from the only master-plate. With control L18 the issue of the Sevenpence value ended. This control with perforated bottom margin is scarce.

PLATE X

1   Eightpence. Eve's Zinco block.

2 to 6

The Motley Trials in pillar frames.

1

2

3

4

5

6

PLATE X

Chapter Twelve

Eightpence

EARLY colour trials were made from Eve's zinco-blocks of the 'Pillar' design with Downey type head. They are known in two shades of mauve or violet, four shades of green, three shades of red, three shades of brown, two shades of maroon, and in grey, orange and ruby black, all on white paper. They are also known in black on five shades of green paper. In these trials the background to the head was a series of very fine faint horizontal dots. Three further trials, one in magenta, one in green and one in red, were taken from these zinco-blocks from which the dotted lines had been removed.

Extensive trials by the Motley process took place in slightly differing types of the 'Pillar' design with a profile head of two different sizes. Early die proofs by this process had a head 12 mm high. There were five varieties of design. In the first there were no stops after 'POSTAGE' and before 'REVENUE', of which the letters 'POSTA' and 'VENUE' were horizontal and 'GE' and 'RE' sloping. A die proof is known in brown dated September 2, 1912. The remaining four designs with this head had stops after 'POSTAGE' and before 'REVENUE', 'POSTA' and 'ENUE' being horizontal and 'GE' and 'REV' sloping. The shading of the background to the head varies in each.

On the first the background was solid. A proof is known in black, and colour trials on paper watermarked 'Simple' Cypher in brown, deep red-brown, violet-black and magenta.

On the second the background was solid at the top left and shaded at the bottom right. A proof is known in black, and colour trials were made on paper watermarked 'Simple' Cypher in pale red-brown, violet-black and orange.

On the third the background was deep at the top and shallow at the base. A proof is known in black dated February 6, 1913, and colour trials were made on paper watermarked 'Simple' Cypher in violet-black. A further series of colour trials from this plate was made on unwatermarked paper in pale blue, bronze-green, yellow-green, yellow-bistre, deep ochre, red-brown, brownish-red, purple-brown, mauve and pink, all of which were overprinted 'ESSAY'. On the fourth the background was evenly shaded and a proof is known in black dated March 19, 1913.

Trials took place, concurrently with the above, with a Motley design, the head of which measured only 11¾ mm. On this plate there was no stop after 'POSTAGE' and before 'REVENUE', of which the letters 'POST' and 'ENUE' were horizontal and 'AGE' and 'REV' sloping. The 'V' of 'REVENUE' was thinner than the rest of the lettering. A proof is known in black dated December 12, 1912. Colour trials were made on unwatermarked paper in deep red-purple, and greenish grey on white paper and in black on orange-buff paper. There was a further series of colour trials, also on unwatermarked paper, all of which were overprinted 'ESSAY'. The trials were in pale carmine, red-brown, dark brown, purple-brown and olive on white paper, and in black on orange-buff, green and pinkish-brown paper, and in purple on blue paper.

Photographs of alternative designs are known dated January 1 and 18 and April 9, 1913, and a composite die was made from these. A die proof in black is known from the approved die. This proof bore two dates, June 5 and 8, 1913.

The stamp was issued on August 1, 1913. The watermark was 'Simple' Cypher, and the perforation 15 × 14. Perforated copies are known overprinted 'Specimen' in upright type measuring 12½ mm from sheets with control C.13. The stamps were printed at first at Somerset House (control C.13) to a limited extent, and thereafter by Messrs Harrison & Sons. This was the only stamp of this series printed on coloured paper. This yellow paper varied slightly in shade. The black ink varied slightly in depth. There were no shades. The controls were C.13, C13, D14, F15, G15, H16, I16, J17 and K18. Watermark Type II was used with all the controls except L18; and Type III was used with controls J17 and L18. Inverted watermarks are known with control F15, and reversed watermarks with controls G15 and H16.

In 1917 and 1918, with control J17 and K18, some of the stamps were printed upon what is known as 'granite paper'. This contained much foreign matter and was a war-time measure. There was only one electro, which had no plate marking. When put to press at Somerset House there was a white dot in the marginal rule above the first stamp in the top row of both panes, but these were filled in for the subsequent Harrison printings. Control K18 with imperforate margin is scarce. With this control the issue of the Eightpence value ceased.

Chapter Thirteen

Ninepence

EARLY colour trials were made from Eve's zinco-blocks of the 'Pillar' design with Downey type head. They are known in three shades of green, three shades of red, two shades of brown, and in mauve, grey, two shades of maroon, orange and ruby-black, all on white paper. They are also known in black on six shades of yellow paper.

The Eve 'Wreath' design was accepted for the Ninepence, Tenpence and One Shilling values. An enlarged photograph of the frame, on which the side shading did not go beyond the middle of the wreath, was sent to Eve on April 25, 1913 to draw in the values. The head was in profile. This design was accepted except for the head. Final die proofs with the improved medal head in black were dated May 6 and 7, 1913.

The printers at first (control B.13) were Somerset House and thereafter Messrs Harrison & Sons. The watermark for the period 1913-24 was 'Simple' Cypher, and the perforation throughout 15×14. Perforated copies are known overprinted 'Specimen' in upright type measuring $12\frac{1}{2}$ mm from sheets with control B.13.

On first issue on June 30, 1913, the stamps appeared in a colour described in the catalogues as 'Agate'. The reason for this is unknown to the Editors. The colour is actually very deep purplebrown, approaching black.

The following is a list of the first series of controls on the Joynson paper: B.13, E14, F15, G15, H16, I16, J17, K17, K18, L18, N19, O19, O20, P20, Q20, R21, S21, S22, all in slight shades of dark purple-brown.

In September 1922 it was decided to change the colour of the stamp, and three imperforate colour trials were made in shades of olive-green, which was the selected colour. Printings in this colour

116

appeared with controls T22, U23 and V23. The Type II watermark is found with controls B.13, E14, F15, G15, H16, I16, J17, O19 (small printing), O20, R21, U23 (small printing) and V23; and Type III with controls J17, K17, K18, L18, N19, O19, O20, P20, Q20, R21, S21, S22, T22 and U23. Inverted watermarks are known with controls B.13, F15, L18, O19, O20, P20, Q20 and U23; and watermarks inverted and reversed with controls G15, J17, O19, P20, Q20, S21, S22 and U23. Control I16 with bottom margin perforated is rather scarce. Control E14 is only known with perforated bottom margin.

Three electros from the first master-plate have been identified and were used for these printings on William Joynson paper.

THE WATERLOW PRINTINGS AND HARRISON (PROVISIONAL) PRINTINGS 1924-35

The Waterlow stamps appeared in December 1924. The watermark was 'Multiple' block cypher, and the perforation 15×14. They were typographed by Waterlow & Sons Ltd. Perforated copies are known overprinted 'Specimen'.

The following is a list of the controls with the colours associated with each: A24, C25, F26, olive-green; I28, olive-green, deep olive-green; J28, olive-green; L29, olive-green, pale olive-green; N30, olive-green, deep olive-green; P31, olive-green, pale olive-green; R32, olive-green; T33, olive-green, deep olive-green. The controls and colours of the Harrison provisional printings were V34, olive-green, deep olive-green; W35, olive-green; X35, olive-green, pale olive-green.

Inverted watermarks are known with controls A24, C25, F26, I28, J28 and P31. Six electros from the second master-plate have been identified. Only controls A24 and X35 are known with perforated bottom margins.

THE PHOTOGRAVURE STAMPS 1935-38

The Ninepence produced by the rotary photogravure process appeared on December 2, 1935. Imperforate colour trials are known in turquoise-blue, bistre and in the accepted colour. The official colour was 'olive-green', described by the printers as 'sage green'. The only cylinder used was 15, and the controls X35, X35 quarter box, X35 half box, X35 three-quarter box and X35 whole box. The controls and cylinder number were in the margin to the left of the 18th row.

Chapter Fourteen

Tenpence

EARLY colour trials were made from Eve's zinco-blocks of the 'Pillar' design with Downey type head. They are known in three shades of brown, three shades of green, two shades of red, three shades of grey, and in mauve, orange, maroon and ruby-black, all on white paper. They are also known in black on six shades of blue paper and three shades of violet paper.

The approved design was the Eve 'Wreath' design, and proofs from the die, which were endorsed 'Soft Die', are known in black dated June 7, 1913.

This value was issued on August 1, 1913. The printers were Somerset House at the outset (control C.13), and thereafter Messrs Harrison & Sons. The watermark for the 1913-23 period was 'Simple' Cypher, and the perforation 15 × 14 throughout. Perforated copies are known overprinted 'Specimen' in upright type measuring 12½ mm from sheets with control C.13, and overprinted 'Cancelled'.

The controls and colours associated therewith were as follows: C.13, D14, F15, G15, H16, I16, J17, K18, M19, O19, Q21, S21, S22, turquoise-blue, pale turquoise-blue; T22, turquoise-blue, deep turquoise-blue; U23, turquoise-blue, deep turquoise-blue, pale turquoise-blue.

Type I watermark was used with control F15, but this is very rare; Type II with controls C.13, D14, F15, G15, H16, I16, J17 (small printing), K18 (small printing), U23; Type III with controls J17, K18, M19, O19, Q21, S21, S22 and T22. Inverted watermarks are known with control H16 and M19, and watermarks inverted and reversed with controls C.13, O19 and Q21. Control C.13 with perforated bottom margin is rare. Two electros from the first master-plate have been identified and were used with William Joynson paper.

THE WATERLOW PRINTINGS AND HARRISON
(PROVISIONAL) PRINTINGS 1924-35

The Waterlow stamps appeared in November 1924. The water-mark was 'Multiple' block cypher, and the perforation 15×14. They were typographed by Waterlow & Sons Ltd. Imperforate copies are known overprinted 'Specimen' in sloping type and per-forated copies overprinted 'Cancelled' in upright type.

The following is a list of the controls, with the colours associated with each: A24, turquoise-blue, greenish turquoise-blue; D25, F26, turquoise-blue, pale turquoise-blue, greenish turquoise-blue; G27, turquoise-blue, deep turquoise-blue, greenish turquoise-blue; J28, turquoise-blue, deep turquoise-blue; L29, shades of deep to pale turquoise-blue; O31, greenish turquoise-blue; Q32, S33, turquoise-blue, deep turquoise-blue. Those of the Harrison provisional print-ing were U34, V34, greenish turquoise-blue; W35, X35, deep dull turquoise-blue, dull turquoise-blue, pale turquoise-blue. Inverted watermarks appeared with controls D25 and F26, but these are rare.

Three electros from the second master-plate have been identified. Control A24, with perforated margin, is scarce. With subsequent controls perforated bottom margins are unknown.

THE PHOTOGRAVURE STAMPS 1936-39

The Tenpence produced by the rotary photogravure process appeared on February 24, 1936. The official colour was 'Cerulean', described by the printers as 'turquoise blue'. The only cylinder used was 3, and the controls Y36, Y36 quarter box, Y36 half box, Y36 three-quarter box and Y36 whole box. The controls and cylinder number were in the margin to the left of the 18th row. Reverse feed is known with printings from the 'stop' pane under control Y36 without boxing. The left margin is imperforate and the bottom margin with a single extension hole. The example seen is believed to be unique.

Chapter Fifteen

One Shilling

EARLY colour trials were made from Eve's zinco-blocks of the 'Pillar' design with Downey type head. They are known in five shades of brown, five shades of green, two shades of red, and in grey, magenta, mauve, maroon, black, ruby-black and orange, all on white paper. Further extensive colour trials were made on coloured paper. These were in art purple on rose and blue paper, turquoise on blue and yellow paper, black on two shades of pink or rose paper, red paper and four shades of cerise paper, in brown on green paper and in bright sage-green on blue paper.

Final die proofs in the Eve 'Wreath' design are known in black dated June 12, 1913.

This value was issued on August 1, 1913. The printers at the outset were Somerset House (control C.13) and thereafter Messrs Harrison & Sons. The watermark for the 1913-23 period was 'Simple' Cypher, and the perforation 15 × 14 throughout. Perforated copies are known overprinted 'Specimen' in upright type measuring 12½ mm from sheets with control C.13, and overprinted 'Cancelled'.

The controls and colours associated therewith were as follows: C.13, D14, E14, F15, bistre-brown, pale bistre-brown, buff; G15, bistre-brown, olive-bistre and a very rare deep bistre-brown in colour varnish or varnished ink, similar to that described above in connection with the Halfpenny Die IB, the One Penny Die IA and Die III, and the Fivepence; H16, bistre-brown, pale bistre-brown, olive-bistre; I16, bistre-brown, pale bistre-brown, olive-bistre, pale olive-bistre, buff and a very rare deep bistre-brown in colour varnish or varnished ink, as above-mentioned in connection with control G15; J17, bistre-brown, olive-bistre, pale olive-bistre; K17 olive-bistre, pale olive-bistre; L18, bistre-brown, olive-bistre, pale

121

olive-bistre; M19, N19, O19, O20, shades of deep to pale olive-bistre; P20, olive-bistre, pale olive-bistre; Q20, bistre-brown, olive-bistre, pale olive-bistre, yellow-brown; R21, bistre-brown, pale olive-bistre, very pale olive-bistre; S21, S22, T22, U22, olive-bistre and pale olive-bistre; U23, olive-bistre; V23, olive-bistre, deep olive-bistre. Shades of pale buff, deep bronze and golden-brown also exist.

Type II watermark was used with controls C.13, D14, E14, F15, G15, H16, I16, J17, K17 (small printing), Q20, R21, U22, U23 and V23; and Type III with controls J17, K17, L18, M19, N19, O19, O20, P20, Q20, R21, S21, S22, T22 and U23. Inverted watermarks are known with controls J17, K17, O19, P20, Q20, R21 and S21; and watermark inverted and reversed with controls D14, F15, I16, L18, N19, O19, P20, Q20, S21 and U22.

Four electros from the first master-plate have been identified and were used with William Joynson paper. Control E14 with imperforate or perforated margin is rare. C.13 and K17 with perforated margin are scarce.

THE WATERLOW PRINTINGS AND HARRISON (PROVISIONAL) PRINTINGS 1924-35

The Waterlow stamps appeared in November 1924. The watermark was 'Multiple' block cypher, and the perforation 15 × 14. They were typographed by Waterlow & Sons Ltd. Imperforate copies are known overprinted 'Specimen'.

The following is a list of the controls, with the colours associated with each: A24, B24, olive-bistre; D25, shades of olive-bistre from deep to pale; F26, olive-bistre, pale olive-bistre; H27, bistre-brown, pale bistre-brown; I28, bistre-brown; J28, shades of bistre-brown from deep to pale; K29, bistre-brown, olive-bistre; L29, olive-bistre, pale olive-bistre; N30, bistre-brown; P31, R32, bistre-brown, deep bistre-brown; S33, olive-bistre. Those of the Harrison provisional printings were U34, greyish olive-bistre; V34, greyish olive-bistre, pale greyish olive-bistre; W35, X35, greyish olive-bistre. Inverted watermarks are known with controls A24, D25, F26, I28, J28 and L29.

Five electros from the second master-plate have been identified. Only controls A24 and V34 are known with perforated bottom margins.

THE PHOTOGRAVURE STAMPS 1936-39

The One Shilling produced by the rotary photogravure process appeared on February 24, 1936. The official colour was 'Raw Umber', described by the printers as 'Sepia'. The following controls and cylinder numbers were used: control Y36 with cylinders 3 and 4; and cylinder 5 with controls Z36 and Z36 quarter box, Z36 half box, Z36 three-quarter box, and Z36 whole box. The control and cylinder numbers were in the margin to the left of the 18th row.

Among the cylinder flaws recorded is one on cylinder 5. To the left of the cylinder number on both 'no stop' and 'stop' panes was a faint, yet clear, portion of an erroneously engraved figure 4.

Chapter Sixteen

The Issue of Stamps otherwise than in Post Office Sheets

CERTAIN values of the stamps were made up for sale at Post Offices in booklet form, and also in coils for automatic slot machines.

Some booklets were made up with plain perforated paper, either unwatermarked or watermarked 'Harrison & Sons London'. These were trials.

From time to time booklets were made up of various denominations in varying combinations. These changes were either necessitated by altered postal rates or were made in an attempt to find a combination most suited to the public demand. The stamps were normally in panes of six, and were bound in coloured covers and interleaved with white paper. In all booklets, except the first three editions and series 4 Editions 3 to 128, postal rates were shown, and trade advertisements appeared either on the covers or on the interleaves. In May 1930 an interleaf of Air Mail labels was included.

The following types of booklets were issued during this period.

1. 2/- booklet. Red cover containing 18 at 1d, 12 at ½d. Die IB, watermark Crown. In Chapter III reference was made to stamps issued in Post Office sheets printed at Somerset House appearing plum under the lamp, and to those printed by Harrison appearing pinkish. Panes from booklets so examined show similar reflections, but this refers to the carmine shades only. At this period no imprint appeared on the back covers of the booklets, and therefore it is not possible to say whether all the One Penny stamps were printed by the contractors or whether, as was the case with the Post Office sheets, the booklet electros of this value were first put to press at Somerset House. The above-mentioned reflections under the lamp are caused by different ink compositions, and the appearance of reflections similar to those obtained from identifiable

124

sheet printings suggests that at least some of these electros were first put to press at Somerset House.

Later booklets contained stamps in pale scarlet, scarlet, bright scarlet and the so-called 'aniline-scarlet'. This latter stamp can be identified by the fact that, under the lamp, it fluoresces brilliant yellow, traces of which can be seen on the back, and the paper gives a bluish reflection associated with highly plate-glazed paper, though, in fact, the plate-glazing is not very marked. This is catalogued as S.G. 333.

This booklet was also made up containing Halfpenny and One Penny stamps of Die IB watermarked 'Simple' Cypher, and also of those stamps of Die III watermarked 'Simple' Cypher.

2. 3/- booklet. Red cover containing 12 at $1\frac{1}{2}$d, 12 at 1d, 12 at $\frac{1}{2}$d stamps of Harrison (1912) issue.

3. 3/- booklet. Red cover containing 18 at $1\frac{1}{2}$d, 6 at 1d, 6 at $\frac{1}{2}$d stamps of the following issues:

  (a) Harrison (1912) issue.
  (b) Waterlow issue.
  (c) P.U.C. issue. These booklets were in buff covers with inscription in red.
  (d) Harrison (1934) provisional typograph issue.
  (e) Photogravure issue in both the intermediate and small size images.

4. 3/6 booklet. Red cover containing 18 at 2d (Die I), 6 at 1d of the Harrison (1912) issue.

5. 3/6 booklet. Red cover containing 12 at 2d (Die I), 6 at $1\frac{1}{2}$d, 6 at 1d, 6 at $\frac{1}{2}$d stamps of the Harrison (1912) issue.

6. 3/- booklet. Blue cover containing 18 at 2d (Die I) of the Harrison (1912) issue.

7. 3/6 booklet. Red cover containing 12 at 2d (Die II), 6 at $1\frac{1}{2}$d, 6 at 1d, 6 at $\frac{1}{2}$d stamps of the Harrison (1912) issue.

8. 3/- booklet. Blue cover containing 18 at 2d (Die II) stamps of the Harrison (1912) issue.

9. 3/- booklet. Blue cover containing 24 at $1\frac{1}{2}$d stamps of the Harrison (1912) issue.

10. 2/- booklet. Blue cover containing 10 at 1½d, 6 at 1d, 6 at ½d stamps of the following issues:

(a) Harrison (1912) issue.
(b) Waterlow issue.
(c) P.U.C. These booklets had buff covers with inscription in blue.
(d) Harrison (1934) provisional typograph issue.
(e) Photogravure issue in both the intermediate and small size images.

11. 5/- booklet. Edition No. 1 was in a green cover, the remainder in buff covers, containing 34 at 1½d, 6 at 1d, 6 at ½d stamps of the following issues:

(a) Waterlow issue.
(b) Harrison (1934) provisional typograph issue.
(c) Photogravure issue in both intermediate and small size images.

12. 3/- booklet. Buff cover with red inscription containing 20 at 1½d, 4 at 1d, 4 at ½d stamps of the Silver Jubilee issue.

13. 2/- booklet. Buff cover with blue inscription containing 12 at 1½d, 4 at 1d, 4 at ½d stamps of the Silver Jubilee issue.

The issues under sub-heads 10 and 11 inaugurated the system of having the first booklet sheet composed of four stamps and two blanks *se-tenant*, upon which stamp advertisements were typographed. Special electros were made for these.

In Edition No. 8 (Waterlow printing) the Post Office notices (Air Mails – Cable via Imperial) were inverted in error. This was not a case of the overprint plate being inverted, for this would not invert the print, but a case of those notices which should be set up upright having been set up inverted, and *vice versa*. In Editions Nos. 12 and 67, the advertisements were for Harmer Rooke & Co., and the upper halves in each case were purposely inverted. In Edition No. 171 the advertisements for MacKinlay's Rubber Sponges were printed in green instead of black.

Among the plate flaws recorded was one on the Harrison (1912)

Halfpenny which appeared on the lower right hand stamp in the booklet panes. It is commonly called the 'New Moon' flaw, and appears like a new moon lying on its side with the convex side uppermost. It has been found in the booklets of sub-head 1, No. 13. Its position on the uncut sheet is from the third vertical row, but its horizontal position cannot be determined.

The cylinders used for printing the photogravure stamps in booklets were the Halfpenny intermediate size E1, small size E4, E5 and E6; the One Penny intermediate size F1, small size F6 and F7; the Threehalfpence, printing full panes, intermediate size G4, small size G20, G24 'no stop' pane only, G27 (rare), G30 and G31; and the Threehalfpence, printing advertisement *se-tenant* panes, intermediate size G7, G9, G10, G15, G16 and G17 (all rare), small size G24 'stop' pane only, G26 and G28.

The *se-tenant* advertisements on the intermediate size cylinders were etched upon them, and consequently appeared in the colour of the stamp. Those on the small size cylinders were typographed as before. Cylinder G24 had a unique layout in that the 'no stop' pane printed complete panes, and the 'stop' pane those for the *se-tenant* advertisements.

For the Jubilee issue the cylinders were the Halfpenny 33 and 35; the One Penny 26 (only two copies known) and 37; and the Threehalfpence 30, 41, 58 (only three or four copies known), 59 and 66.

A very rare variety is known in which a few cylinder number panes were found with watermark inverted. One may well ask how this was possible. It could have been caused by the cylinder being put to press the wrong way round, but the 'shadow' of the stamps proves that this was not the case. Another cause could be that the stamps were not printed in the web; but the appearance of these varieties in consecutive booklets makes this extremely unlikely. The actual cause can therefore only have been that an unfinished unreeling drum of unprinted paper was reeled off on to the reeling drum, which was later put back to press in the unreeling position, thus passing over the printing cylinder in the reverse (paper) direction, thereby causing the watermarks to be inverted. This very rare variety occurs only with the Halfpenny cylinder E4 and the Threehalfpence cylinder G26 (with *se-tenant* advertisement for No. 1 Bond or Commercial Trust).

Stamps are known in booklets obliterated by date stamps, overprinted 'Cancelled' in upright or sloping type, overprinted 'Specimen' in upright or sloping type, overprinted 'Cancelled' in upright type with the centre of the stamp punched out cross-shaped by means of punches. Since the punch was T-shaped and the stamps were folded vertically before punching, the size and shape of the cross varies. A few of these are trial booklets, but the majority are those sent to Advertisers as Voucher Copies which were at first obliterated by date stamp; then, in April 1926, overprinted 'Cancelled' in sloping type (though very occasionally 'Specimen'), and, in February 1928, overprinted 'Cancelled' and punched. The stamps of the Silver Jubilee issue were twice overprinted 'Cancelled' and once punched. Full details concerning the production and issue of stamps in booklets are contained in two series of articles by Colonel J. B. M. Stanton published in the *British Philatelist*, Vols. XXXVII (June to October 1948) and XL (May 1949) to XLI (February 1951).

Prior to the issue of stamps in coils, for use in slot or affixing machines, trial rolls were made up. For this purpose perforated labels took the place of stamps, and these were attached to the core-ends at the inner end and to the wrapper at the outer end. Two types of label were in use. The first was that with the head of T. R. Harrison which was also in use for experimental booklets, and the second bore a coat of arms and the name of the Harrison firm. Other experiments were made with plain paper dummies. These were either unwatermarked or watermarked 'Harrison & Sons London'. Other coils were made up with the actual stamp paper watermarked Crown. Vertical strips were separated from sheets before they were put to press and joined lengthwise. Each strip was of the length of 21 stamps, but only 20 of these were watermarked, since upon the printed sheet no watermark fell in the interpane margin. Each watermarked dummy was overprinted 'Cancelled' diagonally either in green or in red, but there was no overprint upon the unwatermarked dummy. At later stages coils of dummies, either printed or blank, were made up for testing the vending machines. These are described later.

Twenty types of coils for issue in slot or affixing machines were made up. Originally the large coils were of 1,000 stamps and the small of 500, but these were later reduced to 960 and 480 respectively. Subsequently 'Kermode coils' were made up for use in Post Office machines only. The small coil consisted of 1,000 stamps, later reduced to 960, and the large coil was composed of 1,920 stamps. Coils delivered the stamps either lengthwise (top or bottom end first) or sideways (left side first).

At first the coils were made up by joining strips separated from Post Office sheets, but in 1921 experiments took place at Somerset House for the production of continuous coils by reel printing on Grover presses, a system which was adopted during the Waterlow contract, but not for the Twopence Halfpenny and Threepence coils made during the Harrison (1934) contract.

Upon first issue the large coils were priced at 2d over face value and the small coils at 1d over face. Later this was increased to 4d and 2d respectively, but later again reduced, and finally the surcharge was removed altogether. Originally the wrappers were of buff paper printed in the colour of the stamps concerned, but were later of the colour of the stamps with printing in black.

The following is a list of the coils made up:

HALFPENNY

Lengthwise Delivery

(C) Joined strips made up with 1,000 stamps of
    (a) Die II watermark 'Multiple' Cypher.
    (b) Harrison (1912) issue watermark 'Simple' Cypher.

(D) Joined strips made up with 1,000 stamps of
    (a) Die II watermark 'Simple' Cypher.
    (b) Die II watermark 'Multiple' Cypher.
    (c) Harrison (1912) issue watermark 'Simple' Cypher.

    Continuous coils made up with 960 stamps of
    (a) Waterlow issue.
    (b) Photogravure issue.

I

(G) Joined strips made up with 500 stamps of
 (*a*) Die II watermark 'Multiple' Cypher.
 (*b*) Harrison (1912) issue watermark 'Simple' Cypher.
 (*c*) Harrison (1912) issue watermark 'Multiple' Cypher.
Continuous coils made up with 480 stamps of
 (*a*) Waterlow issue.
 (*b*) P.U.C. issue.
 (*c*) Photogravure issue.
(H) Joined strips made up with 500 stamps of
 (*a*) Die II watermark 'Multiple' Cypher.
 (*b*) Harrison (1912) issue watermark 'Simple' Cypher.

KERMODE (small)

Joined strips made up with 1,000 stamps of Harrison (1912)
issue watermark 'Simple' Cypher.
Continuous coils made up with 960 stamps of Waterlow issue.
Coil redesignated (W).
Continuous coils made up with 960 stamps of
 (*a*) Waterlow issue.
 (*b*) P.U.C. issue.
 (*c*) Photogravure issue.

KERMODE (large)

Continuous coils made up with 1920 stamps of Waterlow issue.
Coil redesignated (Y).
Continuous coils made up with 1920 stamps of
 (*a*) Waterlow issue.
 (*b*) P.U.C. issue.
 (*c*) Photogravure issue.

Sideways Delivery

(P) Joined strips (with watermark upright) made up with 480
 stamps of
 (*a*) Harrison (1912) issue watermark 'Simple' Cypher.
 (*b*) Waterlow issue.

Continuous coils (with watermark sideways) made up with
480 stamps of

   (*a*) Waterlow issue.
   (*b*) P.U.C. issue.
   (*c*) Photogravure issue.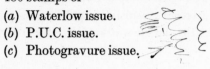

ONE PENNY

Lengthwise Delivery

(A) Joined strips made up with 1,000 stamps of

   (*a*) Die II watermark Crown.
   (*b*) Die II watermark 'Simple' Cypher.
   (*c*) Die II watermark 'Multiple' Cypher.
   (*d*) Harrison (1912) issue watermark 'Simple' Cypher.

(B) Joined strips made up with 1,000 stamps of

   (*a*) Die II watermark 'Simple' Cypher.
   (*b*) Die II watermark 'Multiple' Cypher.
   (*c*) Harrison (1912) issue watermark 'Simple' Cypher.

Continuous coils made up with 960 stamps of

   (*a*) Waterlow issue.
   (*b*) P.U.C. issue.
   (*c*) Photogravure issue.

(E) Joined strips made up with 500 stamps of

   (*a*) Die II watermark Crown.
   (*b*) Die II watermark 'Simple' Cypher.
   (*c*) Die II watermark 'Multiple' Cypher.
   (*d*) Harrison (1912) issue watermark 'Simple' Cypher.
   (*e*) Harrison (1912) issue watermark 'Multiple' Cypher.

Continuous coils made up with 500 (Somerset House) or 480
(other printings) stamps of

   (*a*) Somerset House printings with watermark 'Simple'
       Cypher.
   (*b*) Waterlow issue.
   (*c*) P.U.C. issue.
   (*d*) Photogravure issue.

(F) Joined strips made up with 500 stamps of
    (*a*) Die II watermark 'Simple' Cypher.
    (*b*) Die II watermark 'Multiple' Cypher.
    (*c*) Harrison (1912) issue watermark 'Simple' Cypher.

KERMODE (small)

Joined strips made up with 1,000 stamps of
    Harrison (1912) issue watermark 'Simple' Cypher.
Continuous coils made up with 1,000, later 960, stamps of
    Waterlow issue.
Coil redesignated (X).
Continuous coils made up with 960 stamps of
    (*a*) Waterlow issue.
    (*b*) P.U.C. issue.
    (*c*) Photogravure issue.

KERMODE (large)

Continuous coils made up with 1,920 stamps of
    Waterlow issue.
Coil redesignated (Z).
Continuous coils made up with 1,920 stamps of
    (*a*) Waterlow issue.
    (*b*) P.U.C. issue.
    (*c*) Photogravure issue.

Sideways Delivery
    (O) Joined strips (with watermark upright) made up with 480 stamps of Harrison (1912) issue watermark 'Simple' Cypher.
    Continuous coils (with watermark sideways) made up with 480 stamps of
        (*a*) Waterlow issue.
        (*b*) P.U.C. issue.
        (*c*) Photogravure issue.

THREEHALFPENCE

Lengthwise Delivery

(J) Joined strips made up with 1,000 stamps of Harrison (1912) issue.

(K) Joined strips made up with 1,000 stamps of Harrison (1912) issue.

Continuous coils made up with 960 stamps of

(*a*) Waterlow issue.

(*b*) P.U.C. issue.

(*c*) Photogravure issue.

(L) Joined strips made up with 500 stamps of Harrison (1912) issue.

Continuous coils made up with 480 stamps of

(*a*) Waterlow issue.

(*b*) P.U.C. issue.

(*c*) Photogravure issue.

(M) Joined strips made up with stamps of Harrison (1912) issue.

Sideways Delivery

(N) Joined strips (with watermark upright) made up with 480 stamps of Harrison (1912) issue.

Continuous coils (with watermark sideways) made up with 480 stamps of

(*a*) Waterlow issue.

(*b*) P.U.C. issue.

(*c*) Photogravure issue.

TWOPENCE

Lengthwise Delivery

(Q) Joined strips made up with 1,000 (Harrison) or 960 (other printings) stamps of

(*a*) Harrison (1912) issue. Die I.

(*b*) Waterlow issue.

(*c*) Photogravure stamps.

(R) Joined strips made up with 500 (Harrison) or 480 (other printings) stamps of
  (*a*) Harrison (1912) issue. Die I.
  (*b*) Waterlow issue.
  (*c*) Photogravure issue.
(S) Joined strips made up with 500 stamps of Harrison (1912) issue. Die I.

KERMODE (small)

Joined strips made up with 1,000 stamps of Harrison (1912) issue. Die I.

Sideways Delivery
(T) Joined strips (with watermark upright) made up with 480 stamps of
  (*a*) Harrison (1912) issue. Die I.
  (*b*) Waterlow issue.
  Continuous coils (with watermark sideways) made up with 480 stamps of
  (*a*) Waterlow issue.
  (*b*) Photogravure issue.

TWOPENCE HALFPENNY

Lengthwise Delivery
(F) Joined strips made up with 960 stamps of photogravure issue.

Sideways Delivery
(M) Joined strips (with watermark upright) made up with 480 stamps of Harrison (1934) provisional typograph printing.

THREEPENCE

Lengthwise Delivery
(C) Joined strips made up with 960 stamps of photogravure issue.

Sideways Delivery

(S) Joined strips (with watermark upright) made up with 480 stamps of Harrison (1934) provisional typograph printing.

The One Penny photogravure stamps in coil (E) and the Threehalfpence in coil (L) are known both in the intermediate and small size, the former being very rare. The initial Halfpenny and One Penny photogravure stamps in coils (P) and (O) were printed from reverse sideways cylinders and had the watermark reading downwards. They are very rare. Subsequent stamps were printed from ordinary sideways cylinders.

Among the flaws recorded was one appearing as a coloured blob on the King's nose on the Threehalfpence stamps printed by Messrs Waterlow and made up into continuous coils with sideways delivery (watermark sideways). It appears on every thirteenth stamp. This is rare.

From time to time either blank paper or printed labels the size of stamps were made up in coils for testing the vending machines, one of which attained some philatelic notoriety. This label was printed in green and resembled the shape of a 'poached egg'. It is said that some of these left in a London vending machine were obtained against the insertion of halfpenny coins and that these labels did genuine postal duty. That some of these labels did pass through the post doing duty as Halfpenny stamps there is no doubt, but, since the envelopes or cards bearing the 'poached egg' were often accompanied by a printed request from the Post Office for the recipient to inform the Post Office of the name and address of the sender, it seems clear that the postal duty was not necessarily genuine, and that only the possibility of a genuine sale prevented the Post Office from charging postage due on such communications. Later complete coils of the 'poached egg' found their way into the philatelic market.

PLATE XI

The original Mackennal sketch for the high values.

Chapter Seventeen

The High Values

STAMPS of the values of Two Shillings and Sixpence, Five Shillings, Ten Shillings and One Pound were issued, also a commemorative One Pound stamp for the Postal Union Congress of 1929.

These stamps were printed by the recess process, the general principles of which were the cutting, in *intaglio*, of a soft steel die which was then hardened, the taking up under pressure of the impression of the die on to a soft steel roller, which in its turn was hardened, and the transferring of the roller impression by rocking in the number of impressions on to a flat soft steel plate, and finally the hardening of the latter.

The design for the definitive issue, which was by Mr, later Sir, Bertram Mackennal, and was common to all four values, with lettering by Mr George W. Eve, was adapted from the 1892 issue of Barbados, which depicted the Seal of the Colony and showed Britannia with trident in her outstretched right hand and the shield of the Union Flag on her left arm, drawn through the sea by three horses. In the top left corner was inset, in an ornate circle, the head of King George V which was taken from the Mackennal coinage head.

Details of the commemorative One Pound stamp will be found after those of the stamps of the definitive issue.

The Essays and Progressive Stages of the Making of the Dies and the Die Proofs which were taken therefrom from time to time

Much work was undertaken prior to the issue of the definitive stamps and in the Royal Collection, in that presented to the Royal Philatelic Society, London, by the late Mr H. C. V. Adams already referred to, and in other collections there are many examples of this work.

The Royal Collection contains the original Mackennal essay, and photographs of it exist both before and after the lettering had been painted in by Mr Eve. Later the effect of various heads in the space provided was considered.

The earliest die proof seen by one of the Editors is dated August 24, 1912. The die showed the King's head and lines of the shield, but was incomplete in the upper garlands, centre horse's head and Britannia's right arm and garment.

Further die proofs were taken on August 30 with the garlands complete, but at this stage horizontal lines of shading had been added to the white diagonals of the St Andrew's Cross on the shield. Later die proofs in progressive stages of engraving were taken on September 6, 11, 12 and 13, and at a later date when the dies were finally approved.

But the dies as approved (and there is an example of the One Pound die endorsed 'Approved Die, J.A.C.H.') were heraldically incorrect. Not only were there lines of shading in the St Andrew's Cross diagonals, but space for the white vertical and horizontal portions of the St George's Cross was missing.

To rectify this error, transfer roller impressions must have been taken up from these dies, and upon the latter the lines of the erroneous shield removed and fresh flat dies laid down, which were therefore complete except for the engraving of the shield. That the heraldically correct engraving of the Union Flag was done separately on each die there can be no doubt, since on each individual die these lines differ. Though the differences are small, they are distinct.

A die proof in blue is in existence showing the shield blank except for an irregular S-shaped line upon it.

This, however, cannot have been the original and heraldically incorrect master die with the shield cleared, as this die is known to have been in use on January 28, 1913, some three and a half months after the first correct die had been completed. On that date proofs were taken from the master die in brown, carmine-red, indigo and green, the colours adopted for the four values. These proofs were, of course, without value. Further proofs were also taken on that date from the completed correct dies. Those taken from the master die were undoubtedly colour trials, since they were endorsed 'From Master Plate. Waterlow's Ink.', those from the completed dies being endorsed 'Waterlow's Ink.' only.

The use of the words 'Master Plate' is not understood, since a master plate has no function in the recess process. It may be that these words were inadvertently used for 'Master Die', which could only refer to the heraldically incorrect die, because no master die could exist with the correct shield, since the lines were separately engraved on each individual die.

PLATES AND PRINTERS

Upon completion and approval of the dies for each value, impressions were taken up on transfer rollers and plates laid down at the Royal Mint in ten rows of four impressions each, without vertical or horizontal separating gutters. Marginal markings, which varied from time to time, were added, and the plates were handed over to the printing contractors by whom they were put to press without any control piece.

On first issue in July and August 1913 the contractors were Messrs Waterlow, Bros. and Layton. At this period each plate had marginal crosses engraved above and below the gutter between the second and third vertical rows and to the right and left of the gutter between the fifth and sixth horizontal rows.

In 1915 the contract for printing passed to Messrs De La Rue and Co., and the plates then in use by Waterlow, Layton, with the exception of that used for printing the One Pound value which was discontinued, were handed over to them.

In both these cases the height of the stamp image measured 22 mm.

In 1918 the contract for printing passed to Bradbury, Wilkinson and Co. Ltd, and for this purpose new plates were laid down, but prior to this a dot had been cut on each of the dies below the centre of the design. In the case of the Two Shillings and Sixpence it was 4 mm below, in that of the Five Shillings 3·9 mm below and in that of the Ten Shillings 3·5 mm below. The use of this dot was to assist the workman in aligning the transfer roller correctly when laying down the plates, a principle which had been employed by the American Bank Note Company when preparing plates for printing

PLATE XII

1   The die, nearing completion, but with the shield heraldically incorrect.

2   The completed die for the Half Crown with the shield heraldically correct.

flag

B

Darker hoof

Broken leg

Yellow neck

9 13 12

1

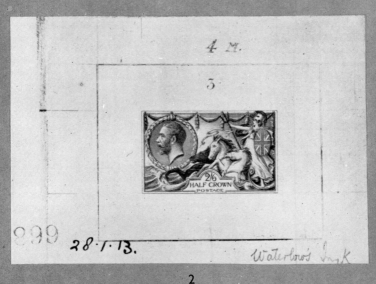

4 M.

3

2/6
HALF CROWN
POSTAGE

668

28·1·13.

Waterloo's Ink

2

PLATE XII

postage stamps. Since this dot was taken up on the transfer roller, in theory as each row was rocked in there would appear a dot below the impressions and in a constant position in relation to the stamp above it, which would give the workman an indication of where to align the top of the roller when laying down the next row below. Consequently this dot is not in a constant position in relation to the stamp above which it appears to occur, its position being dependant upon how close to it the next row was rocked in. It usually appeared just above the stamp or almost co-incident with the top line. Occasionally it appeared between the outer and inner top lines of the stamp.

In practice, however, this dot did not always appear. This indicates that the impressions, though laid down from side to side, were rocked in vertically, and the reason for non-appearance of the dot was incomplete excursion of the roller, that is the transfer impression was not rocked in its entirety.

At the same time, in addition to the marginal crosses mentioned above, further markings were engraved in the margins. Normally there were vertical lines in both side margins approximately opposite the top and bottom rows, and horizontal lines in the top and bottom margins approximately opposite the first and fourth vertical rows.

Whereas the height of the stamp image on the plates put to press by Waterlow, Layton and De La Rue measured 22 mm, that of the Bradbury, Wilkinson plates measured, at this period, 22·5 mm (full). Since these new plates were laid down from the same dies (though by different rollers) this is somewhat difficult to explain. It is, however, well-known that the softened steel of a plate will 'flow' away from the hardened steel roller under pressure during the process of rocking in and it is feasible that the methods in use at the Royal Mint in 1918 to soften the steel caused a temper different from that obtained in 1913 and that this increased the height of the stamp images.

In 1926 printing took place by a new method in which the paper was undamped. This is characterized by the fact that the paper is not in any way toned and appears pure white.

In 1927 a new set of plates was handed over to the contractors.

In this case the height of the stamp image was 23 mm (bare), and none of these plates showed the positional dots which were a feature of the 1918 plates. This was probably due to incomplete excursion of the roller, not when laying down the plates but when taking up the die impression. This may have been intentional since this dot did not appear on any later plates.

In 1934 the contract for printing passed to Waterlow and Sons, Ltd, the reconstituted firm of Messrs Waterlow, Bros. and Layton. However, before laying down any of the plates for their use the dies were considerably deepened. This is most noticeable in the lines of the background to the King's head which hitherto consisted of horizontal lines of shading but now had diagonal lines added.

To prepare a die for deepening, the usual method employed was to take up an impression of the original die on to a roller and transfer this impression to another flat piece of steel destined to become the new die, upon which the process of deepening was carried out, thus leaving the original die intact.

Here arises the question. From which die was this transfer impression taken up? Since the lines on the shield on all the re-engraved values were identical, a new master die must have been engraved. If the transfer was taken up from one of the individual heraldically correct dies, both the lines of the shield and the value inscription would have to have been removed, but, if it was taken up from the old heraldically incorrect master die, only the lines of the shield would have had to be removed. A die proof of this stage has not been seen, nor any proof from the individual dies after transfer of the value inscription, though in the Royal Collection there are four impressions, dated 19.2.34, all of the Five Shillings denomination taken from these dies, but they were colour proofs for each value.

The system of marginal markings upon the plates was altered considerably. These now consisted of short horizontal and vertical lines in all four corners of the plate a considerable distance from the stamp impressions. There were also short vertical lines in the gutter between the second and third vertical rows opposite the tops of these impressions in the upper row, and the bottoms of them in the lower row.

All these marginal markings, at whatever period they were made, being engraved by hand, vary in shape, size and position, and from a study of these lines it is possible to identify the plates, though with the plates laid down from the re-engraved dies this is very difficult, since the corner markings rarely appear on the printed sheets and those within the stamp gutters are cut by the perforation. In the details of the stamps under their respective values which follow, these plates have been given a number, but, like the numbers allotted to the typograph plates, these numbers are purely arbitrary.

Official numbers were, however, given to the high value plates, and these were engraved direct upon the plates, though their position was so high above the top row of stamps that they rarely appear upon the printed sheet. One of the Editors has seen two examples of these numbers, both on De La Rue printings. The first was upon Plate 4 of the Two Shillings and Sixpence and was 'H.V.9'. The second was upon Plate 3 of the Ten Shillings and was some figure, either a 1, 4 or 7, followed by the letters H.V. Unfortunately the margin was not sufficiently wide to show the whole marking.

From this it is clear that each plate, at this period, bore its officially allotted number and since this number was accompanied by the letters 'H.V.', it is presumed that these numbers were allotted irrespective of the denomination of the plate. It is, however, not clear whether these numbers were engraved on the plates issued to Bradbury, Wilkinson. One of the Editors has seen the top half of a sheet from Plate 2 of the Two Shillings and Sixpence, used for the experimental small cypher in column printing, which had a top margin wider than the height of two stamps, upon which no marking appeared.

PAPER AND PERFORATORS

The paper for the definitive stamps was watermarked with a large script Royal Cypher – G v R – surmounted by a crown, a single watermark appearing on each stamp. In the top, bottom and both side margins of each sheet was the watermarked word 'Postage'.

There was, however, an exception to this paper which occurred with an experimental printing of the Two Shillings and Sixpence and Five Shillings denominations printed by Bradbury, Wilkinson. In this case the watermark was similar to that of the Joynson paper used for the low values in 1912, that is a small script cypher in columns, but in this case the watermark was sideways in relation to the stamps. Stamps with this watermark are known only with the overprint 'Cancelled'.

The texture of the paper was normally stout wove, but there were two exceptions to this. The first occurred in the initial printings of the Two Shillings and Sixpence value by Waterlow, Layton. In this case the paper resembled fairly thick parchment. The second occurred with the early printings of all three values by Bradbury, Wilkinson. In this case the paper appeared to be a fine ribbed linen (laid) paper.

The perforation of the stamps, which was 11×12, was by comb-heads with two different pin settings both of which were set to perforate the sheets from top to bottom or bottom to top.

Type I

There was an extension spur of 12 pins on the left of the comb-head and a single extension pin on the right. This machine was only in use by Waterlow, Layton with top feed, the bottom margin being perforated through, the top margin imperforate, the left margin with a single extension hole and the right margin perforated through.

Type II

This comb-head was without extension spur, but at each end was a single extension pin.

(a) When set to perforate from top to bottom the bottom margin would be perforated through and the top margin imperforate.

(b) When set to perforate from bottom to top the bottom margin would be imperforate and the top margin perforated through.

In each case both side margins had a single extension hole.

This machine was in use by De La Rue, Bradbury, Wilkinson, and Waterlow & Sons, all with bottom feed. Top feed was also in use, but only by Bradbury, Wilkinson. The diameter of the pins on the Bradbury, Wilkinson comb-heads were slightly larger than those of the other two contractors.

DIFFERENTIATION OF THE WORK OF FOUR PRINTERS

There is no difficulty in separating the printings made by Waterlow & Sons, since they only printed stamps from plates laid down from the re-engraved dies. Nor is there any difficulty in separating the work of Bradbury, Wilkinson, since stamps printed by them all measured 22·5 to 23 mm in height, as against the 22 mm of the stamps printed by the other two contractors.

Difficulty may, however, be encountered in separating the printings of Waterlow, Layton and De La Rue. But there are two infallible tests which can be applied, both of which concern the perforation. The first is only applicable to marginal blocks since the perforation of all margins, except the left, differs. The second test can be applied to single stamps. The height of the perforation spurs on the De La Rue comb-heads is slightly less than that on the Waterlow, Layton comb-heads. Consequently the upper teeth of the perforation on both sides of the De La Rue stamps are slightly wider than those of Waterlow, Layton,* upon which all teeth were of approximately the same width.

Apart from the differences in colour between these two printings, the following points are of assistance in separating them:

The Waterlow, Layton paper is usually toned, while that of De La Rue is white.

In the Waterlow, Layton printing no colour shows through the back of the stamp whereas in the De La Rue printings it does, especially on the Five Shillings value.

The gum of the Waterlow, Layton printings is generally evenly applied and is pale yellowish or white, whereas on the De La Rue stamps it is sometimes unevenly applied and always yellow.

* It is believed that this was first noted by the late Mr Hiscock, of Messrs Stanley Gibbons and Frank Godden Ltd.

Chapter Eighteen

Two Shillings and Sixpence

DIE proofs in States 1 and 2 are known, undated, in green on card with the figure 3 at the top; and also in State 2 with 4M and 3 at the top in green on card and vermilion on India paper, both the latter being dated 12.11.12. The *Imprimatur* sheet was registered at Somerset House on August 8, 1913.

WATERLOW, LAYTON PRINTINGS

On April 29, 1913, imperforate colour trials on ungummed paper were made in fifteen unadopted colours, namely two shades of light brown, light and dark red, purple, purple-brown, olive-green, blue-green, greenish blue, bright blue, ultramarine, pale ultramarine, orange, orange-red and black, and also in the accepted colours for all four values, namely sepia-brown, rose-carmine, indigo-blue and green.

Imperforate plate proofs were taken in pale dull green on card; in red, blue-green, brown and black on slightly surfaced paper; and in intense black on paper watermarked 'JAMES WEIGLEY 219'.

Very rough proofs in brown, carmine and indigo were taken on thin yellowish paper. These were used to place on top of plates put into storage, presumably to assist in their recognition.

Perforated stamps are known overprinted 'Specimen' horizontally in upright type measuring 12¾ mm; 'Cancelled' in upright type measuring 14¾ mm; and 'Cancelled' diagonally between two lines measuring 22 mm.

The stamps were issued on July 1, 1913, in shades of sepia-brown, brown, blackish-brown, greyish-brown and yellowish-brown.

At least two plates can be identified. On Plate 2, which was not put to press until late in the contract, stamp impression No. 5, that

146

is the first stamp of the second row, was re-entered, the original entry being rocked in too high. The original entry was not completely erased, and marks of the faulty entry can be seen doubling the outer and inner top lines of the bottom line of the stamp in the right half, and also the horizontal and diagonal lines on the shield. Enlarged photographs of double entries are often difficult to follow, and sometimes even misleading, when they cannot be compared with a similar photograph of a single entry. However, in the accompanying illustration the lines of the second have been faded out and the marks of the original faulty entry which remain visible have been accentuated. From a study of this illustration no difficulty should be experienced in recognizing this re-entry. Although this is the only major re-entry occurring on the Waterlow, Layton printings of this value, examples are known of stamps which appear to be doubly printed, owing to a slight shift of the paper during printing, and care should be exercised not to confuse this variety with that of double entry.

On the same plate there are slight marks of double entry on No. 2, the original faulty entry having been slightly to the left of the second entry, with consequent doubling of the top of the right side line and the ball-like ornament.

DE LA RUE PRINTINGS

Perforated colour trials upon gummed watermarked paper were taken in ultramarine, indigo, pale green, purple and grey; and on ungummed unwatermarked paper in bright sepia, bright blue, magenta and the accepted colours for the Two Shillings and Sixpence and Five Shillings values.

Imperforate plate proofs were taken in three shades of dull brown, and in grey-brown, on gummed watermarked paper.

Perforated stamps are known overprinted 'Cancelled' horizontally in upright type measuring 15 mm.

The stamps were issued in 1915. The initial printing was in a tone described as 'Silver grey-brown'. This was followed by the first series of printings in shades of sepia-brown, sepia, brown, grey-brown, blackish-brown and nigger.

PLATE XIII

THE HALF CROWN RE-ENTRIES

1 The re-entry appearing in late Waterlow and early De La Rue printings. (Plate 2, Stamp Impression No. 5.)
The original entry was laid down too low. There are further slight marks of re-entry on the neck of the right-hand horse's head. Further doubling could be expected in the N.E. corner background, but as the second entry was above the first by the distance between the lines of shading, the doubling is coincident with the line above.

2 The major re-entry, Bradbury Wilkinson printings, 22·5 image plate. (Plate 3, Stamp Impression No. 2.)
The original entry was slightly too low and twisted slightly clockwise. Further doubling appears just below every horizontal line of the shield and N.E. background. These have been omitted from the sketch for simplicity.

3 The 'Nissen' re-entry, Bradbury Wilkinson printings, 22·5 image plate. (Plate 2, Stamp Impression No. 3.)
The original entry was slightly too much to the right, the only part affected being the doubling of the vertical lines of the shield.

1

2

3

PLATE XIII

In the second series of printings the stamps appeared in shades of brown, chestnut, cinnamon and vandyk. There was a very coarse printing in deep brown.

In the third series of printings the stamps appeared in shades of grey-brown and mole.

Sheets are known with the watermark inverted, reversed and inverted and reversed, owing to errors of feeding the sheets into the press. Examples of displaced watermark also occur, and stamps can be found with either a portion of the watermarked word 'Postage' or with no watermark at all. The latter is rare.

At least one plate, which had already been at press under the Waterlow, Layton contract, has been identified as in use by De La Rue, together with at least three plates which, so far, have not been identified as previously at press. Plate 2 with the major re-entry on No. 5 was in use by both contractors, though it was taken from press very soon after the commencement of the De La Rue contract. The faulty marks of original entry were still visible, but were very much fainter. It is possible that this may have been caused by a third entry co-incident with the second, which would cause compressional faintness of these marks. In the opinion of one of the Editors this faintness was probably caused by wear of the plate.

Plate 5, which had been at press during the second series of printings, wore very badly, and printings are known, usually in the cinnamon colour, though occasionally in dark brown, in the worn state, which towards the end of its use became so marked that no shading is visible in the sky above the horses.

BRADBURY, WILKINSON PRINTINGS

The stamps were issued in 1918 in shades of chocolate-brown, reddish-brown, brown, yellow-brown, chestnut-brown and sepia-brown.

For convenient reference the early plates with stamp images of 22·5 mm in height are referred to as Type A plates, and the latter ones with stamp images of 23 mm in height as Type B plates, though these plates have been numbered consecutively throughout the whole issue.

There were two experimental printings, both of which were made from Plate 2, one of the A type plates. In each case the stamps were overprinted 'Cancelled' in upright type measuring $15\frac{1}{2}$ mm.

The first was upon repp (or ribbed) paper with the normal watermark, and the second upon the experimental paper with the small cypher in column watermark sideways.

At least eleven plates of the A type have been identified with certainty and there were probably a further two plates. Four plates of the B type have also been identified.

Upon Plate 3 (A type), stamp impression No. 2, the second stamp of the top row, was re-entered. The original entry, which was not completely erased, was rocked in slightly too low and was slightly twisted clockwise. Marks of faulty entry can be seen doubling the inner top frame line throughout its length, both inner and outer frame lines in their upper halves, and the lines, horizontal, vertical and diagonal, of the shield, and some lines of Britannia's garb.

Upon Plate 2 (A type) there is a re-entry, which, though not so prominent as that upon Plate 3, is worthy of illustration. This re-entry, which is on stamp impression No. 3, and was first reported in the *British Philatelist*, Vol. XLIII, page 3, shows the original faulty entry rocked in slightly too much to the right, the doubling appearing in the upper portion of the right inner and outer frame lines. The vertical lines of the shield are all closely double, as are some of the diagonal lines.

There is also a minor re-entry on stamp impression No. 1 on this plate, which shows the doubling of the left outer frame line from the bottom upwards for most of its length.

On Plate 11 there was a minor re-entry on stamp impression No. 4, which shows a slight doubling of the lines of the shield.

No re-entries have so far been seen on the Type B plates.

WATERLOW AND SONS PRINTINGS

These stamps, which were printed from plates laid down from the re-engraved die, were issued in October 1934 in shades of chocolate-brown, brown and red-brown.

As mentioned above, difficulty has been experienced in the identification of these plates, but there is no doubt that more than one plate was in use.

Chapter Nineteen

Five Shillings

DIE proofs in State 1 are known undated in brown on card; and in State 2 in brown, blue and blue-green on card dated 10.10.12; on India paper undated in blue, green, brown and carmine; on thin wove paper in brown, blue and green dated 14.10.12; and on thin paper undated in dark brown, red-brown, carmine and green. The *Imprimatur* sheet was registered at Somerset House on 8.8.1913.

WATERLOW, LAYTON PRINTINGS

Imperforate plate proofs were taken in the colour of issue on white paper. Very rough proofs were taken on thin yellowish paper in the same colour under circumstances similar to those of the Two Shillings and Sixpence.

Perforated stamps are known overprinted 'Specimen' horizontally in upright type measuring $12\frac{3}{4}$ mm; 'Cancelled' in upright type measuring $14\frac{3}{4}$ mm; and 'Cancelled' diagonally between two lines measuring 22 mm.

The stamps were issued on July 4, 1913, in shades of rose-carmine, carmine, rose, rose-pink and crimson.

At least three plates have been identified.

DE LA RUE PRINTINGS

Perforated stamps are known overprinted 'Specimen' horizontally in upright type measuring $12\frac{3}{4}$ mm; and 'Cancelled' in upright type measuring 15 mm.

The stamps were issued in shades of carmine and reddish-carmine. There is also a printing in a very intense red, the ink of which is suffused into the paper.

Stamps are known with watermark inverted and watermark reversed, owing to errors of feeding the sheets into the press.

At least one plate, which had already been at press under the Waterlow, Layton contract, has been identified as being in use by De La Rue, together with one plate which, so far, has not been identified as previously at press. One plate wore very badly and showed practically no shading in the sky above the horses.

BRADBURY, WILKINSON PRINTINGS

The stamps were issued in 1918 in shades of carmine, rose-red, rose-carmine, rose and carmine-red.

There was a small experimental printing from Plate 4, one of the A type plates, upon paper watermarked small cypher in column sideways. The stamps were overprinted 'Cancelled' in upright type measuring $15\frac{1}{2}$ mm.

At least seven plates of the A type and one plate of the B type have been identified.

WATERLOW AND SONS PRINTINGS

These stamps, which were printed from plates laid down from the re-engraved die, were issued in October 1934 in shades of rose-red.

As mentioned above, difficulty has been experienced in the identification of these plates, but there is no doubt that more than one plate was in use.

So far, no re-entries have been found on any of the Five Shillings plates.

Chapter Twenty

Ten Shillings

UNDATED die proofs with the figure 2 at the top are known on card in States 1 and 2 in blue-green and deep olive-green respectively. The *Imprimatur* sheet was registered at Somerset House on 30.7.1913.

WATERLOW, LAYTON PRINTINGS

Imperforate plate proofs were taken in the colour of issue.

Perforated stamps are known overprinted 'Specimen' horizontally in upright type measuring 12¾ mm; 'Cancelled' in upright type measuring 14¾ mm; 'Cancelled' in italic type measuring 12 mm; and 'Cancelled' diagonally between two lines measuring 22 mm.

The stamps were issued on August 1, 1913, in shades of ultramarine, blue, indigo-blue and indigo.

Only one plate has so far been identified.

DE LA RUE PRINTINGS

Perforated stamps are known overprinted 'Cancelled' horizontally in upright type measuring 15 mm.

The stamps were issued in 1915 in shades of blue and grey-blue.

At least two plates have been identified, neither of which has been found in use by Waterlow, Layton.

BRADBURY, WILKINSON PRINTINGS

Perforated stamps are known overprinted 'Cancelled' horizontally in upright type measuring 15½ mm.

The stamps were issued in 1918 in shades of grey-blue. There was also a very pale blue, sometimes called 'Cambridge Blue', which is of considerable rarity.

At least eight plates of the A type have been identified, but only two plates of the B type have so far been isolated. Doubtless more were in use. On laying down these plates a roller flaw occurred which appeared as a break in the 'S' of the word 'Postage'. The cause of this flaw was the temporary lodgment of a small piece of metal from the transfer roller, whilst taking up an impression, in the corresponding depression of the die. Consequently there was no projection in this position on the roller to bite into the plate. This flaw is analogous to the 'O' flaw which occurred on the One Penny of 1840.

Of the eight A type plates identified, two have the complete 'S' and six show the broken 'S' flaw, the two B type plates found having the complete 'S'. Since the B type plates were laid down from different transfer rollers from the two (at least) previous rollers, this shows that the small piece of metal lodged in the die had by this time either come away from the die or had been removed. Consequently it is not possible to say whether the A type plates with the flaw were laid down before or after those without the flaw.

Two major re-entries occur on the A type plates, both of which were first described in the *British Philatelist*, Vol. XLIII, page 3. The first of these was on Plate 2, one of the complete 'S' plates. It is on stamp impression No. 21, that is the first stamp of the sixth row. It is now usually known as the 'Runnals' re-entry, since it was first found by the late Mr H. C. Runnals. The original entry, which was laid down a trifle too high, was only partially erased with consequent doubling of all the horizontal lines, and also some of the diagonal lines, of the shield. The doubling of the lines of shading of Britannia's garb to the right of the shield is very pronounced.

The second re-entry is usually known as the 'Nissen' re-entry as it was discovered by Mr Harry Nissen as a sequel to the discovery of the 'Runnals' re-entry. It occurs on Plate 5, one of the broken 'S' plates, and is on stamp impression No. 1, the first stamp

PLATE XIV

THE TEN SHILLINGS RE-ENTRIES

1   The 'Runnals' re-entry, Bradbury Wilkinson printings, 22·5 image plate, with perfect S. (Plate 2, Stamp Image No. 21.) The original entry was slightly too high and too much to the left. Most of the horizontal lines in the N.E. corner also show doubling.

2   The 'Nissen' re-entry, Bradbury Wilkinson printings, 22·5 image plate, with broken S. (Plate 5, Stamp Impression No. 1.) The original entry was slightly too low and too much to the right. The original and second entries were very close, consequently apparent doubling of the horizontal lines of shading is hardly perceptible.

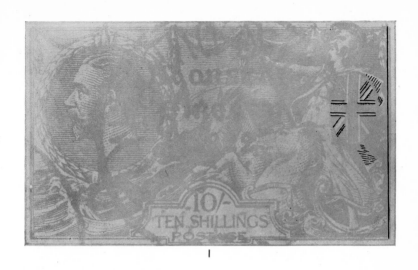

1

2

PLATE XIV

in the top row. In this case the original entry was laid down a trifle too low. Erasure of the original entry was more successfully effected than in the case of the 'Runnals' re-entry and apparent doubling is confined to the horizontal lines, and a few of the diagonal lines, of the shield.

On Plate 9, one of the B type plates stamp impression No. 4, that is the fourth stamp of the top row, the '0' of 10/- appears widely double above and to the right.

WATERLOW AND SONS PRINTINGS

These stamps, which were printed from plates laid down from the re-engraved die, were issued in October 1934 in shades of indigo and blue.

As mentioned above, difficulty has been experienced in the identification of these plates, but there is no doubt that more than one plate was in use.

Chapter Twenty-One

One Pound

UNDATED die proofs of the definitive stamp with the figure 4 at the top are known on card in States 1 and 2 in green and deep olive-green respectively. The *Imprimatur* sheet was registered at Somerset House on 15.8.1913.

WATERLOW, LAYTON PRINTINGS

Imperforate plate proofs were taken in the colour of issue.

Perforated stamps are known overprinted 'Specimen' horizontally in upright type measuring $12\frac{3}{4}$ mm; 'Specimen' in italic type measuring $10\frac{1}{2}$ mm; 'Cancelled' in upright type measuring $14\frac{3}{4}$ mm; and 'Cancelled' diagonally between two lines measuring 22 mm.

The stamps were issued on August 1, 1913, in shades of green and blue-green. Only one plate has been identified.

At the end of the Waterlow, Layton contract the issue of the One Pound stamp was discontinued.

THE POSTAL UNION CONGRESS ISSUE

The stamp was designed by Mr Harold Nelson. His design, which was based on St George and the Dragon, was first submitted by him as an unaccepted essay for the 1924 British Empire Exhibition commemorative stamp. This artist's original sketch embodies both St George and the Dragon, but this allegorical design was placed on the left of the essay with the space reserved for the King's head on the right. The essay was subscribed 'British Empire Exhibition 1924'.

In 1929 Mr Nelson re-submitted this design, though modified, as an essay for the commemorative One Pound stamp. His sketch, which differed only slightly from the accepted design, now showed the allegorical design on the side opposite to that of the original sketch and was superscribed 'Postal Union Congress London 1929'.

Unlike the dies for the definitive stamps, which were engraved at the Royal Mint, the die for this stamp was engraved by Messrs Bradbury, Wilkinson and Co., who also laid down the single plate used in five rows of four impressions each, and printed the stamps upon paper watermarked with a large double-lined crown over the Royal Cypher, a single watermark appearing on each stamp. The perforation was 12 and was effected by a line machine which perforated the horizontal and vertical rows in separate operations.

Die proofs are known in black.

Imperforate colour trials were taken in 16 colours and in the accepted black. These are on cards lettered A to Q.

Imperforate plate proofs in black are known, not only in singles, but also in blocks of four, the latter being for presentation purposes. Perforated stamps are known overprinted 'Specimen' in red in upright type measuring $10\frac{1}{2}$ mm.

The stamps were issued on May 10, 1929, the day of the opening of the Ninth Congress of the Universal Postal Union in London, in black.

There were numerous thin vertical and horizontal lines on the stamps, chiefly through the superscription. In fact no less than 19 out of the 20 stamps show these lines in varying positions.

The stamps were on issue for about two months, after which they were withdrawn, though remaining valid for postage.

Appendix A

The Plating of the Low Values

The Electros, their Markings and Use

As previously mentioned in Chapter I, almost every electro, at some time during its use, bore either some marking deliberately made in the printer's rule or had some characteristic of that rule by which printings made from that electro can be recognized. The lists which follow are threefold.

(A) LIST OF ELECTRO MARKINGS

The first part of this Appendix describes these markings and in it each electro has a number allocated to it, these numbers being purely arbitrary. No official information has been forthcoming on the subject of the number of electros used and this list has been compiled solely from the results of many years' patient research. Further, the Editors do not suggest that these lists are necessarily complete. They are merely a record of what has been identified.

The following notes and illustrations are explanatory of the method used in the description of these markings:

The horizontal rules, whether above or below the panes, have been numbered from left to right and the vertical rules from top to bottom, the latter being followed by an indication of the side on which they are.

In these rules cuts and dots were made. Sometimes they were not made centrally, sometimes cuts did not pass completely through the rule, and sometimes other peculiarities existed. When this occurred a qualifying word has been added to describe the special features. All dots are deemed to be circular unless qualified by a word indicating their shape. Further, each dot or cut has been described as being below one of the letters of the value inscription of the stamp above it, or, if in one of the rules at the side of the pane, it is followed by a figure giving the measurement in milli-metres from the base of the rule to the centre of the cut or dot therein.

Top left: Two small dots (top/base) and cut with central dot. *Top right:* Cut and oval dot. *Bottom left:* Half dot top and half cut base. *Bottom right:* Dot breaking top and dot bulging top.

Some of the electro numbers are followed by small letters *a*, *b*, *c*, *d* or *e*. This description has been adopted to indicate a change in the marking in the rule, whether this constitutes the filling in of a dot, as in the case of an electro which has been tested at Somerset House being handed over to the Contractor, or the addition of a cut or dot to an electro which had already been put to press by the contractor.

The filling in of Somerset House dots is self-explanatory, but no explanation can be given concerning the addition of further dots or cuts, though this may possibly have indicated that the electro had been cleaned during the first Harrison contract. That the electros were removed from the press there can be no doubt, since, with a single exception, referred to under the One Penny value on page 57, after the addition of a cut or dot the electro appeared in the press on the side opposite to that which it originally occupied.

(B) THE USE LIST

This part of the Appendix records the number of each electro, with the control under which printings were made.

Some of the early Halfpenny and One Penny electros made from

Die II of the three-quarter face issue were put to press on paper watermarked Crown, Simple Cypher and Multiple Cypher. In these cases the control, whether narrow or wide, is followed by the type of paper, Simple and Multiple Cypher being abbreviated to GVR (S) and GVR (M) respectively.

(C) THE COMPARATIVE CONTROL POSITION

Sometimes, not only the position of the control, but also the characteristics of the control piece, can be of assistance to the student in allocating a block, which shows neither marking in, nor characteristic of, the rules, to its correct plate.

Where there are only two or three, and in one case four, electros at press under the same control, and the controls are clearly characteristic, they have been listed.

HALFPENNY

ORIGINAL DIE
List of electro markings

1. No marking.
2. Curved cut 20th right side.
3. Cut 19th right side, 10¾.
4. Cut 19th right side, 8¾.
5. Cut 18th right side, 10.
6. Curved cut 17th right side, 13.

These electros were put to press with controls as follows:

1. All wide.
2. All wide.
3. All wide.
4. All wide.
5. All wide.
6. All wide, All narrow.

DEEPENED DIE
List of electro markings

1.
 a. Minute dot under 3rd; cut 20th left side; cut 20th right side.
 b. Added cut 17th left side.
2.
 a. Two minute nicks in either side of 19th left side, 8.
 b. Added cut 20th left side, 12; cut 18th left side, 14¼; cut 20th left side.
3. Cut 17th left side, 9¾.
4. Cut 20th right side, 8¼.
5. Double cut 17th left side; cut under PE of 12th; cut 17th right side.

6. Cut 17th left side; cut 19th right side; cut 17th right side.
7. Cut under 11th; cut 20th right side.
8. Cut 18th left side.
9. Cut 20th left side, 12; cut 19th left side, 13; cut 18th left side; cut 20th right side, $12\frac{1}{4}$; cut 19th right side, $12\frac{1}{4}$.

10.
   a. Cut under P of 11th.
   b. Added cut 19th left side, $10\frac{1}{2}$; cut 19th right side, 12.
11.
   a. Cut under FP of 12th.
   b. Added cut 17th right side.
12. Cut under HA of 12th.

These electros were put to press with controls as follows:

1.
   a. All wide.
   b. All narrow.
2.
   a. All wide.
   b. All wide.
3. All wide.
4. All wide.
5. All narrow.
6. All narrow.

7. All narrow.
8. All narrow.
9. All narrow.
10.
   a. All narrow.
   b. All narrow.
11.
   a. All narrow.
   b. All narrow.
12. All narrow.

REDRAWN DIE
List of electro markings

1.
   a. Small dot under PE of 5th.
   b. Added dot under E of 12th.
2. Small dot under LF of 6th.
3. Big double dot under (N)N of 7th.
4. Pear dot (base) under FP of 8th.
5. Small dot under FP of 9th.
6. Small dot under P of 10th; base of 20th left side completely bevelled off.
7. Small dot under F of 11th.
8. Small dot (top) under FP of 12th.
9. Minute dot 20th left side, 6.
10.
   a. Big dot under F of 5th.
   b. Added single fine diagonal cut 20th left side.

11. Big dot under HA of 6th; fine 'X' cut in 20th left side.
12. Big dot under AL of 7th; fine horizontal 'V' cut in 20th left side.
13. Big oval dot (top) under FP of 8th; minute dot 20th left side.
14. Small dot under PE of 9th; base of 20th left side partly bevelled off.
15. Minute nick under NY of 9th; dot (base) under PE of 11t.h
16.
   a. Dot under FP of 1st; horizontal dash under HALFP of 2nd; dot under NN of 12th.
   b. Added cut under A of 12th.
17. $\frac{1}{2}$ cut (base) and dot under N(N)Y of 12th.

18. Long dot under HA of 12th.
19. 20th left side bent.
20. ½ cut (base) under PE of 9th.
21. ½ cut (base) under N(N) of 10th.
22. Small dot (base) under P of 12th.
23. Dot under PE of 12th.
24. No marking.

These electros were put to press with controls as follows:

1.
  a. B11, B12 narrow Crown.
  b. B13.
2. B11, B12 narrow Crown.
3. B11, B12 narrow Crown.
4. B11, B12 narrow Crown, B13.
5. B11, B12 narrow Crown, B13.
6. B11, B12 narrow Crown, B13.
7. B11, B12 narrow Crown.
8. B11, B12 narrow Crown, B12 wide G v R (S), B13.
9. B.12 G v R (M).
10.
  a. B12 narrow Crown.
  b. B12 wide Crown,
     B12 wide G v R (M),
     B12 wide G v R (S).
11. B12 narrow Crown,
    B12 narrow G v R (M),
    B12 narrow G v R (S),
    B12 wide G v R (S).
12. B12 narrow Crown,
    B12 wide Crown,
    B12 narrow G v R (M),
    B12 wide G v R (M),
    B12 narrow G v R (S),
    B12 wide G v R (S).
13. B12 narrow Crown,
    B12 wide Crown,
    B12 narrow G v R (M),
    B12 wide G v R (M),
    B12 narrow G v R (S),
    B12 wide G v R (S),
    B13.
14. B12 narrow Crown.
15. B12 narrow Crown,
    B12 narrow G v R (M),
    B12 narrow G v R (S).
16.
  a. B12 narrow Crown,
     B12 narrow G v R (M).
  b. B12 narrow G v R (M),
     B12 narrow G v R (S), B13.
17. B12 narrow Crown, no control Crown,
    B12 wide G v R (S), B13.
18. B12 narrow Crown,
    B12 narrow G v R (M),
    B12 narrow G v R (S).
19. B12 wide G v R (S), B13.
20. B12 wide G v R (S), B13.
21. B12 wide G v R (S), B13.
22. B12 wide G v R (S), B13.
23. B12 wide G v R (S), B13.
24. B13.

FIRST HARRISON CONTRACT, 1912 TO 1923
List of electro markings

1.
  a. Dot above 1st in upper and lower panes; minute dot under H of 2nd.
  b. Dots above 1st filled in; added cut under (N)N of 1st.

2.
  a. Dot above 2nd in upper and lower panes; indents at base of 1st and 12th.
  b. Dots above 2nd filled in; added cut under FP of 3rd.
  c. Added dot under E of 3rd.

3.

a. Dot above 3rd in upper and lower panes; minute tick (outer) 17th left side, 14.

b. Dots above 3rd filled in; added small dot 17th left side, 11.

c. Added big cut under P of 1st.

4.

a. Dot above 4th in upper and lower panes.

b. Dots above 4th filled in; added sloping cut (base) under FP of 4th; small dot 18th left side, 12½.

5.   Dot under HA of 1st.

6.

a. Dot (top) under PE of 1st; small ½ cut (top) under H of 6th.

b. Added dot under NN of 1st.

7.

a. ½ cut (base) under LF of 1st; small dot 20th left side, 18¾.

b. Added dot under PE of 2nd.

8.   ½ cut (top) under LF of 2nd.

9.

a. Irregular cut under E of 3rd.

b. Added 2 dots 20th left side, 10, 12.

10.

a. Small dot 19th left side, 10½.

b. Added dot under HA of 1st.

11.

a. Cut within 9th rule at left.

b. Added cut 20th left side, 12¾.

12.

a. Dash at right of 2nd.

b. Added dot under PE of 3rd.

c. Added sloping cut under FP of 3rd.

13.

a. Dot under FP of 1st.

b. Added dot under PE of 1st.

c. Added dot (inner) 20th left side, 9¾.

14.

a. Dot under P of 2nd.

b. Added dot under EN of 2nd.

c. Added dot under LF of 3rd.

d. Added ½ dot (top) under PE of 3rd; 2 dots 18th left side, 10, 12¼.

15.   Dot (base) under PE of 1st.

16.

a. Dot under PE of 2nd.

b. Added 2 dots 19th left side, 10¾, 14.

c. Added cut under N(N) of 1st.

17.   Dot under PE of 3rd.

18.   Dot under FP of 4th.

19.   3 dots (left dot minute) under LFPE of 2nd.

20.

a. 3 dots (centre dot minute) under LFP of 3rd.

b. Added dot under A of 1st.

21.

a. 2 dots (top/base) under FPE of 4th.

b. Added 2 dots 19th left side.

c. Added cut under LF of 3rd.

22.   2 dots (base/top) under FPE of 4th; cut under HA of 11th; 3 diagonal cuts 19th left side.

23.

a. Dot under H of 1st.

b. Added cut under HA of 4th.

24.   Dot under H of 2nd.

25.   Dot under H of 3rd.

26.   Dot under H of 4th.

27.   2 dots under NN of 1st.

28.

a. 2 small dots under PEN of 2nd.

b. Added dot under P of 1st.

29.   2 dots under ALF of 3rd.

30.   2 dots under HALF of 4th.

31.

a. Double ½ cut (top/base) under HA of 2nd.

b. Added dot covering base of above cut.

32.

  a. Dot under P of 1st.

  b. Added fine double cut under PE of 3rd.

33. Dot under PE of 3rd.

34. Cut under PE of 1st; dot under NN of 9th.

35. Cut under E of 2nd.

36.

  a. Cut under PE of 3rd.

  b. Added 3 dots under HALFP of 3rd.

37. Cut under LF of 4th; minute $\frac{1}{2}$ cut (outer) 20th right side, $5\frac{1}{2}$.

38.

  a. 4 dots from left to under right of F of 4th.

  b. Added cut under PE of 1st; dot 20th left side, $11\frac{1}{2}$; 2 dots 17th left side, $6\frac{1}{2}$, 12.

39.

  a. Dot (top) under PE of 1st; right side of 4th complete.

  b. Added small oval dot under P of 3rd.

40. Dot (central) under PE of 1st; right side of 4th broken.

41. Large dot under P of 2nd.

42. Dot (base) under FP of 1st.

43.

  a. Very fine $\frac{1}{4}$ cut (base) under (N)N of 3rd.

  b. Added $\frac{1}{2}$ dot (top) under E of 10th.

44. Dot (base) under PE of 2nd.

45.

  a. Large dot 19th right side, $7\frac{1}{4}$.

  b. Added small dot 20th left side, $11\frac{1}{2}$.

46.

  a. Cut under N(N) of 1st.

  b. Added cut 20th right side, $11\frac{1}{4}$; large dot (breaking outer) 18th right side, 11.

47. No marking.

48. Big dot 17th right side, 11.

49.

  a. Small dot under PE of 9th.

  b. Added small dot under P of 2nd.

50. Dot (breaking base) under P of 2nd.

51.

  a. Large dot 17th right side, $8\frac{1}{2}$.

  b. Added dot under PE of 1st.

  c. Added 2 minute dots under LF, NN of 2nd.

52.

  a. Large dot under E of 9th.

  b. Added small dot 20th left side, 14.

53. Small dot 17th right side, $4\frac{1}{2}$.

54.

  a. Dot (top) under FP of 2nd.

  b. Added dot under E of 2nd.

55. Dot (base) under E of 1st.

56. Small dot (central) 18th right side, $11\frac{1}{2}$; small dot (inner) 17th right side, 10.

57. $\frac{1}{2}$ dot (top) under N of 9th; big dot (breaking inner) 17th right side, $10\frac{1}{2}$.

58. Dot under F of 10th.

59. 19th left side scooped out (outer), 8–12, with dash to right of it.

60. 4 dots under AL, FP, and 2 touching each other under E of 3rd.

61. Dot (breaking outer) 19th left side, $6\frac{3}{4}$, 4 dots from left end to left of F of 4th.

62. Dot (base) under PE of 1st.

63. Large dot (breaking outer) 18th right side, 10, small dot (central) 17th right side, 10.

64. Slanting cut 19th right side, 4.

65. Large dot 19th left side, $8\frac{3}{4}$,

66.
   a. Small dot (central) 19th left side, $9\frac{1}{2}$.
   b. Added 2 fine cuts 19th left side, $11\frac{1}{2}$, 13.

67. Dot (inner) 18th right side, 11.

68. Dot (inner) 20th left side, $11\frac{1}{2}$.

69. 2 cuts 19th left side, 7, $9\frac{1}{2}$.

70. $\frac{1}{2}$ dot (base) under P and nick under NY, both of 4th.

71. Large oval dot under PE of 2nd.

72. Oval dot under FP of 3rd.

73. Elongated dot and 2 oval cuts 19th left side, $11\frac{1}{4}$, 13.

74. Oval dot (widely breaking top) to right of P of 2nd.

75. Oval dot (only just breaking top) under PE of 2nd.

76. Small dot (outer) 18th left side, 11; nick 10th left side, $7\frac{1}{2}$; nick opposite interpane gutter left side, $13\frac{1}{2}$.

77. 2 large dots 19th left side, $10\frac{1}{2}$, 13.

78. Minute fine nick (outer) 19th left side, $8\frac{1}{4}$.

79. Base of 2nd rule cut away from under ENNY to right end.

80. Large dot (central) 19th left side, $9\frac{1}{4}$.

81. $\frac{1}{2}$ cut and $\frac{1}{2}$ dot (outer) 19th left side 11, $13\frac{1}{2}$.

82. Small dot (outer) 20th left side.

83. 2 cuts under E and (N)N of 11th.

These electros were put to press with controls as follows:

1.
   a. B.13.
   b. C13, C14, D14.

2.
   a. B.13.
   b. C13, C14, D14.
   c. E14.

3.
   a. B.13.
   b. C13.
   c. C13, C14, D14.

4.
   a. B.13.
   b. C13, C14, D14.

5. C13, C14, D14.

6.
   a. C13, C14.
   b. E14, F15, G15.

7.
   a. C13, C14, D14.
   b. D14.

8. C13, C14, D14.

9.
   a. C13, C14.

   b. E14.

10.
   a. C13, C14, D14.
   b. F15, G15.

11.
   a. C13, C14.
   b. C14, D14.

12.
   a. C14, D14.
   b. D14, E14.
   c. E14.

13.
   a. D14, E14.
   b. E14.
   c. E14.
   d. E14, F15.

14.
   a. D14, E14.
   b. E14, F15.
   c. F15.
   d. G15.

15. E14, F15.

16.
   a. E14.

b. F15.

c. G15, H16, J17.

17. E14, F15.

18. E14, F15.

19. E14, F15, G15, H16.

20.

a. E14, F15, G15.

b. G15, H16.

21.

a. E14, F15, G15.

b. G15.

c. G15.

22. E14, F15, G15.

23.

a. F15, G15.

b. G15, H16.

24. F15, G15.

25. F15, G15, H16.

26. F15, G15.

27. G15, H16, I16.

28.

a. G15, H16, I16, J17.

b. J17.

29. G15, H16, J17.

30. G15, H16, I16.

31.

a. G15, H16, I16, J17.

b. J17.

32.

a. H16.

b. H16, I16, J17.

33. H16, I16, J17.

34. H16, I16, J17.

35. H16, I16, J17.

36.

a. H16.

b. I16, J17.

37. H16, I16.

38.

a. I16, J17.

b. J17.

39.

a. J17.

b. J17, K17, K18, L18, M18, M19.

40. J17.

41. J17.

42. J17, K17, K18, L18, M18.

43.

a. J17.

b. K17, K18, L18, M18.

44. J17, K17, K18.

45.

a. J17, K17, K18.

b. L18, M18.

46.

a. J17.

b. J17, K17, K18, L18, M18, M19.

47. J17, K17.

48. J17, K17, K18, L18.

49.

a. J17.

b. K17, K18, L18, M18, M19.

50. J17, K18.

51.

a. K17, K18.

b. K18, N19.

c. Q21 narrow, R21, T22, U22, U23.

52.

a. L18, M18, M19.

b. M19, N19.

53. M18, M19.

54.

a. M19.

b. N19.

55. M19, N19, P20, Q20, Q21 narrow.

56. M19, N19.

57. M19.

58. M19.

59. M19, N19, O20, P20.

60. N19.

61. N19, P20.

62. N19.

63. N19.

64. N19.

65. N19, P20, Q20, Q21 narrow.

66.

a. O20.

b. T22, U22, U23.

67. O20, P20.

68. P20, Q20, R21, S21, S22, T22, U22, U23.
69. Q21 narrow.
70. Q21 narrow, S21, S22, T22.
71. Q21 narrow, Q21 wide, R21, S21, S22, U22.
72. Q21 narrow, Q21 wide, R21, S21, S22, T22.
73. Q21 wide, R21, U22.
74. R21, T22, U22, U23.
75. S22, T22, U22, U23.
76. T22.
77. U22, U23, V23.
78. U23, V23.
79. U23.
80. U23, V23.
81. U23, V23, W23.
82. V23.
83. V23.

WATERLOW CONTRACT AND HARRISON PROVISIONAL PRINTINGS
List of electro markings

1. Dot under N(N) of 3rd.
2. Dot under EN of 1st.
3. Minute dot (inner) 20th left side, 10.
4. Minute dot 19th left side, 8.
5. Dot under PE of 2nd; projection below rule under L of 1st; dot (outer) left side, $12\frac{3}{4}$.
6. Base of rule under 2nd cut away under NNY to right end.
7. Dot 19th left side, $9\frac{1}{2}$.
8. $\frac{1}{2}$ dot (top) under E of 3rd.
9. Dot 18th left side, 12.
10. Dot (top) under F of 4th.
11. $\frac{1}{2}$ dot and $\frac{1}{2}$ cut (top) under E of 2nd.
12. $\frac{1}{2}$ dot (top) under PE of 3rd.
13. Split at right end of rule under 2nd; dot (inner) 19th left side, $7\frac{1}{2}$.
14. 2 dots under PEN of 3rd.
15. Dot (outer) 20th left side, $6\frac{1}{2}$.
16. Small $\frac{1}{2}$ cut (base) under L of 1st.
17. 2 dots 19th left side, $10\frac{1}{2}$, $13\frac{1}{2}$.
18. Dot under F of 2nd.
19. Large dot (outer) 20th left side, $11\frac{1}{2}$.
20. Dot (base) under FP of 1st.
21. Dot under P of 3rd.
22. Small dot 20th left side, $11\frac{1}{2}$, the base of which bends inwards.
23. Big dot 19th left side, 12.
24. Nick at left of 3rd rule.
25. Minute dot at base of 20th left side.
26. Indistinct dot 19th left side, 16.
27. Nick at right of 3rd rule.
28. Minute dot (inner) 20th left side, $7\frac{1}{2}$.
29. $\frac{1}{2}$ dot (outer) 19th left side, 11.
30. Indents (base) under H and L of 1st.
31. Left end of 1st rule very thick and curves upwards.
32. Cut at top of 1st left side with dot half way down, dot above 4th.
33. Very fine cut 19th left side, 13.

These electros were put to press with controls as follows:

1. A24, B24, C25, D25.
2. A24, C25, D25.
3. A24, B24, C25.
4. A24, H27.

5.	B24, C25, D25, E26.	19.	I28, J28, K29, L29.
6.	B24, C25, D25, E26.	20.	I28, J28, K29, L29.
7.	B24, C25.	21.	I28, J28, K29, L29.
8.	C25, D25, E26, G27, I28, J28, K29.	22.	J28, K29, L29, N30.
		23.	J28, K29, L29.
9.	C25.	24.	M30, N30, Q32.
10.	C25.	25.	M30, Q32.
11.	D25, E26, F26, G27, I28.	26.	N30, O31, P31.
12.	D25, F26, G27, I28.	27.	P31, Q32, R32, S33, T33.
13.	F26, H27, I28.	28.	P31.
14.	F26, G27, H27.	29.	S33, T33.
15.	F26, G27, H27.	30.	U34, V34.
16.	F26, G27.	31.	U34, V34.
17.	G27.	32.	U34.
18.	I28, J28.	33.	V34.

THE POSTAL UNION CONGRESS ISSUE
List of electro markings

1. $\frac{1}{2}$ dot (base) under E of 1st.
2. $\frac{1}{2}$ dot (base) under GR of 2nd.
3. $\frac{1}{2}$ dot (top) under ES of 3rd.
4. Dot 20th left side, 7.
5. Dot 19th left side, 7.
6. Dot (inner) 19th left side, 20.
7. No marking.
8. Large dot (breaking top) under 4th.

These electros were put to press with controls as follows:

1. K29, L29.
2. K29, L29.
3. K29, L29.
4. K29, L29.
5. K29, L29.
6. K29, L29.
7. K29, L29.
8. L29.

ONE PENNY
ORIGINAL DIE
List of electro markings

1.
  a. No marking.
  b. Added cut under EP of 2nd; cut under NN of 7th; dot 19th right side.
2.
  a. No marking.
  b. Added cut under P of 1st.
3. Dot 20th right side, 12$\frac{1}{2}$.
4. 'U' mark under E of 3rd.
5. Dot 18th right side, 10$\frac{1}{2}$.
6. Dot 17th right side, 9$\frac{1}{2}$.
7. Dot under E of 11th; fine dot 20th right side.
8. Cut under E of 11th.
9. $\frac{1}{2}$ dot 20th right side, 9$\frac{1}{2}$.
10. Cut 19th right side, 10; left of 11th rule cut away.
11. Cut under E of 9th.

12.
  a. ½ dot 19th right side, 10.
  b. Added cut under (P)E of 11th.

13. Nick (outer) 20th right side; cut under E of 10th.

These electros were put to press with controls as follows:

1.
  a. A.11.
  b. All wide.
2.
  a. A.11.
  b. All wide.
3. All wide, All narrow.
4. All wide.
5. All wide.
6. All wide.
7. All wide.
8. All wide.
9. All wide.
10. All wide.
11. All wide, All narrow.
12.
  a. All wide.
  b. All wide.
13. All wide, All narrow.

DEEPENED DIE
List of electro markings

1. No marking.
2. Cut 20th right side, 9.
3.
  a. No marking.
  b. Added oval cut 20th right side, 11½.
  c. Added cut 17th right side.
4. Cut 20th right side, 14.
5. Cut 20th right side, 13.
6. ½ cut (outer) 20th right side, 12.
7. Cut under PE of 12th; cut 20th right side, 10.
8.
  a. ½ cut (base) under E of 11th; cut 19th right side, 13½.
  b. Added cut 20th right side, 11¾.
9.
  a. No marking.
  b. Added cut 19th right side, 16.
10. Cut 19th right side, 11½.
11. Cut 19th right side, 8¾.
12. Cut 19th right side, 7¾.
13. Cut 18th right side.
14. Cut 17th right side, 9.
15.
  a. No marking.
  b. Added minute dot under EN of 9th.

These electros were put to press with controls as follows:

1. All narrow.
2. All narrow.
3.
  a. A.11.
  b. All narrow.
  c. All narrow.
4. All narrow.
5. All narrow.
6. All narrow.
7. All narrow, All wide.
8.
  a. All narrow.
  b. All narrow, All wide.
9.
  a. A.11.
  b. All narrow.
10. All narrow.
11. All narrow.

12. All narrow.
13. All narrow.
14. All narrow, All wide.

15.
  a. A.11.
  b. All narrow.

THE REDRAWN DIE
List of electro markings

1.
  a. No marking.
  b. Added dot under EP of 5th.

2.
  a. No marking.
  b. Added dot (base) under NE of 6th.

3.
  a. No marking.
  b. Added dot under NN of 7th.

4.
  a. Scoop (base) under right of 8th.
  b. Added small dot under NE of 8th.

5.
  a. No marking.
  b. Added dot under PE of 9th.

6.
  a. Dot above 1st in top row.
  b. Dot above 1st filled in; added dot under PE of 1st; dot under EP of 10th.

7.
  a. No marking.
  b. Added dot under EP of 11th.

8.
  a. No marking.
  b. Added dot under EP of 12th.

9.
  a. Dash under PE of 11th.
  b. Added dot under EP of 11th.

10.
  a. Dash under PE of 12th.
  b. Added dot under (N)E of 12th.

11. Cut under PE of 9th.
12. $\frac{1}{2}$ cut under PE of 10th.
13. Cut under PE of 11th.
14. Cut under (P)E of 12th.
15. Small dot 19th right side, $9\frac{1}{4}$.

16.
  a. Two small dots 20th right side, $10\frac{1}{2}$, 16.
  b. Added dot under P of 12th.
17. Dot under P of 9th.
18. Dot under PE of 10th.

These electros were put to press with controls as follows:

1.
  a. B11.
  b. B11.

2.
  a. B.12.
  b. B11.

3.
  a. B11.
  b. B11, B12 narrow Crown.

4.
  a. B11.
  b. B11, B12 narrow Crown.

5.
  a. B11.
  b. B11, B12 narrow Crown.

6.
  a. B.11, B.12.
  b. B11, B12 narrow Crown.

7.
  a. B11.
  b. B11, B12 narrow Crown.

8.
  a. B.11, B.12.
  b. B.12, B11, B12 narrow Crown.

9.
  a. B12 narrow Crown.
  b. B12 narrow Crown.

10.
- *a.* B12 narrow Crown.
- *b.* B12 narrow Crown.

11.   B12 wide Crown,
B12 wide G v R (M),
B12 wide G v R (S), B13.

12.   B12 wide Crown,
B12 wide G v R (M),
B12 wide G v R (S), B13.

13.   B12 wide Crown,
B12 wide G v R (M),

      B12 wide G v R (S).

14.   B12 wide Crown.

15.   B12 wide Crown, B13.

16.
- *a.* B12 wide Crown,
B12 wide G v R (M),
B12 wide G v R (S).
- *b.* B13.

17.   B13.

18.   B13.

FIRST HARRISON CONTRACT, 1912 TO 1923
List of electro markings

1.   No marking.

2.
- *a.* Dot under PE of 1st.
- *b.* Added $\frac{1}{2}$ dot (inner) and dot 20th left side, 5, 8.

3.
- *a.* Dot under EN of 2nd.
- *b.* Added 2 dots under ON, EP of 3rd.
- *c.* Added dot and $\frac{1}{2}$ dot (outer) 20th left side, 9, $10\frac{1}{2}$.

4.
- *a.* Small dot under (P)E of 3rd.
- *b.* Added minute dot 3rd at left.

5.
- *a.* Dot under PE of 4th.
- *b.* Added dot under NN of 4th.
- *c.* Added dot under NE of 1st.

6.   2 dots under NE, (P)E of 1st; dot 18th right side, 10; marginal rule under 11th thin.

7.   Dot under PE of 3rd; dot 17th right side, 10; nick left base of 12th; marginal rule under 11th thin.

8.
- *a.* Slanting internal cut under PE of 1st.
- *b.* Added small dot under (P)E of 5th.

9.   Dot 20th left side, $13\frac{1}{2}$.

10.
- *a.* 2 big dots under (O)N, EN of 2nd.
- *b.* Added long dot under EP of 2nd.

11.
- *a.* Dot (breaking right) 18th right side, 10.
- *b.* Added small dot 18th right side, $4\frac{3}{4}$.

12.   Dot (central) 18th right side, $11\frac{3}{4}$.

13.   Dot (breaking right) 19th left side, 8.

14.
- *a.* Dot 19th left side, 12.
- *b.* Added 2 cuts to left of O ON of 2nd.

15.   Dot 17th right side, $8\frac{3}{4}$.

16.   Dot 20th left side, $7\frac{3}{4}$.

17.   Triangular dot under EN of 2nd.

18.   Triangular dot under PE of 3rd.

19.   Irregular dot, which is large and sometimes plain, but at other times hardly visible (top) under EN of 4th small dot above 11th upper pane.

20.   Dot 18th right side, $10\frac{1}{2}$.

21. Dot 18th right side, 8.
22. Dot (bulging right) 17th right side, 11.
23. ½ cut (base) and ½ dot (top) under (N)N of 1st.
24. 2 small dots under ONE of 2nd.
25. 2 dots at left and under PE of 4th.
26. Dot (breaking left) 18th right side, 11½.
27. Small dot (central) 18th right side, 12½.
28. Dot (bulging right) 18th right side, 11.
29.
   a. Dot (left) 20th left side, 12½.
   b. Added cut to left of O of 1st.
30. Flat oval dot under EN of 1st.
31. Dot (breaking base) to left of P of 2nd.
32. ¾ dot (base) under O of 3rd.
33. Dot under ON of 4th; dot 18th right side, 12.
34. Dot 18th right side, 8.
35. Dot 17th right side, 10.
36. Curved dot under PEN of 1st.
37. Wide ¾ cut (base) under PEN of 2nd; slanting ¾ cut (base) under PE of 3rd, right end of which is damaged; dot 20th left side, 8¾.
38. Curved dot under PE of 3rd.
39. Curved dot under EP of 3rd; curved dot under PE of 4th.
40. Dot under EP of 3rd; dot 18th left side, 13; dot 19th left side, 11½.
41. Dot under NE of 4th; dot under P of 8th; ½ cut (inner) 17th left side.
42. Dot under PE of 6th.
43. Dot under EP of 3rd; dot under P of 7th; dot 17th

left side, 11¼; dot 18th left side, 13; dot 19th left side, 11.
44. Dot under E(N) of 1st; dot under PE of 5th; dot 20th left side, 10½.
45. Large dot (breaking base) under EN of 2nd; dot 20th left side.
46. Irregular slanting cut under EPE of 1st; curved dot under EP of 3rd.
47. Small dot under PE of 2nd.
48. Curved dot under N(N) of 2nd; large oval dot (breaking base) under NE of 3rd.
49. Dot under EP of 2nd; minute dot under (O)N of 12th.
50. ½ dot (base) under EN of 2nd; dot 19th left side, 10.
51. ½ dot (top) under PE of 3rd.
52. Curved dot under EN of 3rd; nick (outer) and dot 19th left side, 15½, 11.
53.
   a. Large dot (breaking top) under EP of 3rd; dot 19th right side, 11.
   b. Added large dot (breaking base) under EN of 1st.
54. Indent (base) under ON of 5th; dot (breaking inner) 19th left side, 10.
55. Dot 20th left side, 11.
56. Small oval dot under PE of 1st.
57. Dash under EN and dot under (N)N of 1st; dot and irregular ½ cut (base) under EP of 2nd; dot (base) under NE of 3rd; 4 cuts 19th right side, 9½–11.
58. Large dot (breaking top) under PEN of 2nd.
59. Oval cut under EP of 2nd.
60. Dot under P of 2nd; 2 oval cuts under PE of 3rd.

61.
  a. Dot and oval dot under P, EN of 2nd; large dot (breaking top) under NE of 4th.
  b. Added large dot (top) under (N)N of 4th.
62. Irregular dot under EP of 4th.
63. Dot under P of, and dash to the right of, 4th; nick (outer) 20th left side, 10.
64. Nick (base) at right end of 10th.
65. Indent (base) under NN of 11th.
66. 'X' cut 17th right side, $14\frac{1}{2}$; 'X' cut and straight cut 18th right side, $13\frac{1}{2}$, $12\frac{1}{2}$.
67. 'X' cut 17th right side, 10; 'X' cut 18th right side, $10\frac{1}{2}$; 2 dots over 2 cuts 19th right side, 9, 13.
68. Dot (breaking base) under PE of 1st.
69. Dot (base) under EN of 1st; dot 20th left side, $13\frac{3}{4}$.
70. Dot under EN of 2nd.
71. $\frac{1}{2}$ dot (top) under PE of 10th.
72. Nick (base) at right end of 11th.
73. Dot 18th right side, $9\frac{1}{2}$.
74. Dot (base) under EP of 2nd; dot (central) 19th left side, 14.
75. Dot (breaking base) to left of P of 10th.
76. Horizontal 'V' cut 19th right side, 12.
77. Dot under (P)E of 1st; dot (outer) 19th left side; $\frac{1}{2}$ dot (inner) 20th left side, $11\frac{3}{4}$.
78. Cut at right of 1st.
79. Dot under PE of 1st.
80. Dot (top) under N(N) of 2nd; nick (outer) and dot 19th left side, $15\frac{1}{2}$, $10\frac{1}{2}$.
81. Dot under (N)E of 10th.
82. 3 dots under PE, NN, to right of Y of 3rd.
83. 4 dots under EN, NY, to right of Y of 4th.
84. $\frac{1}{2}$ dot (base) at extreme left of 11th.
85. 2 nicks (outer) and dot 19th left side, 15, 12, $10\frac{1}{2}$.
86. Dot under (N)N of 1st.
87.
  a. Dot (breaking inner) 20th right side, 12.
  b. Added dot under PE of 10th.
88. Dot 17th right side very low.
89. Nick (base) at right of 11th.
90. Dot 17th right side.
91. Minute (almost invisible) nick 19th right side, $12\frac{1}{2}$.
92. 3 cuts 20th right side, 8, $12\frac{1}{2}$, 17.
93. 4 half cuts (outer) 20th right side, 5, $8\frac{3}{4}$, $12\frac{1}{4}$, $15\frac{1}{2}$.
94. Minute dot (inner) 20th left side, 12.
95. Dot (centre) 18th right side.
96. Left of 12th thins at left.
97. Dot under (P)E of 1st; dot (outer) 20th left side, 9; 2 nicks (outer) 19th left side, 12, 15.
98. Nick (base) at right end of 12th.
99. Tall dot 20th right side.

These electros were put to press with controls as follows:

1. C12, C13, C14.
2.
  a. C12, C13.
  b. C13.
3.
  a. C12, C13.
  b. C13.
  c. C13.

4.
  a. C12, C13.
  b. C13, C14.
5.
  a. C12, C13.
  b. C13.
  c. C13, C14.
6.   C12, C13.
7.   C12, C13.
8.
  a. C13.
  b. C13, C14.
9.   C13, D14.
10.
  a. C13.
  b. E14.
11.
  a. C13.
  b. C13.
12.   C13, C14, E14.
13.   C14.
14.
  a. C14, D14.
  b. E14.
15.   C14, E14.
16.   C14, D14, F15.
17.   D14, E14.
18.   D14.
19.   D14, E14.
20.   D14.
21.   D14.
22.   D14, E14.
23.   E14.
24.   E14.
25.   E14.
26.   E14.
27.   E14.
28.   E14.
29.
  a. E14.
  b. F15.
30.   F15.
31.   F15, H16.
32.   F15.
33.   F15, G15.
34.   F15.
35.   F15, G15.

36.   G15.
37.   G15.
38.   G15, H16.
39.   G15.
40.   G15, H16.
41.   G15, H16.
42.   G15.
43.   G15, H16, I16.
44.   H16.
45.   H16.
46.   I16.
47.   I16.
48.   I16.
49.   I16, J17, K17.
50.   I16.
51.   I16.
52.   I16.
53.
  a. I16, J17.
  b. J17.
54.   I16.
55.   I16, J17.
56.   J17.
57.   J17.
58.   J17.
59.   J17.
60.   J17.
61.
  a. J17.
  b. J17.
62.   J17.
63.   J17, K17.
64.   J17.
65.   J17, K17, K18.
66.   J17, K17.
67.   J17.
68.   K17.
69.   K17.
70.   K17.
71.   K17, K18, M19.
72.   K17, K18.
73.   K17, M19.
74.   K18.
75.   K18, L18, N19, O19, O20, R21, S21.
76.   K18.
77.   M19.

M

78.	M19.		88.	P20.
79.	N19.		89.	R21.
80.	N19.		90.	S21, T22.
81.	N19.		91.	S22, T22, U22, U23.
82.	N19. P20.		92.	T22, U22, U23, V23.
83.	N19.		93.	T22, U22, U23, V23.
84.	N19.		94.	T22.
85.	P20.		95.	T22.
86.	P20.		96.	T22.
87.			97.	U22.
	a. P20, Q20, Q21 narrow, R21.		98.	V23, W23, W24.
	b. R21, S21, S22, T22, U22.		99.	W23, W24.

WATERLOW CONTRACT AND HARRISON PROVISIONAL PRINTINGS
List of electro markings

The list of these electros is very small. Doubtless many other electros were made, but the fact that the control is on the right of the sheets and most cuts were towards the left, together with the lack of complete bottom strips, makes identification of these electros very difficult.

1. 1 cuts left side, vertical position not known.
2. Small dot at right of 11th.
3. Dot (inner) 20th right side.
4. ½ cut (outer) 20th right side.
5. Nick at right of 10th.
6. Horizontal dash at right of 11th.
7. Nick at left of 11th.
8. Base of 20th right side bent in.

These electros were put to press with controls as follows:

1. B24 (experimental paper).
2. F26.
3. F26, G27.
4. G27, H27.
5. K29, M30, N30.
6. Q32, R32, S33, T33.
7. U34.
8. V34.

THE POSTAL UNION CONGRESS ISSUE
List of electro markings

1. Dot 20th right side; scoop 19th right side.
2. No marking.

These electros were put to press with controls as follows:

1. K29, L29.
2. K29, L29.

THREEHALFPENCE
FIRST HARRISON CONTRACT, 1912 TO 1923
List of electro markings

1.
 a. Dot above 1st in upper and lower panes.
 b. Dots above 1st filled in.

2.
 a. Dot above 2nd in upper and lower pane; scoop under THR of 10th.
 b. Dots above 2nd filled in; added very fine cut 1st top row; nick 1st right side which is split at top; scoop (outer) 2nd right side.
 c. Added minute dot under L of 1st.
 d. Added dot 20th right side.

3.
 a. Dot above 3rd in upper and lower pane; indent below right of 3rd.
 b. Dots above 3rd filled in; added very fine cut 2nd top row; scoop (outer) 2nd right side; no split 1st right side.
 c. Added minute dot under L of 2nd.

4.
 a. Dot above 4th in upper and lower panes.
 b. Dots above 4th filled in.

5.
 a. Dot (base) to left of T of 1st.
 b. Added ½ dot (inner) 19th right side.

6.
 a. Large dot (breaking base) to left of T of 2nd.
 b. Added ½ cut (base) under (P)E of 2nd.

7. Dot (top) to left of T of 3rd.
8. Dot (base) to left of T of 4th.

9. Large diamond dot under T of 1st.
10. 2 dots 19th left side, 9, 10.
11. Dot (outer) 20th left side, 11.
12. 2 cuts 20th left side, 5, 6½.
13.
 a. 2 cuts 19th left side, 6½, 7; 20th left side bulges at top and lower middle.
 b. Added ½ cut (base) under HA of 2nd.
14. Cut 20th left side, 10.
15. Small dot under AL of 2nd.
16. Small dot under AL of 3rd; dot 17th left side, 11½.
17. Large oval dot (base) under H(A) of 1st.
18. Large oval dot under L of 2nd; oval dot 19th left side, 11½.
19. ½ cut (outer) 19th left side, 9½.
20.
 a. Cut 20th left side, 6.
 b. Added ½ cut under TH of 1st.
21. Large ½ dot under AL of 2nd.
22. ½ dot (base) under F of 11th.
23. No marking.
24.
 a. Dot (outer) 19th left side, 6.
 b. Added nick (base) under EN of 2nd.
25. Cut 19th left side, 5½.
26. Oval (blurred) cut 20th left side, 15.
27. Small dot (outer) 19th left side, 9½.
28. Large dot (base) under L of 2nd.
29. ½ dot (outer) 20th right side (one of the PENCF plates).
30. Minute dot under FP of 2nd.

31. $\frac{1}{2}$ dot (inner) 19th left side, 12.
32. $\frac{1}{2}$ dot (outer) 20th left side, 9, lower end of 20th thin.
33. $\frac{1}{2}$ dot (outer) 20th left side, 10$\frac{1}{2}$.
34. Dot (inner) 20th left side, 13.
35. Fine dot 20th left side, 8$\frac{3}{4}$.
36. Large circular dot (base) under (E)H of 1st.
37. Small nick (base) to left of T of 2nd.
38. Tall dot 19th left side, 10$\frac{1}{2}$.
39. Dot (outer) 20th left side, 11$\frac{1}{2}$; $\frac{1}{2}$ dot (outer) 19th left side, 10.
40. 2 cuts 18th right side.
41. $\frac{1}{2}$ dot (outer) 20th left side, 5.
42. Outer side of 20th left side damaged, 4–5.

These electros were put to press with controls as follows:

1.
   a. A.12 narrow, A.12 wide.
   b. C13.
2.
   a. A.12 narrow, A.12 wide.
   b. C13, D14.
   c. F15, G15, H16, J17.
   d. J17, K18, 18 (only), L18.
3.
   a. A.12 narrow.
   b. C13, D14.
   c. F15, G15, H16, J17, K18, L18.
4.
   a. A.12 narrow.
   b. G15, H16, K18.
5.
   a. K18, L18, M19.
   b. M19.
6.
   a. K18, L18.
   b. M18, M19.
7. K18, L18, M19, N19.
8. K18, L18, N19.
9. L18, M18, M19.
10. L18, N19.
11. L18, M19, N19.
12. L18, O19, Q21 narrow, Q21 wide, T22.
13.
   a. M18, M19, N19.
   b. N19.
14. M18, M19, N19.
15. M19, N19.
16. M19.

17. N19, O19, O20, T22.
18. N19, O19, O20, Q21 narrow, T22, U23.
19. N19.
20.
   a. N19, O19, Q20, Q21 wide, T22, U22, U23.
   b. U23.
21. N19, O19, O20, Q20, Q21 wide.
22. N19, Q20, T22.
23. N19, Q20, Q21 narrow.
24.
   a. N19, O19, O20, Q20.
   b. Q21 narrow, T22.
25. O19, Q20, T22, U23.
26. O19, O20, Q21 wide, T22.
27. O19, O20, Q21 narrow, T22, U22, U23.
28. O19, O20.
29. Q21 narrow, Q21 wide.
30. T22.
31. T22, U22, U23.
32. T22, U22, U23.
33. T22, U22, U23.
34. T22, U22, U23.
35. T22, V23.
36. V23.
37. V23, W23.
38. V23.
39. V23, W23, W24.
40. W23.
41. W23.
42. W23.

Comparative control positions

A.12 narrow.   Electro 1. A below centre of second E. Control slopes slightly down, ·95–1·00.

Electro 2. A below right loop of R. Top of 2 slightly damaged. Control slopes slightly down, 2·00–2·10

Electro 3. A below centre of first E. Control slopes down, ·80–1·00.

A.12 wide.   Electro 1. Dot between A and 12 low. A below RE. Control level, 2·20.

Electro 2. A below left vertical of H. Control level, 1·80.

C13.   Electro 2. Figure 1 below (P)E(N). Control slopes evidently down, 3·60–4·00.

Electro 3. Figure 1 below (P)E(N). Control slopes slightly down, 1·30–1·40.

D14.   Electro 3. Heavy control much damaged.

K18.   Electro 4. Base of upright of K thin. Lower diagonal of K thick and defective at base.

Electro 8. Base of lower diagonal of K blunted. Top right of figure 8 very defective.

WATERLOW CONTRACT AND HARRISON PROVISIONAL PRINTINGS
List of electro markings

1. Dot (base) under PE of 1st.
2. Small dot (base) under HA of 2nd.
3. Small dot (base) under AL of 3rd.
4. Small dot 20th left side, 14.
5. Fine dot 19th left side, 15½.
6. ½ dot (outer) and full dot 18th left side, 21, 10.
7. 19th (inner) left side scooped out, 4–6.
8. ½ cut (outer) 19th left side, 8½.
9. Dot and ½ dot (inner) 19th left side, 9½, 10½.
10. ½ dot (outer) 20th left side, 5.
11. Dot under A of 4th.
12. Line under 1st bevelled at left.
13. Dot 20th left side, 10½.
14. Oval dot 19th left side, 8.

15. 19th left side bulges in middle; 20th left side thins at base.
16. Base of 20th left side bent inwards.
17. Dot 20th left side, 10.
18. Fine dot (inner) 20th left side, 11.
19. ½ cut (outer) 19th left side, 14.
20.
  a. Large dot (top) under LF of 1st.
  b. Added fine dot under EN of 3rd.
21.
  a. Dot (top) under AL of 2nd.
  b. Added dot 20th left side, 10.
  c. Added minute dot under A of 1st.

22.
   a. Notch (base) to right of (C)E of 2nd.
   b. Added minute dot under L of 1st.
23. Minute dot under EH of 2nd.
24. Small dot under F of 3rd.
25. Fine dot under L of 4th.
26. Large and small dot 20th left side, both 6½.
27. Dot 19th left side, 8; small nick (base) under FP of 3rd.
28. Scratch under NC of 2nd.
29. Double nick at left of 2nd.
30. Scratch under NC of 3rd.

31. Double notch (base) under EN of 2nd.
32. Vertical score 20th left side.
33. ½ dot (base) under HA of 3rd.
34. Small dot (top) under HA of 3rd.
35. Oval dot under EE of 3rd.
36. Dot (base) under HR of 3rd.
37. 2 dots, top and bottom of 20th left side, 19½, 3.
38. 2 dots, top and bottom (outer) of 19th left side, 21, 3.
39. 2 dots top and bottom of 19th left side (in a different position to Plate 38).

These electros were put to press with controls as follows:

1. A24,
   A24 experimental paper, B24, C25, D25.
2. A24, B24, C25, D25.
3. A24, B24, C25, D25, D25 experimental paper, F26.
4. A24, B24.
5. A24.
6. A24.
7. B24, C25, D25.
8. B24, E26.
9. C25.
10. C25, D25, F26.
11. D25, E26.
12. E26, F26, G27.
13. E26, F26, G27, H27.
14. E26, F26, G27.
15. E.26, E26, H27, I28.
16. F26, G27.
17. H27, I28.
18. H27, I28, J28.
19. I28, J28.
20.
   a. J28, K29, L29.

   b. M30.
21.
   a. J28, K29, L29.
   b. L29, O31.
   c. O31.
22.
   a. J28.
   b. L29, M30.
23. L29.
24. L29, M30.
25. L29.
26. M30, N30.
27. M30, N30, O31.
28. M30, N30, O31, Q32, R32.
29. N30, O31, P31, Q32, R32.
30. N30.
31. O31, P31, Q32.
32. O31, P31, Q32, R32
33. S33.
34. S33, T33.
35. S33, T33.
36. S33, T33.
37. T33.
38. T33, U34, V34.
39. V34.

P.U.C. ISSUE
List of electro markings

1. ½ cut (base) at right of 2nd.
2. ½ cut (top) at right of 3rd.
3. Internal score in 20th left side.
4. Base of 3rd ragged.
5. No marking.

These electros were put to press with controls as follows:

1. K29, L29.
2. K29, L29.
3. K29, L29.
4. K29.
5. K29, L29.

TWOPENCE
DIE I
HARRISON 1912–23 PRINTINGS
List of electro markings

1.
  a. No marking.
  b. Added dot above 2nd in upper and lower panes.
  c. Dots above 2nd filled in.

2.
  a. Dot above 6th in upper and lower panes; dash under E of 2nd.
  b. Dots above 6th filled in.

3. Cut under PE of 1st.
4. Cut under WO of 2nd.
5. Minute mark (outer) 19th left side, 10.
6. Large dot 20th left side bulging line at left, 12.

7.
  a. Dot 19th left side, 11.
  b. Added dot 19th left side, 7½.

8. Fine dot 20th left side, 13.

9.
  a. Nick (inner) 20th left side, 2.
  b. Added oblique dot 20th left side, 14.

10. 2 dots, one large one small, 20th left side, 13, 14.

11. Fine dot (base) under EN of 2nd.
12. Outer base of 19th left side bevelled off.
13. Large pear-shaped dot 19th left side, 11½.
14. Scoop (outer) 19th left side, 8½–11.
15. Elongated dot 19th left side, 10½.
16. Fine dot (or nick) (base) under W of 1st; nick (outer) base of 19th left side, 2; large dot (central) 19th left side; 4 small dots (central) 1st right side, 6, 8, 10, 12; scoop (outer) 2nd right side, 10–12; scoop (outer) 15th right side, 4–6; nick (base) 9th right side, 6.
17. Nick (outer) 20th left side, 10.
18. Oval cut 20th left side, 11.
19. ½ dot (inner) 20th left side, 8.
20. Oval cut 19th left side, 14.
21. Oval dot 19th left side, 11½.

These electros were put to press with controls as follows:

1.
   a. No control.
   b. C.13.
   c. D14, J17, K17, M19, O19, O20, P20, S21.
2.
   a. C.13.
   b. O20, P20.
3. No control, C14, D14, F15, G15, H16, I16, J17, K17, L18, M19, N19, O19, P20, Q20.
4. No control, C14, D14, F15, G15, H16, I16, J17, K17, O19, O20, P20.
5. O20, P20.
6. P20, Q20, Q21 narrow, S22.
7.
   a. P20.

   b. P20, Q21 narrow, S21.
8. P20.
9.
   a. P20.
   b. Q21 narrow, R21, S22, T22.
10. P20, Q20, Q21 narrow, Q21 wide, R21, S21.
11. P20, Q21 wide, R21, S21.
12. P20, Q21 narrow, R21.
13. Q20, R21, S22.
14. Q21 narrow.
15. Q21 narrow, R21, T22.
16. Q21 wide, R21, S21, S22, T22.
17. R21, S21, T22.
18. R21, S21, S22, T22.
19. R21, S21, S22, T22.
20. S21, S22, T22.
21. S21, S22.

DIE II

HARRISON 1912–23 PRINTINGS
List of electro markings

1. Oval cut 19th left side, 13.
2. Dot (outer) 20th left side, $13\frac{1}{2}$; $\frac{1}{2}$ dot (base) under P of 1st.
3. No marking, lower part of 20th left side thins.
4. Dot 20th left side, 13.
5. Dot 19th left side, 13; fine

vertical scratch 20th left side, which is slightly damaged, 11.
6. Dot central 10th under P; dot (central) 18th right side, 13; rule under 11th damaged from left to below CE.

These electros were put to press with controls as follows:

1. S21, S22, T22, U22, U23, V23.
2. S21, S22, T22, U22, U23.
3. S22, T22.
4. T22, U23, V23, W23, W24.
5. T22, U23, V23, W23, W24.
6. T22.

WATERLOW CONTRACT AND HARRISON PROVISIONAL PRINTINGS
List of electro markings

1. Base of 20th left side rounded off.
2. Left of rule under 1st pointed below.

3. Minute dot 20th left side, 11½; rule under 1st slightly scooped out under OP.
4. Large dot 20th left side, 13.
5.
   a. Dot 19th left side, 13.
   b. Added minute dot under P of 2nd.
6. Dot 19th left side breaking right, 8½; base of rules under 1st, 2nd and 3rd very irregular.
7. ½ dot (inner) 20th left side, 10½, with minute dot to the left of it and lower portion of rule very irregular.
8. Dot, with offshoot dot, above it and to right of it; 20th left side, 13; nick to left of 1st at base.
9. Minute dot (base) under P of 2nd; dot 19th left side, 11¾.
10. Large dot (breaking top) under P of 1st.
11. ½ dot (top) under P of 2nd.
12. Nicks (base) at right and left of 2nd; dot 19th left side, 11½.
13. Dot (bulging sides) 20th left side, 12.
14. Indent (base) under to right of E of 2nd; 2 dots 19th left side, 11, 13.
15. No marking.
16. Indent (base) under C of 1st.

These electros were put to press with controls as follows:

1. A24, B24, C25.
2. A24, B24, F26, L29, M30, N30, P31, Q32, R32.
3. B24, D25, F26, H27, I28, K29, L29.
4. B24, C25, D25, E26.
5.
   a. D25, E26, I28, J28.
   b. J28, K29, L29.
6. F26, G27, H27, I28, J28.
7. F26, G27, H27, K29, M30.
8. J28, K29, L29.
9. J28, K29, L29.
10. M30, N30, O31, P31.
11. M30, N30, O31, P31, Q32, R32.
12. N30, Q32, R32, S33, T33, U34.
13. N30, O31, R32, T33.
14. O31, Q32, R32, S33, T33.
15. U34, V34.
16. V34.

TWOPENCE HALFPENNY
HARRISON 1912–23 PRINTINGS
List of electro markings

1.
   a. Dot above 1st in upper and lower panes; rules on left side irregular.
   b. Dots above 1st filled in.
2.
   a. Dot above 2nd in upper and lower panes.
   b. Dots above 2nd filled in.
   c. Added oval dot under PE of 1st.
3.
   a. Dot above 3rd in upper and lower panes; base of 20th left side bent inwards.
   b. Dots above 3rd filled in.

4.
- a. Dot above 5th in upper and lower panes; 20th right side damaged.
- b. Dots above 5th filled in.

5.
- a. Base of rule under 2nd pointed at right.
- b. Added minute nick at left of 1st; minute nick top of right of 2nd.

6. Oval dot (top) under FP of 2nd.
7. 20th left side bevelled at base.
8. Circular dot (low) under PE of 1st.
9. ½ cut (base) under FP of 2nd.
10. Cut under (P)E of 1st.
11. Cut under LF of 2nd.

The electros were put to press with controls as follows:

1.
- a. A.12.
- b. C13, C14, D14, E14, G15, H16, I16, J17, J.17, K17, L18, M18, N19, O19, O20, R21.

2.
- a. A.12.
- b. C13.
- c. I16, J17.

3.
- a. A.12.
- b. C13, I16.

4.
- a. A.12.
- b. I16.

5.
- a. E14, G15.
- b. G15, H16.

6. I16, J17, O20, Q21.
7. L18, O19, O20, Q21, S21, S22, T22, U23, V23.
8. N19, O19, O20, P20, Q21, R21, S22, T22, U23.
9. N19, O20, Q21, R21, S21, S22, T22, U23.
10. S21, S22, T22, U23, V23.
11. S21, S22, T22, U23, V23.

Comparative control positions

A.12.   Plate 1. Control slopes down to right, ·8–1·2.
         Plate 2. Control almost level, ·8–·9.
         Plate 3. Right of top of figure 2 flattened.
         Plate 4. Control level, 1·2.
C13.   Plate 1. Right lower loop of figure 3 blunted, 1·9.
         Plate 2. Control level, 1·3.
         Plate 3. Marks in top point of C, 1·0.
E14.   Plate 1. Top of figure 4 pointed at right, 2·8.
         Plate 5. Top of figure 4 perfect, 2·8.
G15.   Plate 1. Control level, 1·3.
         Plate 5. Control level, ·9.
I16.   Plate 1. Serif of figure 1 perfect.
         Plate 4. Serif of figure 1 bifurcated.

WATERLOW CONTRACT AND HARRISON PROVISIONAL PRINTINGS
List of electro markings

1. No marking.
2. Outer side of 20th left side very irregular; rule under 1st curves slightly up towards left end.
3. Dot (inner) 20th left side, 13.
4. Cut under LF of 2nd.
5. Large dot (outer) 19th left side, 11.
6. Dot under PE of 1st.
7. Dot 20th left side, 10.
8. Minute dot 19th left side, 11.
9. 20th left side bends in at base; rule under 1st splays out at left end; minute dot under NY of 2nd.
10. Dot 20 left side, 7; minute dot under right '2½' of 2nd.
11. Scratch in rule under Y of 1st.
12. ½ cut under PE of 1st.
13. Base of 20th left side has an inward projection.

These electros were put to press with controls as follows:

1. B24, C25, E26, I28, K29, M30, N30, Q32, S33, T33, V34, W35.
2. B24, C25, H27, I28, M30, N30, O31, Q32, R32, S33, T33, V34, W35.
3. D25, E26, G27.
4. E26, G27, I28.
5. E26, G27, I28.
6. G27, H27.
7. I28, K29.
8. I28.
9. I28, K29, N30, Q32, R32, S33.
10. K29.
11. T33, V34.
12. V34, W35.
13. V34, W35.

THE P.U.C. ISSUE
List of electro markings

1. ½ dot (inner) 20th left side, 13.
2. ½ dot (outer) 19th left side, 10½.

These electros were put to press with controls as follows:

1. K29, L29.
2. K29, L29.

THREEPENCE
HARRISON 1912–23 PRINTINGS
List of electro markings

1.
  a. Dot at left and dot centrally above 1st in upper pane; dot centrally above 1st in lower pane.
  b. Dots above 1st filled in.

c. Further dots cut above right of 1st in upper and lower panes; right of line under 2nd broken at base.

d. Left of line under 3rd broken at base.

e. Added horizontal dash under PE of 2nd.

(*Note:* It is thought that the dots cut in state *c.* were never filled in as specimens have been seen in the 'misty' shade associated with printings under controls C13, J17 and L18.)

2.

a. Dot above 4th in upper and lower panes.

b. Dots above 4th filled in.

3.

a. Dot above 2nd in upper and lower panes; minute $\frac{1}{2}$ dot under right of 5th.

b. Dots above 2nd filled in.

c. Added cut 20th left side, 12.

4.

a. Dot above 3rd in upper and lower panes.

b. Dots above 3rd filled in.

c. Added $\frac{1}{2}$ dot (base) under EP of 2nd.

5. Diamond dot under EP of 2nd.

6. Cut under E(E) of 1st.

7. Cut under E(E) of 2nd.

8. Minute $\frac{1}{2}$ dot (outer) 19th left side, $5\frac{3}{4}$.

9. Dot (inner) 20th left side, $12\frac{1}{4}$.

10. Dot 19th left side, $12\frac{1}{2}$.

These electros were put to press with controls as follows:

1.
a. A.12 narrow.
b. C13 (red-violet).
c. C.13, C13 (blue-violet), D14, F15, G15, H16.
d. I16, J17, L18.
e. M18, N19, Q21 narrow.

2.
a. A.12 wide.
b. C13 (red-violet), C13 (blue-violet), E14, F15, G15, H16, I16, J17, L18, M18, N19, Q21 narrow, R21, S21, S22, T22, U22, U23, V23.

3.
a. A.12 narrow, B.13.
b. C13 (red-violet), E14.
c. E14, F15, H16, I16.

4.
a. B.13.
b. F15, G15.
c. M18, N19, O19, O20, P20.

5. M18, N19, O20, P20, Q21 narrow, R21, U23, V23

6. R21.

7. R21.

8. U22.

9. U23, V23, W23.

10. U22, U23, W23.

Comparative control positions

A.12 narrow.	Plate 1. Top serif of 1 well formed.
	Plate 3. Top serif of 1 malformed.
B.13.	Plate 3. Serifs of B thin, dot circular.
	Plate 4. Serifs of B thick, dot oval.
D14.	Plate 1. Nick in right of loop of D; vertical stroke of 4 malformed.
	Plate 2. Very small serif to figure 1.

E14.   Plate 2. White dot in top serif of figure 1.
            Plate 3. Right of top serif of figure 1 defective.
G15.   Plate 2. Control perfect.
            Plate 4. Top and base of figure 1 and right of figure 5
                     defective.
H16.   Plate 1. Control perfect.
            Plate 2. Left top of H slightly defective.
U22.   Plate 2. Control perfect.
            Plate 9. Top of first figure 2 blunted.
U23.   Plate 2. Control level, 2·50.
            Plate 9. Control level, 1·40.

WATERLOW CONTRACT AND HARRISON PROVISIONAL PRINTINGS
List of electro markings

1.
   a. Tiny nick (base) to right of 2nd.
   b. Added cut 20th left side, 10.
2.   20th left side heavy and irregular.
3.   Big dot 19th left side, 12¾.
4.   ½ dot (inner) 20th left side, 12½.

5.   Minute dot 20th left side, 11.
6.   Minute dot (inner) 19th left side, 9.
7.   No marking.
8.   No marking.
9.   Dot 19th left side.

These electros were put to press with controls as follows:

1.
   a. B24.
   b. B24, C25, D25.
2.   B24, C25.
3.   D25, G27, R32.
4.   E26, G27, I28, K29, M30, P31, R32, V34.

5.   E26, I28, K29, M30, N30, P31, S33, T33.
6.   I28, K29, M30, N30, P31.
7.   M30, N30, P31, R32, S33, T33.
8.   S33, T33.
9.   V34.

Comparative control positions

Owing to there being two plates, Plates 7 and 8, without marking, the comparative positions of the S33 and T33, neither of which are very diagnostic, are recorded.

S33.   Plate 7. Control well to left.
            Plate 8. Control to left, centre of S under T.
T33.   Plate 7. Control to left.
            Plate 8. Control well to left, left of T under left of rule.

FOURPENCE

HARRISON 1912–23 PRINTINGS
List of electro markings

1.

    a. Dot above 1st in upper and lower panes.

    b. Dots above 1st filled in.

    c. Added small dot under RP of 1st.

    d. Dot under RP of 1st enlarged.

    e. Rule under 3rd bevelled off at left.

2.

    a. Dot above 2nd in upper and lower panes.

    b. Dots above 2nd filled in.

    c. Added small dot under RP of 2nd.

    d. Dot under RP of 2nd enlarged.

3. No marking.

4. Dot under RP of 1st, rule under 3rd perfect.

These electros were put to press with controls as follows:

1.

    a. B.13.

    b. C13, D14.

    c. F15, G15.

    d. G15, H16, I16.

    e. I16, J17, K17, K18, N19, O20, Q21 narrow, R21, S21, S22, T22, U22, U23, V23.

2.

    a. B.13.

    b. C13, D14.

    c. F15, G15.

    d. G15, H16, I16, J17, K18, M18, N19, O20, Q21 narrow, R21, S21, S22, T22, U22, U23, V23.

3. H16, I16, J17, M18, S22, U23.

4. N19, R21, S21, S22, T22, U22, U23, V23.

Comparative control positions

B.13. Plate 1. Base of figure 1 well formed.

    Plate 2. Base of figure 1 malformed at left.

C13. Plate 1. C irregular at right of bottom curve; lower right curve of figure 3 irregular.

    Plate 2. C slightly blunted at base; lower curve of figure 3 blunted at right.

D14. Plate 1. Diagonal of figure 4 damaged towards the top meeting the upright below the level of its top.

    Plate 2. Figure 4 well formed.

WATERLOW CONTRACT AND HARRISON PROVISIONAL PRINTINGS
List of electro markings

1. Base of 2nd bevelled off at right, but repaired with G27 control.

2. Base of 20th left side splays out to left.

3. 2 cuts 20th left side, 17, 18½.

4. Dot under RP of 1st; base of 2nd ragged at right.
5. Dot at top of 19th left side; base of 2nd pointed, but not ragged, at right; small diagonal mark or line between base of 20th left side and left of 1st, not always visible.

6. No marking; base of 20th left side bent very slightly in.
7. No marking. 19th and 20th left side bulge outwards at their centres.
8. Dot under P of 2nd; base of 20th left side bent in.

These electros were put to press with controls as follows:

1. B24, C25, E26, G27, I28, K29, Q32, R32, T33.
2. B24, C25, E26, G27, M30, O31.
3. E26, G27, I28, K29, M30, O31.
4. Q32.
5. Q32, R32, T33, V34, W35.
6. R32, V34, W35.
7. V34, W35, X35.
8. X35.

FIVEPENCE

HARRISON 1912–23 PRINTINGS
List of electro markings

1.
 a. Dot above 1st in upper and lower panes; left end of line under 1st thick.
 b. Dots above 1st filled in.
 c. Added 1½ sloping cuts under EN of 1st.

2.
 a. Dot above 2nd in upper and lower panes; minute dot at left of 6th.
 b. Dots above 2nd filled in.
 c. Added sloping cut under P of 2nd.
3. No marking.

These electros were put to press with controls as follows:

1.
 a. B.13.
 b. C14, D14, F15, G15, H16.
 c. H16, I16, J17, K17, L18, N19, O19, Q21 wide, R21.

2.
 a. B.13.
 b. C14, D14, F15, G15, H16.
 c. H16, I16, J17, K17, L18, Q21 wide, S21, S22.
3. I16, Q21 wide, R21, S21, S22, T22, U23, V23.

Comparative control positions

B.13. Plate 1. Serifs of B thin, left side of upright straight.
Plate 2. Serifs of B thick, left side of upright bulges outwards.

C14. Plate 1. C thick and malformed.
      Plate 2. C thin and well formed.
D14. Plate 1. Base of figure 1 nicked at right; figure 4 well formed.
      Plate 2. Base of figure 1 well formed. Horizontal arm of figure 4
                bulges at right of vertical stroke.
F15. Plate 1. Serif of figure 1 small and flat.
      Plate 2. Serif of figure 1 well formed.
G15. Plate 1. Thin control; right of figure 5 under right of rule.
      Plate 2. Thick control; right of figure 5 below to right of rule.
H16. Plate 1. Serif of figure 1 well formed.
      Plate 2. Hardly any serif to figure 1.

The H16 positions refer to the printing before the electro was marked
with cuts.

WATERLOW PRINTINGS
List of electro markings

1.
  a. No marking.
  b. Added dot 19th left side, 10.

2.
  a. Base of 20th left side bent
     inwards.
  b. Added dot 20th left side, 14.
3. Dot 20th left side, 9.

These electros were put to press with controls as follows:

1.
  a. A24, C25.
  b. F26, H27, I28, K29, L29,
     M30, O31, Q32, S33, T33,
     U34, V34, X35.

2.
  a. C25.
  b. C25, F26, H27, I28, K29,
     L29, M30, O31, Q32, S33,
     U34, V34, X35.
3. C25.

SIXPENCE

Plate markings similar to those in use with the contractors were not
made on plates put to press at Somerset House, though their system of
placing dots in the rules above both panes was in use with the Sixpence
value as it was with their initial printings of the other values. With the
Sixpence value alternate plates were marked with a dot above the 1st
and a dot above the 2nd.

The following is a list of the rule characteristics of the Sixpence value
on electros put to press:

ELECTROS WITH INTERPANE PILLARED MARGIN

1. No marking.
2.
  a. No marking.

  b. With control L.18 a small
    dot developed in the rule
    below (P)E of 2nd.

3. Base of 20th left side splayed out.
4. Left of rule under 1st thin with right end thickened.
5. 20th left side thins at base.

6. 19th and 20th left side and 1st, 2nd and 3rd rules thin.
7. Small projection under X of 1st.

ELECTROS WITHOUT INTERPANE MARGIN

8. No marking.
9. Rule under 1st thin at left and thick at right; rules under 2nd and 3rd irregular.
10. Minute dot under EN of 2nd.
11. Nick under N of 2nd.
12. Rule under 2nd chipped below left end.
13. Protrusion at top of 1st under C.
14. Two small diagonal nicks under PE, C of 2nd.
15. Minute dot under P of 2nd.
16. Tiny nick under to left of S of 2nd; rule under 1st thinner at left than at right.
17. Tiny nick under I of 1st.

18.
a. No marking.
b. With control X35 the rule under 3rd gradually became worn in its right half, finally showing a nick under N of 3rd which is irregular at right.
19. 19th and 20th left side bevelled at their adjacent ends.
20. 2 cuts 1st left side.
21. Rules 19th and 20th left side thin.
22. Cut 1st left side; shallow (horizontal) nick (base) under CE of 1st; horizontal mark in 2nd under E(N).

These electros were put to press with controls as follows:

ON JOYNSON PAPER

1. C.13 (dull lilac), C.13 (red-purple), D,14 (the so-called 'comma' variety), E.14, F.15, G.15, H.16, I.16, L.18.
2.
a. C.13 (dull lilac), C.13 (red-purple), D.14, E.14, F.15, G.15, H.16, I.16, J.17, K.17.
b. L.18, M.18, N.19, O.19, P.20, Q.20 (15 × 14), Q.20 (14 × 14).
3. J.17, K.17, Q.20 (15 × 14)

Q.20 (14 × 14), R.21 (14 × 14), R.21 (15 × 14), S.21, T.22, U.22, V.23, W.23.
4. L.18, L 18 (the so-called 'dot omitted' variety), M.18, N.19, O.19, P.20, Q.20 (15 × 14).
5. L.18, T.22.
6. R.21 (14 × 14), R.21 (15 × 14), S.21, T.22, U.22, V.23, W.23, A.24, B.24.
7. S.21, T.22, U.22, U.23, V.23, W.23, A.24, B.24.

N

ON SAM. JONES PAPER

7. B.24.
8. B.24, C.25,
    D.25 (coated paper), E.26,
    F.26, G.27, I.28, L.29, M.30,
    N.30, R.32, O.31, P.31, Q.32,
    S.33, T.33.
9. B.24, C.25, G.27, H.27, I.28,
    J.28, K.29, M.30, P.31.
10. C.25, D.25 (coated paper),

    D.25 (unsurfaced paper),
    E.26, F.26, G.27, H.27.
11. E.26, J.28, K.29.
12. K.29, L.29, M.30, N.30.
13. L.29, N.30, R.32.
14. N.30, O.31, P.31.
15. O.31, T.33.
16. R.32, S.33, T.33.
17. S.33, T.33.

ON JOHN ALLEN PAPER

16. V34, W35, X35,
    Y36 (unsurfaced paper),
    Y36 (coated paper),
    Z36 (unsurfaced paper).
18. V34, W35, X35,
    Y36 (unsurfaced paper),
    Y36 (coated paper),
    Z36 (coated paper),
    Z36 (unsurfaced paper).

19. X35,
    Y36 (unsurfaced paper),
    Z36 (unsurfaced paper), A37.
20. X35, Z36 (unsurfaced paper),
    A37, B37, C38.
21. Z36 (unsurfaced paper), A37,
    C38.
22. Z36 (unsurfaced paper), A37,
    B37, C38, D38.

SEVENPENCE

List of electro markings

1.
  a. Dot above 1st in upper and
     lower panes; 20th left side
     somewhat thick.
  b. Dots above 1st filled in.
  c. Added small dot under
     (VE)N of 1st.

2.
  a. No marking, but 20th left
     side somewhat thinner.
  b. Added small dot under NP
     of 2nd.
3. No marking.

These electros were put to press with controls as follows:

1.
  a. C.13.
  b. C13, D14.
  c. F15, G15, H16, J17, L18.

2.
  a. C.13, C13, D14.
  b. F15, G15, H16.
3. H16, J17.

Note: It would appear that Plate 2 was put to press at Somerset
House without the usual dots being cut above the upper and lower
panes.

Comparative control positions

C.13.   Plate 1. Figure 1 under PE.
         Plate 2. Figure 1 under E.
C13.   Plate 1. Control level, 2·00.
         Plate 2. Control level, 1·00.
D14.   Plate 1. Figure 4 damaged at top.
         Plate 2. Figure 1 damaged at base.

EIGHTPENCE

Only one electro is known to have been in use. In the *a.* state there was a dot above the 1st in the upper and lower panes. In the *b.* state these dots were filled in. Its use was as follows:

1.
  a. C.13.

  b. D14, F15, G15, H16, I16, J17, L18.

NINEPENCE

HARRISON 1912–23 PRINTINGS
List of electro markings

1.
  a. Dot above 1st in upper and lower panes.
  b. Dots above 1st filled in.
  c. Added dot (top) under EN of 1st.

2.
  a. Dot above 2nd in upper and lower panes.
  b. Dots above 2nd filled in.
  c. Added dot (base) under P of 2nd.
3. No marking.

These electros were put to press with controls as follows:

1.
  a. B.13.
  b. E14, F15, G15, H16, I16, J17, K17, K18, L18, N19.
  c. N19, O19, O20, S21, S22, T22, U23.

2.
  a. B.13.
  b. E14, F15, G15, H16, I16, J17, K17, K18, L18.
  c. N19, O19, O20, P20, Q20, R21, S21, S22, T22, U23, V23.
3. N19, O19, O20, P20, Q20, R21, S21, S22, T22, U23, V23.

WATERLOW CONTRACT AND HARRISON PROVISIONAL PRINTINGS
List of electro markings

1. Irregular cuts 19th left side, 11.
2. Sloping cut 20th left side, 13.
3. Minute dot 20th left side.
4. Minute dot 19th left side.
5. No marking. Thick rules.
6. No marking. Thin rules.

These electros were put to press with controls as follows:

1. A24, C25, F26, I28, J28, L29, N30, P31, R32, T33.
2. A24, C25, F26, I28, J28, L29, N30, P31, R32, V34, W35, X35.
3. J28, L29, N30, P31, R32, T33, V34, W35, X35.
4. V34, W35.
5. W35, X35.
6. X35.

TENPENCE

HARRISON 1912–23 PRINTINGS
List of electro markings

1.
  a. Base of 20th left side bends inwards; dot above 1st in upper and lower panes.
  b. Dots above 1st filled in. With F15 two very small dots appeared (but not always clear) under PE of 1st.
  c. Added large dot under P of 2nd.

2.
  a. No marking.
  b. Added large dot under PE of 1st.

These electros were put to press with controls as follows:

1.
  a. C.13
  b. D14, F15, G15, H16, I16, J17, K18, M19.
  c. M19, Q21 wide, S21, S22, T22.

2.
  a. D14, G15, K18, M19.
  b. M19, O19, Q21 narrow, S21, S22, T22, U23.

WATERLOW CONTRACT AND HARRISON PROVISIONAL PRINTINGS
List of electro markings

1. Dot under PE of 1st.
2. Minute dot (base) under E of 1st; dot under PE of 2nd.
3. No marking.

These electros were put t o press with controls as follows:

1. A24, D25, F26, J28, L29,
    O31, Q32, S33, U34, V34,
    W35.

2. A24, D25, F26, G27, J28,
    L29, O31, Q32, S33, U34,
    V34.

3. G27, W35.

ONE SHILLING

HARRISON 1912–23 PRINTINGS
List of electro markings

1.
  a. Dot above 1st in upper and
      lower panes.
  b. Dots above 1st filled in.
  c. Added dash at left of 2nd.
  d. Added cut under S of 1st.

2.
  a. Dot above 2nd in upper and
      lower panes.
  b. Dots above 2nd filled in.
  c. Added cut under S of 2nd.
3.   No marking.
4.   Cut 19th left side, 18½.

These electros were put to press with controls as follows:

1.
  a. C.13.
  b. D14, E14, F15, G15, H16,
      I16, J17, L18, M19.
  c. M19.
  d. M19, N19, O19, O20, P20,
      Q20, R21, V23.

2.
  a. C.13.
  b. D14, E14, G15, I16, J17,
      K17.
  c. M19, N19, O19, O20.
3.   O19, O20, P20, Q20, R21,
      S21, S22, T22, U22, U23,
      V23.
4.   R21, S21, S22, T22, U22,
      U23, V23.

Comparative control positions

C.13. Plate 1. Figure 1 under first L of SHILLINGS, 1·80.
      Plate 2. Figure 1 under LL of SHILLINGS.
D14. Plate 1. Control well formed.
      Plate 2. D very thick, base of figure 1 pointed and defective.
G15. Plate 1. Control to right, right of figure 5 under right of rule.
      Plate 2. Control to right, right of figure 5 beyond right of rule.
I16. Plate 1. Control to right, right of 6 under right of rule.
J17. Plate 1. Figure 7 slightly defective at point and thin, 1·10.
      Plate 2. Figure 7 well formed and thick, ·90.
R21. Plate 3. Control to left. R without top serif.
      Plate 4. Control to right.
S21. Plate 3. Diagonal white mark in figure 2.

S22. Plate 3. Small white tick in right of neck of 2nd figure 2.
T22. Plate 3. Left of top of T malformed.
      Plate 4. T well formed.
U22. Plate 3. Control level, 4·30.
      Plate 4. Control level, 2·80.
U23. Plate 3. Control thick and central.
      Plate 4. Control well to left and well formed.
V23. Plate 3. Point of figure 2 well formed.
      Plate 4. Point of figure 2 blunted.

WATERLOW CONTRACT AND HARRISON PROVISIONAL PRINTINGS
List of electro markings

1. Base of 20th left side tends to bend inwards.
2. Cut 19th left side, 19; base of 20th left side thins two-thirds the way down.
3.
    a. Dot 20th left side, 12½.
    b. Added large dot 20th left side.
4.
    a. ½ dot (inner) 19th left side, 18; small nicks at each end of rule under 2nd.
    b. Added dot (outer) 19th left side, 6.
5. Cut under S of 1st.

These electros were put to press with controls as follows:

1. A24, B24, D25.
2. A24, B24, D25, U34.
3.
    a. F26, H27, I28, J28, K29, L29, N30, P31, R32.
    b. S33, U34, V34, W35, X35.
4.
    a. F26, H27, I28, J28, K29, L29, N30, P31, R32, S33.
    b. U34, V34.
5. V34, W35, X35.

Appendix B

The Plating of the High Values

THE principle employed in the plating of the recess-printed high values is very similar to that used for the plating of the Line-Engraved One Penny stamps of 1840 and later; that is, the joining together of overlapping pieces showing the same diagnostic characteristics. But dissimilarity necessarily exists from the fact that there is nothing on these stamps to assist the plater in determining the position of any one stamp on the plate. Consequently reliance can only be placed on marginal pieces which show markings thereon to fix the position on the sheet.

It may be possible, when examining stamps or non-marginal pieces printed from the Bradbury, Wilkinson plates with positional dots, to allocate these to their correct positions, but this could only be done by comparison with known pieces, since the exact position of the dot defies identification by written description.

The study of these plates is still in its infancy, but the Editors consider that such information as has so far been acquired is worthy of record, though they have confined themselves in these notes to the description of salient features which are not common to more than one plate. Doubtless other plates were put to press, but, unless a plate can be identified with certainty, it has not been included.

It must be emphasized that the numbers which the Editors have allotted to the plates are purely arbitrary. These numbers have been allotted consecutively for each value; but it would appear that the official numbers of the plates were based upon the current numbers of the plates, irrespective of values.

The following notes on the individual values may be of use to readers.

TWO SHILLINGS AND SIXPENCE

1. The 22 mm Image Plates
(Put to press by Waterlow and De La Rue.)

In the list that follows the first measurement is the distance between the centre of the cross in the upper margin and the top of the stamps in the upper row. The second measurement, where shown, is the length of the horizontal arm, both of which are in millimetres. In determining this latter length the Editors have been much handicapped by the fact that so many of the blocks examined have been divided down the vertical line of the cross and consequently show either only the left or the right portion of the horizontal line.

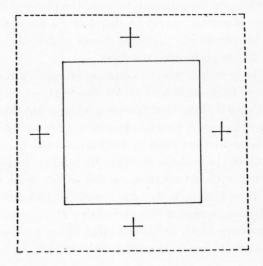

The marginal crosses on plates with the 22 mm images.

Plate 1	12·1 mm
Plate 2	12·25 mm, 12·5 mm
Slight re-entry No. 2	
Major re-entry No. 5	
Plate 3	12·4 mm
Plate 4	12·5 mm

The plate was officially engraved with the number H.V.9.

Plate 5   12·25 mm, 13·0 mm

This plate became very worn.

These plates are known as having been put to press by contractors as follows:

Plate 1	Waterlow
Plate 2	Waterlow, De La Rue
Plate 3	De La Rue
Plate 4	De La Rue
Plate 5	De La Rue

Plate 2 was used for the printing by De La Rue which was overprinted 'Cancelled'.

2. The 22·5 mm Image Plates
(The Type A dot Plates.)

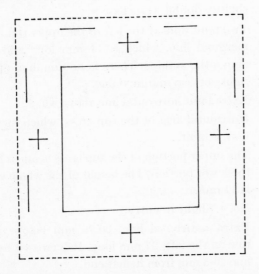

The marginal crosses and vertical and horizontal marginal lines on plates with both the 22·5 and 23 mm images.

Plate 1. The horizontal arm of the top cross slopes down to the right.

Plate 2. No. 1. Minor re-entry; No. 3. The 'Nissen' re-entry.

Extra horizontal marginal line 19·75 mm above No. 3, 33 mm long.

Plate 3. No. 2. Major re-entry.

Extra horizontal marginal lines below No. 38, 29 mm long, and No. 39, 13 mm long. No cross in bottom margin below the gutter between Nos. 37 and 38.

Plate 4. The vertical arm of the top cross measures 8·5 mm; the horizontal arm 8 mm; the centre of the cross is 13·25 mm above the stamps in the top row.

Plate 5. Extra horizontal marginal line, 21 mm above No. 3, 25 mm long.

Plate 6. Two dots at the left of the upper right horizontal marginal line, which is 13 mm long and 20 mm above the stamps. The upper right vertical marginal line is slightly double at its base.

Plate 7. Two faint dots at the left of the upper right horizontal marginal line, which is 11 mm long and 19·75 mm above the stamps. There is no doubling of the upper right vertical marginal line.

Plate 8. Extra faint horizontal line above No. 2.

Plate 9. Horizontal arm of the top cross, which measures 11·5 mm, is faint.

Plate 10. The upper portion of the top cross is much longer than the lower portion. The height of the whole vertical line is 11 mm.

Plate 11. No. 4. Slight re-entry.

Plate 12. Extra horizontal line, 20·75 mm below the bottom row on the left, 37 mm long. It is crossed by a vertical line 20·5 mm from its left end.

Plate 13. Strong extra horizontal marginal line 29·5 mm below No. 39, 21 mm long.

3. The 23 mm Image Plates
(The Type B no dot plates.)

Plate 1. No. 8 has a fine horizontal line over it.

Plate 2. The upper left horizontal marginal line measures 12 mm and is 20 mm above the stamps.

Plate 3. The upper left horizontal marginal line measures 19 mm and is 21 mm above the stamp.

Plate 4. The upper left horizontal marginal line measures 8 mm and is 20 mm above the stamp.

FIVE SHILLINGS

1. 22 mm Image Plates
(Put to press by Waterlow and De La Rue.)

At least four plates have been identified by the distance between the centre of the top cross and the top of the stamps. These are as follows:

Plate 1	12 mm
Plate 2	12·25 mm
Plate 3	6 mm
Plate 4	12·75 mm

These plates are known put to press by Contractors as follows:

Plate 1	First Waterlow printing
Plate 2	Second Waterlow printing, De La Rue
Plate 3	Waterlow
Plate 4	Waterlow, De La Rue

2. The 22·5 mm Image Plates
(The Type A dot plates.)

Plate 1. The right-hand horizontal arm of the top cross is double.

Plate 2. The upper vertical arm of the top cross is double. Extra horizontal marginal line 20·5 mm above No. 2.

Plate 3. The upper right horizontal line is 21·5 mm above the stamps, and is 25 mm long.

Plate 4. The lower left vertical marginal line is double at its base. There is a very faint extra horizontal marginal line 20 mm below No. 39 and is 42 mm long.

Plate 5. There is a dot to the left of the upper right horizontal marginal line which is 11 mm above the stamps and 20·75 mm long. The upper right vertical marginal line is double at its top.

Plate 6. There is a dot to the left of the upper right horizontal marginal line which is 10·5 mm above the stamps and 20·5 mm long. There is no doubling of the top of the upper right vertical marginal line.

Plate 7. There is a dot towards the left end on the upper right horizontal marginal line which is 10 mm above the stamps and 20 mm long.

TEN SHILLINGS

1. 22 mm Image Plates
(Put to press by Waterlow and De La Rue.)

Owing to lack of material only two plates have been identified with certainty though more may have been in use. The identification can be effected by the distance of the centre of the bottom marginal cross below the stamps. These are:

Plate 1	12·25 mm
Plate 2	12 mm

Plate 1 has been found put to press by Waterlow and Plate 2 by De La Rue.

Further plate identification can be effected by means of the upper marginal cross and printings from two plates have been found, both of which were put to press by De La Rue. But owing to the lack of connecting material it is not possible to say that either of these two plates is the same as or different from the two plates noted above. The particulars of identification are as follows:

Plate A. The centre of the top marginal cross is 12 mm above stamps and there is a dot to the left of its horizontal arm.

Plate B. The centre of the top marginal cross is 12·55 mm above the stamps and there is no dot to the left of its horizontal arm. This plate bore the official engraved notation in the top margin of some indecipherable number followed by the letters H.V.

2. The 22·5 mm Image Plates

(The type A dot plates.)

Identification of these plates is difficult, though it is assisted by some of the plates having a perfect 's' in 'POSTAGE' whereas in others that letter is broken.

Of these plates, with the perfect 's', only two have been identified, whereas eight plates with the broken 's' can be separated.

Perfect S. Plates

Plate 1. The centre of the top marginal cross is 9·5 mm above the stamp.

Plate 2. The centre of the top marginal cross is 9·25 mm above the stamp. No. 21. The 'Runnals' re-entry.

Broken S. Plates

Plate 3. The centre of the right marginal cross is 9·5 mm to the right of the stamps. The centre of the bottom marginal cross is 12·75 mm below the stamps. The lower left vertical marginal line is 11·25 mm long and 21·25 mm to the left of the stamps.

Plate 4. The centre of the right marginal cross is 9·75 mm to the right of the stamps. The centre of the top marginal cross is 12·25 mm above the stamps. The upper left horizontal line is 21·5 mm long and 21 mm above the stamps.

Plate 5. The centre of the top marginal cross is 12·5 mm above the stamps. The upper left horizontal marginal line is 15·5 mm long and 20·25 mm above the stamps. No. 1. The 'Nissen' re-entry.

Plate 6. The centre of the top marginal cross is 12 mm above the stamps.

Plate 7. The centre of the top marginal cross is 12·5 mm above the stamps. (No re-entry No. 1.)

There is one plate on which the base of the lower right vertical marginal line is double, with a dot to the left of it near the base. It is not known which plate this is, but it is not Plate 3.

3. The 23 mm Image Plates

(The Type B no dot plates.)

Plate 8. The upper right vertical marginal line is 18 mm long and 17·75 mm to the right of the stamps.

Plate 9. The upper right vertical marginal line is 15 mm long and 17·25 to the right of the stamps. No. 4. The '0' of '10/-' appears to be double.

ONE POUND

The One Pound value of 1913 and the 1929 Commemorative appear each to have been printed from a single plate.

Appendix C

The Quartz Lamp

Notes on its philatelic use in connection with the
Stamps of King George V

THE differentiation of colours is a formidable task because so much depends upon a clear and unequivocal nomenclature when allocating stamps to their printings or separating the work of the various printers. To the above difficulty is added the sensatory peculiarities of each pair of eyes.

Occasionally colour blindness, total or partial, is met with in the human eye, when the colour sensations do not fully react upon the brain. Less extreme cases are much more common and in them the sensitivity to the colours is only slightly impaired; hence, as often has been asserted, hardly any pair of eyes ever 'see' the same stamp in exactly the same hue, for one of the primary colours will predominate, even if only to a slight extent.

The colour of a stamp, as seen by the eye, is dependent upon the wave-length of that light which is reflected from its surface. White light can be split up into the colours of the spectrum – or more commonly speaking, the rainbow – which are red, orange, yellow, green, blue, indigo and violet; red having the longest wave-length and violet the shortest. This splitting up may be effected not only by optical means, but also occurs when white light impinges upon pigments or dyestuffs since it is not all of the wave-lengths that are reflected; some of them are absorbed. Consequently when a substance absorbs all but the light of the red wave-length, these being reflected, we 'see' this substance as red. Further, when a substance is viewed under white light and it absorbs all the wave-lengths, it appears to the eye as black, since no rays are reflected.

Apart from the detection of forgery and the repair of stamps, considerable assistance may be obtained from the quartz lamp in the recognition of certain stamps and their allocation to specific printings. This assistance is obtained from three phenomena which appear when stamps are viewed under the lamp: these are the apparent change of colour, an imparted brilliance (or 'flash-up'), and fluorescence.

The quartz lamp consists of a reflector in which is housed a metallic gas-actuated mercury vapour quartz tube through which an electric current passes and which emits not only an extremely bright light, but also a large range of the ultra-violet rays which are invisible to the human eye. For philatelic use the reflector is covered with a filter screen to cut out many of the wave-lengths emitted by the tube. As it is said that different makes of lamp show slightly different results, it should be mentioned that the make of lamp upon which these notes are based is the Hanovia Sun Ray lamp screened with a Wood's glass filter stained with nickel-iron and cobalt.

The lamp is often loosely referred to as the 'ultra-violet' lamp or sometimes, erroneously, as 'black light', but it is neither of these. The tube emits most of the frequencies in each of the colour bands. It emits green, blue, violet and the range of the invisible ultra-violet strongly, this latter, and this latter alone, being the true 'black light'. The filter passes the majority of the emitted frequencies. Of the ultra-violet it excludes the real ultra-violet, though passing the 'near ultra-violet', that is those invisible rays with a wave-length shorter than and close to the violet, but in having to subdue their brilliance to enable feeble fluorescence to be seen, red light has to be introduced. This is, however, emitted by the metallic actuating gas in the tube.

The three phenomena mentioned above, together with their visual effect, are recorded in detail under the separate headings which follow.

APPARENT CHANGE OF COLOUR

This is probably the most important of the three phenomena seen, especially when studied in conjunction with the imparted brilliance, for it is these which enable much of the work of different printers and their various printings to be recognised.

To the unaided eye many stamps appear similar, and in some cases so similar that separation of the various printings by colour alone is virtually impossible with any degree of certainty. But no two printers used pigments or dyestuffs of exactly the same chemical composition. Further, the composition varied from printing to printing. Although, when these stamps are viewed by the full range of frequencies of white light, there is no appreciable difference of colour, that is of reflected wave-lengths, this is not so when they are viewed under the lamp. Therefore, different printings appear in different colours, neither of which is the same as that when the stamps are viewed by white light. Consequently contrasts, these being sometimes widely contrasting, are obtained and this renders it possible to differentiate easily various printings, and in many cases to separate different printings by the same contractor.

Further assistance is obtained from this phenomenon in the study of the paper upon which the stamps are printed.

The surface of the printing paper falls into three categories. These are (1) unsurfaced, (2) coated and (3) plate-glazed.

Under the lamp unsurfaced paper appears yellowish brown, which can be described as 'dirty-looking'. Coated paper appears a bright bluish violet, though there are two exceptions to this. These are described under the individual stamps so printed. The apparent change of colour of plate-glazed paper is dependent upon the degree of plate-glazing, but it is never 'dirty-looking', nor a bright bluish violet. It always appears very clean with a greater or lesser degree of bluish violet colour. As compared with unsurfaced paper, it can be described as pale bluish violet, and, when compared with normal coated paper, as very clean white.

IMPARTED BRILLIANCE OR 'FLASH-UP'

These stamps are all in the carmine group. The effect of this phenomenon is that the whole surface of the stamp appears to rise up and glow which gives the appearance of the stamp 'flashing-up' in a pinkish or reddish colour in varying degrees of brilliance.

FLUORESCENCE

This phenomenon is a transient luminescence caused by stimulation by the ultra-violet rays raising the electron to a higher energy level in the molecule. The electron returns to its original level in stages of intermediate orbits, thus giving off energy, and in this case the energy is partly in the form of the creation of light.

It should always be borne in mind that fluorescence, unlike 'flash-up', is an actual creation of light which is emitted by certain dyestuffs under stimulation. Consequently, again unlike 'flash-up', it can be seen under true 'black light'.

The property of fluorescence under ultra-violet rays is confined to certain dyestuffs of the aniline group. Though this group contains some thousand dyes, few possess this property. Philately is only concerned with two of these dyestuffs. These are both derivatives of aminobenzine (phenylamine) which is pure aniline. Though aniline itself is not fluorescent, it is the starting point from which many dyes, some of which possess this property, have been produced.

Of the two dyestuffs under consideration the first is resorcinphthalein, the fluorescin of commerce, which was mixed with the green pigment for two small printings of the halfpenny stamp. The fluorescent emission in this case is either green or yellowish green.

The second is the dye tetrabromoresorcinphthalein, the eosin of commerce, which is produced by the action of bromine upon fluorescin, which was mixed with the red pigments used in the production of some of the early George V stamps.

The general effect of fluorescence as seen by the eye is, in the case of fluorescin, an intensification of the green colour combined, to a greater or lesser degree, with the introduction of a golden colour, and in the case of eosin the changing of the red colour of the stamp to a golden colour. In both these cases, since the luminescence is transient, no chemical reaction takes place.

The golden colour varies from brilliant gold to dull brownish gold dependent upon the percentage of eosin in use, its degree of contamination by the pigment and its dilution.

Full details of these three phenomena, in so far as they affect the viewing of the stamps of King George V, have been recorded in the preceding chapters dealing with the individual values.

The Editors feel that it is unfortunate that the word 'aniline' has for a long time been used not only in connection with S.G. 333 and 343, but also with some of the Edward Harrison and Somerset House printed stamps, since aniline itself was not used in the printing of those stamps and is not, in itself, fluorescent under the quartz lamp. Incidentally the 'anil' in 'aniline' is derived from the anil shrub *Indigofera Tinctoria*, from which the very fugitive blue vegetable dye indigo is extracted and from which the aniline group was originally obtained, though the modern method is by extraction from coal-tar.

NOTE

It is realized that some of the statements made in this Appendix, particularly with regard to certain dyes and their effect on the eye under the quartz lamp, may be regarded by some experts as controversial. Nevertheless the Editor responsible believes that the explanations given will provide the student with information which is adequate.

Appendix D

Essays for Colour only – not Design

As will have been seen from Chapters II to XV, these essays were extensive, the experiments being conducted not only in the inks of three colour-makers, but also, it is believed, at the Stamping Department at Somerset House. Further, in many cases more than one design has been used for the colour tests. These designs were the Mackennal sketches and the Eve zinco-blocks, whether half-tone or line, the frames of which resembled stamps, though not necessarily the accepted frames for the value concerned.

Two lists follow. The first is a list of the official colour code of each experiment followed by the official name of the colour where known. Where the latter is not known the apparent colour has been shown within brackets.

It should be noted that the 'M.H.' series of experiments has not been included. These were made at a much later date from either actual approved dies, or dies which were essays for design.

The second is a list, value by value, of the designs in use with each colour trial.

These lists have been prepared from specimens of the essays in the Royal Collection and other specialized collections.

THE MANDERS BROS. ESSAYS

Each essay bears the letters MB at the top.

MB1	Rose-pink 21544	MB10	(Violet)
MB2	Red 21543	MB11	(Very pale yellow-ochre)
MB3	Orange 21541	MB12	Mauve 21641
MB4	Brown 21542	MB13	Purple 20757
MB5	Dark green 21540	MB34	Red-brown 20815
MB6	Light green 21539	MB39	Deep purple
MB7	(Olive-bistre)	MB46	Grey-green 20836
MB8	(Pale blue)	MB48	Brown 21691
MB9	(Very pale blue)	MB49	Red 21816

MB52	Crimson 21793	MB84	Brown 22065
MB53	Red 21924	MB86	Claret 22027
MB61	Blue Stamp 21869	MB87	Violet 22032
MB66	Royal Blue 21724	MB89	Grey 22053
MB69	Blue-violet 21860	MB90	Bartolozzi Brown
MB70	Purple 21731	MB91	Dutch Brown 22208
MB72	Yellow Stamp 21768	MB92	Pearl Grey 22191
MB73	Violet-grey 21867	MB93	Grey-green
MB75	Olive-brown 21804	MB94	Payne Grey 22199
MB76	Red 22020	MB95	Magenta 22236
MB77	Deep red 22021	MB97	Violet
MB78	Crimson 22022	MB101	Red
MB79	Blue 22033	MB106	Mauve 22427
MB80	Steel blue	MB108	Bistre-brown 22244
MB82	Sage-green 22049		

THE SLATER AND PALMER ESSAYS

Each essay bears the letters SP at the top.

SP1	(Reddish-brown)	SP60	Maroon No. 170
SP2	(Rose-red)	SP66	Blue No. 162
SP3	(Green)	SP81	Special Stamp Brown No. 164
SP4	(Purple-brown)		
SP5	(Bright blue)	SP83	Special Stamp Brown No. 128
SP6	(Grey)		
SP7	(Deep blue)	SP84	Special Ruby-brown Stamp No. 155
SP8	(Blue)		
SP10	Blue No. 102	SP86	Mid cadmium yellow
SP23	Vermilion C	SP87	Special deep cadmium yellow
SP25	Vermilion E		
SP26	Vermilion F	SP88	Orange No. 126
SP36	Green No. 118	SP92	Ruby-black No. 160
SP39	Green No. 120	SP93	Verdant green
SP40	Green No. 154	SP95	Art purple No. 225

THE WINSTONE ESSAYS

Each essay bears the letter W at the top.

W1	(Red)	W9	Mauve 17
W2	Red 23	W10	Red 52; also known endorsed Mauve 20
W3	(Carmine-pink)		
W4	(Pale red)	W11	No. 12 Purple
W5	(Pale blue)	W12	No. 22 Purple
W6	Blue 18	W13	No. 33 Deep green
W7	(Pale dull blue)	W14	No. 32 Mid green
W8	Blue 29		

W15	Pale green No. 31, which is only known on white paper; also known endorsed Brown No. 15, but only known on yellow paper
W16	No. 25 green
W17	Dark brown No. 35
W18	Brown No. 15
W19	No. 34 Light brown
W20	Orange No. 16
W21	Green No. 24
W22	Green No. 13
W23	Green No. 10
W24	No. 30 Blue
W25	No. 28 Purple
W26	No. 19 Slate-grey
W30	Blue No. 1; also known endorsed Blue No. 4
W35	Green No. 7
W40	Red No. 37
W41	Dark brown No. 39
W44	Green No. 42
W56	Green No. 26
W64	Bright purple No. 46
W65	Bright purple No. 47.
W66	Bright purple No. 48
W70	Red No. 52.
W90	Yellow L.P. No. 49
W91	Amber L.P. No. 50
W93	Tyrian Plum No. 56
W98	Quick drying black

THE ESSAYS BELIEVED TO HAVE BEEN MADE BY THE STAMPING DEPARTMENT AT SOMERSET HOUSE

Each essay bears the letters SD at the top.

SD1	No. 1 Red
SD2	Red 52
SD3	Green
SD4	(Deep purple)
SD5	Brown
SD6	Blue; also known endorsed deep blue
SD7	Yellow
SD8	(Olive-green)
SD9	(Orange-vermilion)
SD10	Light blue
SD11	Green
SD12	Maroon
SD13	Grey
SD14	Black
SD15	Purple
SD16	Sage-green
SD18	Grey
SD19	Bright sage-green

ESSAYS WITH THE CODE LETTER H, THE MEANING OF WHICH IS NOT KNOWN

H5   Turquoise No. 45282

The above-recorded colours were used to print essays from dies and zinco-blocks as follows:

HALFPENNY

From the Mackennal Sketch die.

SP   36, 39, 93   SD   3
W   15, 22, 23, 35, 44

ONE PENNY

From the Mackennal Sketch die.

MB   52, 53, 76, 78, 101   W   2, 10, 40, 70
SP   25, 26   SD   1, 2

THREEHALFPENCE

From the Mackennal Sketch die.

MB   48, 73, 77, 86, 87, 90, 91, 95   SD   4, 12
W   41, 64, 66, 93

TWOPENCE

From the Mackennal Sketch die.

MB   61, 64, 69, 70, 72, 90, 91, 95;   W   17, 19, 65, 66, 70, 93; on
     on yellow paper 61, 90   yellow paper 19, 93
SP   81, 83, 84, 86, 87; on yellow   SD   5
     paper 81

TWOPENCE HALFPENNY

From the Mackennal Sketch die.

MB   66, 79, 80   W   6, 30, 35
SP   10, 66   SD   6

THREEPENCE

From the Eve half-tone zinco-blocks, wreath design with small head.

MB   1, 2, 3, 4, 5, 6, 7, 8, 9, 10, 11,   W   1, 2, 3, 4, 5, 6, 7, 8, 9, 10, 11,
     12   12, 13, 14, 15, 16, 17, 18,
SP   1, 2, 3, 4, 5, 6, 7, 8   19, 20, 21, 22, 23, 24, 25,
                                               26; on yellow paper 15

From the Eve half-tone zinco-blocks, wreath design with large head.

MB   1, 2, 3, 4, 5, 6, 7, 8, 9, 10, 11,   W   1, 2, 3, 4, 5, 6, 7, 8, 9, 10, 11,
     12   12, 13, 14, 15, 16, 17, 18,
                                               19, 20, 21, 22, 23, 24, 25,
                                               26; on yellow paper 18

From the Mackennal Sketch die.

MB   61, 69, 70, 72, 90, 91; on   W   17, 19, 64, 65, 66, 90, 93; on
     yellow paper 61, 70, 90   yellow paper 19, 66, 93
SP   81, 83, 84, 86, 87; on yellow   SD   7, 16, 18
     paper 81

FOURPENCE

From the Eve line zinco-block, wreath design.

MB   12, 46, 49, 75, 77, 82, 84, 89,   W   56, 91
     91, 92, 93, 94   SD   8, 16
SP   23, 40, 60, 88, 92

FIVEPENCE

From the Eve line zinco-block, wreath design.

MB   12, 46, 49, 75, 77, 82, 84, 92,   W   91
     93, 94   SD   9, 10, 17
SP   23

SIXPENCE

From the Eve line zinco-blocks, wreath design.

MB   12, 13, 39, 46, 49, 75, 77, 84,   W   56
     89, 92, 94   SD   15
SP   23, 40, 60, 88, 92

SEVENPENCE

From the Eve line zinco-blocks, wreath design.

MB   12, 46, 49, 75, 77, 84, 89, 91,   SD   10, 19
     92, 94, 95, 97, 106, 108   On Jones green paper No.
SP   6, 23, 40, 60, 88, 92, 93   17. 5
On Jones Rose paper No. 80.   On Spicers Blue paper 6440.
95   19
On Jones Blue paper No. 91.   H   On Jones Blue paper No. 91.
95   5
W   56, 98   On Jones yellow paper No.
     139.   5

From the Eve half-tone zinco blocks, pillar design with small head.

MB   1, 2, 3, 4, 5, 6, 7, 8, 9, 10, 11,   W   1, 2, 3, 4, 5, 6, 7, 8, 9, 10, 11,
     12, 49, 75, 89, 91   12, 13, 14, 15, 16, 17, 18,
SP   1, 2, 3, 4, 5, 6, 7, 8   19, 20, 21, 22, 23, 24, 25, 26

From the Eve half-tone zinco-blocks, pillar design with large head.

It is not known which colour-maker made these trials, but they are known in two shades of red, brown, purple-brown, violet, olive-green, blue and grey-black. Nor are their code numbers known.

EIGHTPENCE

From the Eve line zinco-blocks, pillar design with fine dotted background.

MB 12, 46, 49, 75, 77, 84, 91, 92, 97

SP 23, 40, 60, 88, 92

W 56

On coloured paper 98 on Green No. 1; on Green No. 2; on Green No. 3; on Green No. 4; on Green No. 5

SD 11, 12

From Eve zinco-blocks as above with the background cut away.

It is not known which colour-maker made these trials, but they are known in magenta, red and green. Nor are their code numbers known.

NINEPENCE

From the Eve line zinco-blocks, pillar design.

MB 12, 46, 49, 75, 77, 84, 92

SP 23, 40, 60, 88, 92

W 56

On coloured paper 98 on Golden-yellow. Jones No. 131; on Amber; on Crown

watermark yellow; on Lemon Jones No. 79; on Deep Canary Jones No. 139; on Yellow Spicers No. 6468

SD 12

TENPENCE

From the Eve line zinco-blocks, pillar design.

MB 12, 34, 46, 75, 77, 84, 92, 94

SP 23, 40, 60, 88, 92

W 56

On coloured paper 98 on Spicers Blue No. 6440; on Jones Blue No. 58; on Jones

Blue No. 91; on Blue No. 1; on Blue No. 2; on Blue No. 3; on Jones Violet No. 136; on V.W. Pur gummed (pale mauve); on Mauve

SD 13

ONE SHILLING

From the Eve line zinco-blocks, pillar design.

MB 34, 46, 75, 77, 84, 92, 94, 95, 106, 108

SP 23, 40, 60, 88, 92, 93

On Jones Rose No. 80. 95

On Jones Blue No. 91 95

W 56, and 98 on white paper

On coloured paper

98 on Spicers pale pink No. 6444; on Jones Rose No. 80; on Jones Red No. 141;

Spicers Cerise No. 6442; Cerise No. 78 Jones; Cerise No. 1; Cerise No. 2

SD 5, 14, 19

On Jones Green No. 17. 5

On Spicers Blue No. 6440. 19

H On coloured paper only

On Jones Blue No. 91. 5

On Jones Yellow No. 139. 5

Two further series of trials took place for colour which consisted of an impression taken from the Edward VII die and one of the Georgian designs in use for the above trials, both in the same ink, the purpose of these being to show any difference which might be apparent between prints from the rough Georgian designs and the finished Edward VII design.

It should be noted that the prints from the Edwardian Fourpence and Sevenpence do not show the fringe which appeared above and to the right of the die proofs, although faint traces of spots of colour do appear. However, there can be no doubt that these were impressions from the dies as an albino impression of the remainder of the fringe is clearly visible.

These essays are as follows:

1. With wide space between the two impressions.

½d green (This trial has no code		3d	S.P.4. On yellow paper
number, but is endorsed 'green'.		4d	W.20
It is probably S.D.3)		6d	M.B.39
1d	S.D.1	7d	S.P.6
2½d	W.5		

2. With close space between the two impressions.

½d	S.D.3	4d	S.D.8
1d	S.D.2	6d	S.D.15
2½d	S.D.6	7d	S.D.10
3d	S.D.7		

Appendix E

The Eve Correspondence

THIS correspondence between the authorities and the artist has fortunately been preserved. It contains much which throws light on various aspects of the preparatory stages.

Letter (11) records the request for the 'electro blocks' from which the colour scheme for the entire issue was prepared. The use of these has been referred to both in individual Chapters and in Appendix D.

Letter (13) contains a reference to a 'young engraver'. Presumably this is H. P. Huggill, who is again mentioned in Letter (19).

It has been stated that Huggill had engraved the Fourpence value. It should here be realized that it was not the Fourpence as printed, but the Fourpence as originally intended but subsequently issued as Fivepence, to which this statement refers.

There is no evidence in either this letter or any later one as to who did in fact engrave the 'Pillar Die'. The Fourpence which was to have been in this design was issued in the Mackennal design on January 15, 1913, and the Fivepence, which was the first of the pillar designs to be issued, did not appear until about five and a half months later, when the first of the wreath design stamps was issued.

From what appears in the correspondence it would seem that Huggill's work on the Fourpence was not considered satisfactory and that both the pillar and wreath master dies were engraved by Harrison.

A few letters of no significance have been omitted; otherwise the correspondence has been printed in its entirety. It opens with the following letter from the General Post Office:

(1)

General Post Office, London
1st July, 1910

Sir,

I have been directed by the Postmaster General to invite a small number of artists, including yourself, to submit one or more designs for the frames of the first stamps to be issued with the head of His present Majesty. The designs are required by the 30th July. It is proposed to pay to each artist whose designs are not accepted a single fee of ten

219

guineas, the designs becoming the Postmaster General's property. For
any designs which he decides to adopt, a fee of 50 guineas would be paid
for the first and of 30 guineas for each subsequent design by the same
artist.

The drawings should not be larger than will go into a circle 9 inches in
diameter; it is not material how much smaller they are than this. At
least one of them should be of a finished character. The printed stamps
will be of the same size and shape as the current issues of values of $\frac{1}{2}$d. to
1/–.

A portrait of the King will be separately obtained and the designs for
the frame should merely give an outline of the head in profile to indicate
the space it is intended to fill which should be about the same as, or only
very slightly smaller than, in the present penny stamps, the profile
facing in the same direction. For your guidance I am to state that the
treatment of the head will be similar to that adopted in the current
issues; the background, however, will be solid in all cases and not
shaded.

At least one design must consist of a frame for the portrait with a lion
couchant beneath it. The words 'Postage and Revenue' should also
appear, though the lettering may be small. No other words, letters or
figures should be introduced. It is desirable that a royal crown, of the
same type as in the present stamps, should be included, but this is not
essential if it is inconsistent with the general character of the artist's
design.

The Postmaster General will be glad to learn that you will assist him
by the submission of designs. He will be happy to furnish any further
particulars that you may desire, and will be obliged if you will treat as
confidential those that are embodied in this letter.

I am, Sir,
Your obedient Servant,
Matthew [Nathan?]

(2)

5 Sheen Gate Mansions
East Sheen, S.W.
4th July, 1910

Sir,

I reply to your letter of the 1st inst., for which I am much obliged.
I beg to say that I shall be glad to submit designs for the frames of the
first stamps to be issued with the head of His present Majesty, in accordance therewith.

I assume that it will be necessary to indicate the value, or leave a space for it, in addition to the words 'Postage and Revenue', and also that the absence of shading in the background of the head need not extend to the treatment of the frame. For the sake of certainty, however, I venture to trouble you with queries on these points. One other query occurs to me, namely whether it would be permissible to use the Royal Cypher.

I am, Sir,
Yours faithfully,

Geo. W. Eve

The Secretary
General Post Office

(3)

General Post Office, London
6th July, 1910

Sir,
       I find that the following sentence was omitted to be included in my letter of the 1st instant with reference to the subject of designs for the new stamps.

'Every design must embody in an easily visible manner the denomination of the stamp in numerals thus: – 1d., either once or repeated, but not necessarily in words also.' Will you kindly note this additional instruction?

As regards the other points raised in your letter of the 4th instant, I am to state that except as restricted by my former communication the treatment of the frame is left entirely to your discretion and that the use of the Royal Cypher would not be in accordance with the sentence in that communication limiting the letters and figures to be introduced into the design.

I am, Sir,
Your obedient servant,

Matthew [Nathan?]

G. W. Eve, Esq.

(4)

General Post Office
London
3th October, 1910

Dear Sir,
       With reference to the enclosed designs for new postage-stamps submitted by you, Mr Herbert Samuel would be much obliged if you

would be so good as to let him have reduced copies of the size of ordinary postage-stamps.

Yours faithfully,

W. Price

G. W. Eve, Esq.

(5)

General Post Office, London
28th October, 1910

Sir,

I am directed by the Postmaster General to acknowledge the receipt of your letter of the 27th instant, forwarding drawings and copies of your designs for the new stamps.

With regard to design B, the drawing and reduced copy of which are enclosed, the Postmaster General desires the ribbons across the label (on which the words 'Twopence' are shown) to be omitted; and he will be glad to know whether you desire to make any consequential alteration in the design.

I am to request that you will be so good as to reply at the earliest possible moment.

I am, Sir,
Your obedient Servant,

W. G. Kirkwood

G. W. Eve, Esq.

(6)

Pressing

General Post Office, London
28th January, 1911

Sir,

I am directed by the Postmaster General to inform you that he is advised by Mr W. Ellison-Macartney, the Deputy Master of the Mint, who is undertaking the preparation of the dies for the George V postage stamps, that it will be necessary to make certain *modifications* in the *two* designs which you submitted in October last, and which have been approved provisionally for the frames of the stamps of the values from 4d. to 1/- inclusive, in order to fit them to the approved effigy of His Majesty.

The Postmaster General will be much obliged, therefore, if you will be good enough to place yourself in communication with the Deputy

Master of the Mint, in order that these modifications may be effected at the earliest possible moment.

I am, Sir,
Your obedient servant,
W. G. Kirkwood

G. W. Eve, Esq.

Marginal Note. Wrote Deputy Master of the Mint 29th. Saw Mr Ellison Macartney 31st Jan. Informed Secretary G.P.O. same date.

(7)

Royal Mint
7th February, 1911

Dear Sir,

I have just heard from the Postmaster General that a decision has not yet been arrived at as to whether the series of stamps for which you have made the designs are to be printed in mono-colour or bi-colour. If the latter, the designs which have been accepted will require further modification than that discussed with you recently. As the decision may not be arrived at for some days, I write to say that perhaps you had better await it in order to avoid throwing away your time on work which may have again to be altered.

I am,
Yours faithfully,
William Ellison Macartney

G. W. Eve, Esq.
5 Sheen Gate Mansions
East Sheen, S.W.

(8)

5 Sheen Gate Mansions
East Sheen, S.W.
13th March, 1911

Dear Sir,

Herewith I beg to return the Postage Stamp design with the rearranged wording. I venture to suggest that if 'bi-colour' is employed it would be desirable that the King's Portrait should be in one colour and the whole of the frame in the other.

I remain, Dear Sir,
Yours faithfully,

Geo. W. Eve

W. Ellison Macartney

(9)

Royal Mint
15th March, 1911

Dear Sir,

Yours of the 13th instant with enclosed design received. I am glad to say that 'bi-colour' is to be abandoned. I think you have another design, if so, I shall be glad to have it as soon as possible.

Yours faithfully,
William Ellison Macartney

Geo. W. Eve, Esq.
5 Sheen Gate Mansions
East Sheen, S.W.

(10)

The Royal Mint
March 17, – 11

Dear Sir,

You are quite right. After I had posted the letter to you I remembered that we had settled to make the alteration on the die.

Yours faithfully,
William Ellison Macartney

Geo. W. Eve

(11)

The Royal Mint
31st March, 1911

Dear Mr Eve,

The Post Office has just rung me up to say that they want electro blocks of the series of stamps from your two designs, as amended, to take prints from them with a view to determine the colour scheme to be adopted for the entire issue of stamps. As you are aware the lettering and figures were added to your drawings and I do not know that you wish these characters to be retained. They are too thin in comparison with previous issues and the general effect when printed in colour will of course be in part dependent on the forms of these letters and figures.

I enclose a photograph down to stamp size of your latest 9d. stamp and a photo from a good set of characters which we are using for the coinage: also a present penny with these letters to the same size. Should you approve the adoption of such letters for the series of stamps and if not can you put me in the way of getting the characters you wish.

As the Post Office is in a hurry it will be a help if you can reply by the bearer.

Yours truly,

Edward Rigg

(12)

The Royal Mint
5th April, 1911

Dear Mr Eve,

I have now got the series of prints which I promised and enclose herewith samples of them as you may like to look them over. I am retaining the original drawings and you can have them when you call here as you propose. I can then also give you as many of the blank prints for filling in as you require. You doubtless remember that the 5d. stamp design is also to be used for the 4d., 6d., and 7d., Stamp. The 9d. design is to be used for the 8d., 9d., 10d., and 1/- Stamps, and all are to be monocolour.

You are sure to be rather busy with your removal (what awful weather for the purpose) and I really do not think you need come here in regard to the question of printing and if you wish it I will forward the other items by post. The main points to bear in mind so far as I know are that the letters and figures should be bold and stand out well and I suppose I should pass on to you an instruction we have from the Post Office, which seems to me somewhat needless, that the figure and 'pence' must be separate words, thus FIVE PENCE, not FIVEPENCE!

Of course the engraver must see to it that the engraving is sufficiently deep to ensure that there is no contact in rapid printing with the hollows, causing a part which should be white to take up any of the colour.

The enlargement of the current stamp will show you that the tints in your designs will have to be interpreted in lines and the engraver must make new drawings from yours the same size and we will then photograph his drawings down to stamp size, after you have approved them, and from these photographs he will do his engraving.

Yours truly,

Edward Rigg

(13)

The Royal Mint
24th April, 1911

Dear Mr Eve,

As requested in your letter of the 22nd I send a supply of prints from the two designs for stamps for you to fill in the lettering and figures.

P

You will remember that in the 9d. design we arranged to remove the 'et' before 'Revenue' but you have already done this in the other.

A young engraver has been recommended to us who is studying at the South Kensington School of engraving and after he had done a very promising trial piece I gave him your design, or rather a print of it, to redraw with a view to engraving, thickening the lines so that when reduced by photography they would be about the correct size for surface printing. This drawing has now reached me and I enclose it herewith together with the print from which it is produced. Will you kindly examine it and let me have it back with any comments? If approved I think that this can be used for the engraver for in any case the letters and figures would not be inserted and he can modify the Revenue side in accordance with your latest drawing. Are we to understand that the space surrounding the frame and where the lettering is to be left solid as under 'One Penny' of the current stamp? Of course the letters and figures will all stand up white as at present.

I shall be glad to see you at any time that may be convenient about the stamps and shall be glad if you will let me have the enclosed drawing and its original with your comments at your early convenience.

Yours truly,

Edward Rigg

(14)

The Royal Mint
27th April, 1911

Dear Mr Eve,

We are being seriously pressed by the Post Office to have adhesive stamps ready before the Coronation and they specially refer to those from 4d. to 1/–. These as you will remember are your designs and Mr Macartney wishes me to write and ask if you will kindly let us have the lettered photographs I sent you with the least possible delay. The drawing I sent on the 24th instant is even more pressing as the frame must first be finished and the several dies made before the letters and figures can be inserted. Would it be convenient for you to come down here tomorrow or Saturday morning about 11 o'clock, or if you prefer it tomorrow afternoon, but I have an appointment then which will occupy a good deal of time and should prefer not then if it can be avoided.

Yours truly,

Edward Rigg

(15)

The Royal Mint
2nd May, 1911

Dear Mr Eve,

As arranged I have had the two designs for the 6d. and 9d. stamps photographed down to the correct stamp size and I enclose prints herewith together with your original drawings. Will you let me know whether you approve of them in this form as regards thickness of letters and figures and we shall then be in a position to go ahead as soon as opportunity offers.

Please return your own drawings.

Yours truly,

Edward Rigg

(16)

116 Adelaide Road, N.W.
4th May, 1911

Dear Mr Rigg,

On the reduced stamp design that you kindly sent me the figures look a little too insistent but this is probably due to difference of tone. The lettering seemed to want a little strengthening in the thin parts. I have then altered them accordingly. If you agree the rest of the series can be modelled on these. I return the drawing herewith.

Yours faithfully,

Geo. W. Eve

(17)

The Royal Mint
15th May, 1911

Dear Sir,

In the absence of Mr Rigg I have to forward an amended drawing of the 4d. stamp, and also a photograph of it reduced to stamp size. The photograph from which the drawing was made is also enclosed.

Yours faithfully,

W. J. Hocking

Geo. W. Eve, Esq.

(18)

116 Adelaide Road, N.W.
18th May, 1911

Dear Sir,

With regard to the drawings and photographs of the 4d. stamp which in Mr Rigg's absence you have kindly sent me, I have to submit the following remarks: –

The tint of the upper part of the background is much too dark. It was intended to be as light as the necessities of surface printing would permit and about the weight of the lightest tint on King Edward VII stamp. The tint should be carried through the crown. In the latter the line of the arch should be more marked and the jewel more accurately copied from the original.

The background at bottom is intended to be solid graduating to the top and equal on both sides. The drawing of the border and the drawing and proportions of the lettering are not well copied and the sides of the border are very unequal, a slight discrepancy in the original being exaggerated rather than corrected in the line drawing.

In some respect, no doubt, allowance has been made for cutting down to the actual engraving but it will be well to note the preceding points.

It will be desirable to add a tint to the Shamrocks in the badges as I have now indicated even though it may ultimately be dispensed with. I shall be glad to call on Mr Rigg when he returns if my doing so will in any way facilitate the work.

Yours faithfully,

Geo. W. Eve

(19)

Royal Mint
London, E.
25th May, 1911

Dear Mr Eve,

Mr Hocking has given me your letter of the 18th instant to him with its enclosure and I note your criticisms on the drawing of the 4d. stamp. The lines are certainly too heavy as you say: they are not carried behind the crown because they are not in the copy you pencilled here and I said it was to be copied exactly. With a view to get the drawing correct I write to suggest that, if you can make it convenient, you call here at such time as you fix on Monday next and if you will let me have a reply by an early post tomorrow I will write to Huggill and ask him to come here at the same time so that you can talk over the points with him. There does not seem to be much difference in the matter of urgency between this and the 9d. stamp and I propose getting Harrison to work on this latter while Huggill goes on with the former. If Huggill's work is all right well and good but if a failure we must I suppose pass this also over to Harrison when he has done the 9d. one. We close on Saturday for the King's birthday.

Yours faithfully,

Edward Rigg

(20)

Operative Department
Royal Mint, E.
13th July, 1911

Dear Sir,

With reference to the 4d. Stamp which Mr Huggill is about to engrave, it is found that the opening in the framework is too small to permit of the head adopted for the other designs being used, and in the absence of Mr Rigg who is on the continent, the Deputy Master wishes me to write and ask if it was intended that a small head should be used. This would mean considerable delay as a new head would have to be engraved; the alternative would be to modify the framework. I enclose a photograph of the design reduced to stamp size with an impression of the head attached.

Yours faithfully,

H. W. L. Evans

G. W. Eve, Esq.

Note on back of letter. Slightly enlarge oval downwards and sideways. ? drop FOUR PENCE and thicken lower line – respace words. Figures are too thick and ? too large. Which letters should be thicker without losing the character. ? remove tint behind letters and figures.

(21)

7 Marjorie Grove
Clapham Common, S.W.
3.8.11

Dear Sir,

I have just received from the Mint and here enclose, a stamp size photograph of the 4d. stamp design for your approval and the original drawing with which to compare it.

I am sorry that I cannot, owing to a chill, bring the photograph to you myself but will be glad to know whether there are any alterations to be made in the general design and 'colour'. The Mint regret that they could not send a lighter print but assume that I shall be guided by you regarding the weight of line, etc.

Yours sincerely,

H. P. Huggill

G. W. Eve, Esq.

(22)

40 Lavengro Road
West Norwood, S.E.
Aug. 20, – 11

Dear Mr Eve,

Enclosed is a reduced photo of your design for 9d. stamp. Before proceeding to cut it, I would be glad to know if there is any modification or alteration you would like carried out.

The effects of tint and solid black behind caduceus at sides is shown, also the tint behind word 'Postage'.

I would like you to make marginal notes of which sides you prefer and also of anything else you may require attended to.

Yours sincerely,

J. A. C. Harrison

(23)

Royal Mint
London, E.
8th September, 1911

Dear Mr Eve,

Among the various points discussed when you were here yesterday I forgot to tell you that a proposal has been made by the Inland Revenue people to consider the wisdom of replacing the tinted background now in use for the penny and other stamps by a white or solid background. I enclose a series of stamps issued by De La Rues showing the same head in a variety of settings for you to consider, and perhaps in due course you will let me know whether you have any very definite wishes in the matter. Of course I cannot say what view the powers that be will take and I presume the King's approval would be needed for any such modification.

Yours truly,

Edward Rigg

(24)

40 Lavengro Road
West Norwood, S.E.
Sept. 14/11

Dear Mr Eve,

I expect you are wondering when you will see a proof of 9d. stamp.

One reason for its not being ready yet is that I have been engaged on some experimental revisions on 1d. and ½d. stamps and another reason is that I took a few days holiday last week as I was feeling the need of a change.

I hope to bring it for your inspection about the middle of next week. Perhaps you will drop me a line if you are back home again.

Yours sincerely,

J. A. C. Harrison

(25)

40 Lavengro Road
West Norwood, S.E.
20.10.11

Dear Mr Eve,

I am sorry I could not keep the appointment made for this morning. I have got the die ready for your criticism, but shall not be able to see you about it before Wed. next as the G.P.O. are pressing for the ½d. and 1d. plates, both of which require some more work done before they are ready for reproduction.

Yours sincerely,

J. A. C. Harrison

(26)

Royal Mint
London, E.
13th November, 1911

Dear Mr Eve,

If you can lay your hands on them without trouble will you kindly let the bearer have the two negatives of your designs to stamp size of which you spoke on Saturday. I want some prints and your negative is better than that we took from my old large photo.

No further developments.

Yours truly,

Edward Rigg

(27)

Royal Mint
London, E.
Dec. 10.11

Dear Mr Eve,

I am being pressed by the Inland Revenue for the frames to submit to the Postmaster General. How are you getting on? Can you let
me hear early this week?

Yours faithfully,

William Ellison Macartney

12 Dec. (new drawing in course of a fortnight)

(28)

General Post Office
London
21st June, 1912

Sir,

With reference to your letter of the 7th ultimo, I am directed by
the Postmaster General to forward herewith a warrant for £42 in payment of your fees in respect of work executed for the Royal Mint in
connexion with the frame adopted for postage stamps of the denominations 4d. to 7d. inclusive.

I am, Sir,
Your obedient Servant,

Walter G. Gates

G. W. Eve, Esq.

(29)

Stamping Department
Inland Revenue
Somerset House
21st September, 1912

Dear Eve,

Thank you for the 'Colour Dictionary'. I have not been in any
way inconvenienced by its temporary absence!

Here is the provisional Colour Scheme for the new designs (of postage
stamps) so far as I am acquainted with it. In it there are, as you will see,
at present four blanks – for the 8d., 9d., 10d., and 1/– rates – and where
four other distinctive 'self' colours (will the Artist please forgive the
'breeder's' colour vocabulary?) are to come from I do not see clearly.
There's 'Grey', of course – *one of the best of stamp colours* – unappro-

priated, *so collar that* forthwith for the stamp of *yours* t'will suit best! And Bistre, or Bronze, or Copper Bronze, for another – how would *that* do? And (say) Venetian Red or Chestnut for yet another? and 'what say' to Rose Pink, or Salmon, or Carmine, as a last choice?

But if you have any leaning (to say naught of a *preference*) for colour on *coloured papers* in 'Evin's' name speak *now*. Let's have your list forthwith – as full a one as you like – and I'll get 'essays' of the lot in about the time it takes to 'get on' to a 'number' by the Post Office Telephone system.

Yours sincerely,

Seymour Bennett

(Enclosure)

POSTAGE STAMPS OF THE NEW DESIGN
SUGGESTED COLOUR SCHEME

½d.		Green
1d.	Mander /25692	Scarlet
1½d.	Provisional	Brown
2d.		Orange
2½d.		Blue i.e. Bright Blue, Royal Blue, Deep Blue or the like
3d.		Mauve, Lilac or the like
4d.		Light Blue
5d.		Magenta
6d.		Purple
7d.		Raw Umber
8d.		
9d.		
10d.		
1/–		

Stamping Department
21st Sept. 1912

(30)

116 Adelaide Road, N.W

SUGGESTED COLOUR SCHEME

8d.	Bistre	or	Copper Bronze
9d.	Venetian Red	or	Indian Red, Dark Green
10d.	Grey		
1/–	Carmine	or	Maroon, Claret

Black on Rose paper

,,   ,, Yellow ,, , Lemon & Orange

,,   ,, Buff

,,   ,, Green

23rd Sept., 1912

(31)

Royal Mint
London, E.
2nd October, 1912

My dear Eve,

Referring to Lewis's visit to you yesterday I think you will be interested to know that I saw Mr Atterbury here last evening and all those criticisms are wiped out from one cause or another except one, namely the tint lines on the King's nose, and these we have rectified today. I am sending fresh proofs tonight and quite count on the stamp being passed in a day or two. It has taken them nearly a month to make out a lot of queries which we have thus disposed of very quickly and it is evident that a little consultation would have saved a lot of time.

Yours truly,

Edward Rigg

(32)

Stamping Department
Inland Revenue
Somerset House
7th October, 1912

My dear Eve,

Have you yet been able to discuss with the Mint people the remarks I made to you on the 8d. design?

I enclose the only copy – a distinctly dirty one – of the black print of the Die which I yet have, and a statement of our comment thereon, which perhaps you would like to see prior to my sending on anything officially. Kindly return them to me at your early convenience.

I called at your house with them last evening but found you at Church! At least I 'found you out!'

Yours sincerely,

Seymour Bennett

Geo. W. Eve, Esqre,
116 Adelaide Road, N.W.

(Enclosure)

POSTAGE STAMPS ON NEW DESIGN: H.M. GEORGE V
ISSUES

Print in black from Die for 8d. Stamp

The main portion of the line representing the top of the band of jewels in the lower part of the crown is missing. It is presumed that this is intentional?

The pearls on the top of the crown are so arranged that the space between the orb and the nearest pearl to the left of it is wider than the corresponding space on the right, and in that wider space a dot has been placed.

It would be an improvement if the margin of white (or colour) before 'P' in POSTAGE and after 'E' in REVENUE were somewhat widened.

The 'P' in POSTAGE is dwarfed by the 'o', and the spacing of the letters in the words POSTAGE and REVENUE is not regular. The four 'E's are not alike. The first 'E' in REVENUE appears to be more distorted than is necessary.

The lines surrounding the '8's are too fine for successful printing on gummed paper, they are too frail to resist the impact of a spot of hard gum.

The lines under the eye, on the nose and on the forehead are broken. The two short lines which should be on the nose directly in front of the eye are entirely missing.

The beard is more pointed than it is in designs for other stamps having this head.

Most of the tint lines round the head are carried right up to the lines of the pillars, but those which run from the eyebrow, the mouth and the nape of the neck are not.

The following defects exist in this print, but as only one print in black on ivory enamelled card has been supplied (instead of at least six) it cannot be determined whether they are severally due to the engraving, or to the paper, or to the printing: –

The 'o' in POSTAGE is broken.

Nick in the 'G' in POSTAGE.

White spots on the Crown.

Break in the point of nose.

Irregular tint lines in front of mouth and beard.

Broken tint lines in front of neck.

S.B.
7.10.12

(33)

Stamping Department
Inland Revenue
Somerset House
16th October, 1912

My dear Eve,

We are *all* extremely sorry to hear that you are not feeling quite so well. We hope that very soon, as the result of the care which you are wise enough to take, that you will be able to report that 'all is well'.

I think the enclosed is the Motley print which you want? If it is not, please let me know and I will see that you have the one that you do require.

Atterbury purposes calling on you to-morrow (Thursday) morning a little before 10 o'clock to have a chat with you:

(*a*) Upon the proposed revision of the design for the 4d. and the 8d. series, in consequence of the Postmaster General objecting that the Head is too large for the border. A smaller head is suggested, and

(*b*) As to why the *daffodil* (instead of the *leek*) appears in the Insurance Stamps as the emblem of Wales! The Marquess of Tullibardine has put down a Parliamentary question on this point, and I have told our people that you are by far the best authority (probably the *sole* authority) upon whom to rely in giving their answer.

With warmest good wishes,
Yours sincerely,

Seymour Bennett

Geo. W. Eve, Esqre,
116 Adelaide Road, N.W.

(34)

Royal Mint
London, E.
25th October, 1912

My dear Eve,

I believe you have already heard from Atterbury that the P.M.G. has raised further questions in regard to the 4d. and 1/– designs from the same old point of the head of the King being too large, and this notwithstanding the fact that he has himself submitted the former to the King and had it approved. We have an official letter from Somerset House enclosing copy of one they have from the Post Office requesting that fresh designs may be submitted with a smaller head, which of course involves engraving a new head to suit these designs: the letter specifically asks for a head 'slightly smaller' than the present one.

Knowing as we do that the King prefers the head to be on the large side I have tried to get through with a fairly large one and enclose a number for you to try in the frames also enclosed. These latter are photographs from your latest designs four diameters in size. You will doubtless remember that the number used for identification represents the percentage which the diameter of the head measured from the tip of the nose to the back of the head in a horizontal direction is of the width of the frame and on this basis the present head is 47.4. The new ones, 46 and 45 respectively are taken from the large hand drawing made by Harrison for the head on the new penny, which we know as the medal head and it is more recent than the other, the coinage head, and generally considered better. It is important to bear in mind that whichever head is chosen it must be suitable for both designs and I gather that they are most nervous about the 8d. design on account of the straight sides of the opening.

The tint lines round the head are approximately as in the new penny but the Post Office raise the question of darkening them round the forehead, &c., after the manner of King Edward's effigy: this I don't think the King will approve. Also they talk of giving 'a little more body in certain parts of the frame' but this does not press. Please put such head as you prefer in the two frames and let me have the lot back: we will then photograph them down to stamp size for submission.

I was very sorry to hear from Atterbury that you were not so well again but trust that this trouble has now passed away.

Yours truly,

Edward Rigg

P.S. Other sized heads are enclosed merely for comparison.

E.R.

(35)

General Post Office
London
31st October, 1912

Sir,

I am directed by the Postmaster General to forward herewith a warrant for £26 5s. in payment of the account which you recently sent to the Controller of Stamps in respect of your services in connection with the attempted production by Mr Motley's process of the 4d. and 8d. Postage Stamps.

I am, Sir,
Your obedient Servant,
Walter G. Gates

G. W Eve, Esq.

(36)

Royal Mint
London, E.
2nd November, 1912

My dear Eve,

I now enclose a series of photographs, all on the four diameter basis, to correspond with the cut out mounted photographs of the 4d. and 8d. stamps that you already have.

Two prints of the 'medal' head as you wished, with all tint lines removed and of the 46 size.

Two prints of the 'coinage' head already in use on the 1½d., 2d., and 3d., stamps which have been issued.

One print of the 1½d., stamp enlarged to the same size so that you may judge of the margin which is in use.

I send the second item because it has occurred to me that as you are proposing to enlarge the frames to take 46 if you go a step further and make the enlarging so as to take the 47.4, that is the one here referred to, we can save a lot of time, avoid engraving another head very near to the one existing, and avoid reducing the head which seems to be against the King's wishes. These photographs as you will see also have all the tint lines removed.

Yours truly,

Edward Rigg

(37)

Royal Mint
London, E.
9th November, 1912

My dear Eve,

Replying to your letter of the 6th the prints I sent you of heads without tint lines were from the same negatives as the former ones except that the lines had been painted out: so I don't understand your finding them less clear.

Very well! If the P.M.G. and the I.R. chose to stick to the triflingly smaller head they may as well, but I utterly dissent from the scheme. This is not likely to distress either of them but I none the less decline to act Sancho Panza to their Don Quixote!

Please don't think of troubling with a second drawing as a consequence of my suggestion.

Yours truly,

Edward Rigg

(38)

Royal Mint
London, E.
22nd November, 1912

My dear Eve,

I send herewith two prints of each of the large (four diameter) photographs of your two new designs and three each of those stamp size as arranged. Also your original drawings and the print of the maple leaves. Please let me know if you are sending any of these to Somerset House or are we to make further prints for submission.

Yours truly,

Edward Rigg

(39)

Royal Mint
London, E.
28th November, 1912

My dear Eve,

I enclose a print from each of the negatives taken today of your amended drawings and have sent three prints from each to Atterbury as you wished. I am keeping the originals in case we have to do any more photographs from them.

I cannot pretend that they please me and the lines seem to be quite needlessly coarse assuming the printing is placed in competent hands, but after all is that going to be the case!

Yours truly,

Edward Rigg

(40)

Royal Mint
London, E.
14th December, 1912

My dear Eve,

I think you forgot the enclosed when you were here last night so I forward them in case they are wanted.

I have seen Mr Mackennal this morning and you will be glad to hear that he is sending the letter to Mr Macartney today to say that the King prefers *the head on the new penny* and that, providing it is not overdone, there will not in his opinion be any objection to the darkening of the background in the upper parts.

Yours truly,

Edward Rigg

(41)

General Post Office
10th April, 1913

Sir,

I am directed by the Postmaster General to forward herewith a Warrant for £10. 10s. in payment of the account which you recently sent to the Controller of Stamps in respect of services rendered in the preparation of the proofs showing the effect of different styles of 'surround' for the 8d. postage stamp.

I am, Sir,
Your obedient servant,
(Sgd)
for the Secretary

G. W. Eve, Esq.

(42)

Royal Mint
London, E.
23rd April, 1913

My dear Eve,

I enclose some of the series of letterings which you last did for the stamps and please let me know, if possible by return, if you are satisfied that these same designs shall be used for the stamps we now have in hand: of course the 5d. 6d. and 7d., which were intended for the wreath design now have to go with the pillar and conversely as to the 9d. 10d. and 1/–. The similar drawings for 6d., and 7d., are for the moment missing and Harrison has that for 8d. But if you want them I can tomorrow send impressions from the dies we made and were thrown aside.

Yours truly,

Edward Rigg

(43)

Royal Mint
London, E.
25th April, 1913

My dear Eve,

As requested in your letter of yesterday I send herewith four prints of the pillar design, for the 5d., 6d., 7d., and 8d., stamps respectively and three of the wreath design for the 9d., 10d., and 1/– stamps. Will you please draw in the figures and, if you think needful, the lettering on these prints and let me have them back with the least possible delay as S.H. is bustling about them. Please do the 5d. and 9d., first and send me them in advance as these dies are actually waiting for the lettering: the others will be got from a roller taken off these dies so will not be wanted at present. Please also note that the word PENCE has been engraved in these two dies already so we don't want it altered.

One of the prints is very dark but perhaps it will serve and for the reduction to stamps size we shall get the letters all right and this is all that matters.

Yours truly,

Edward Rigg

P.S. I learn by telephone that FIVEPENCE is already engraved in the Pillar Die. E.R.

(44)

Stamping Department
Inland Revenue
Somerset House
5th July, 1913

My dear Eve,

The Sachems of Somerset House (opposite Shorts) entirely concurred in your opinion that the black print on lemon tinted paper is distinctly more satisfactory for the 'Pillar' design than it is for the 'Wreath'.

Accordingly, our Board officially 'moved' the Postmaster General with the view to his also 'finding salvation', and I am very glad to be able to tell you that in reply, he has written that he 'concurs' and approves 'the substitution of black on tinted paper (E.27) in the "Pillar" design for the 8d. stamp, and azure (E.6) in the "Wreath" design for the 10d. stamp, for the colours, approval of which was notified in the Post Office letter of the 20th ultimo.'

So far, so well!

And, I trust, that you and Mrs Eve and the Scion are also well, and flourishing?

Very sincerely yours,

Seymour Bennett

Geo. W. Eve, Esqre
116 Adelaide Road
Hampstead, N.W.

(45)

General Post Office
London
28th October, 1913

Sir,

I am directed by the Postmaster General to inform you that he proposes to introduce at an early date a system of accounting for surcharges on postal packets by means of 'postage due' labels; and he will be glad to learn whether you will assist him by preparing a design for such labels.

A fee of 30 guineas would be paid if any design which you submitted were adopted, or a fee of 10 guineas in the event of no design of yours being approved. In either case any design submitted would become the Postmaster General's property.

The labels will be issued in four denominations, viz: – $\frac{1}{2}$d., 1d., 2d., and 5d. The same design will be used for all four denominations, the numerals and words denoting value alone being different. The labels will be of the same dimensions as the 1d. postage stamp, but the short edge of the stamp will be from top to bottom and the long edge from left to right. The colours of the labels will probably be the same as those of the corresponding denominations of postage stamps, viz., $\frac{1}{2}$d., green, 1d. red, 2d., orange and 5d. fawn.

A set of specimens of the postage due labels issued in certain other countries is enclosed. I am to request that you will be good enough to return it with your reply or when submitting a design.

The postage due labels to be issued in this country should, like the enclosed specimens, bear no portrait. The value of the labels should be shewn by a numeral, which should be very prominent, and also in words in much smaller type. The only other lettering on the labels should be the words 'Postage Due'.

It would be convenient if, in addition to a complete design of, say, the 2d., label, specimens could be furnished of the numerals for the three other denominations shewing the style you suggest.

The Postmaster General will be glad to learn at an early date whether you will prepare a design, and if so, on about what date you anticipate that it will be submitted. He will be much obliged if you will treat the matter as urgent.

I am,
Sir,
Your obedient servant,
Walter G. Gates

Index

Index

ILLUSTRATIONS

Showing the designs
of the Postage Stamps
issued in the reign of
King George V

(1911)

(1912)

(1912–13)

(1913)

(1924)

(1925)

THE RECESS PRINTED STAMPS

(1929)

THE SURFACE PRINTED STAMPS

(1929)

THE PHOTOGRAVURE PRINTED STAMPS

(1934–36)

(1935)